Negotiation Dynamics
to Denuclearize North Korea

Negotiation Dynamics
to Denuclearize North Korea

Cohesion and Disarray

Edited by

SU-MI LEE AND TERENCE ROEHRIG

SUNY
PRESS

Published by State University of New York Press, Albany

For information, contact State University of New York Press, Albany, NY
www.sunypress.edu

Library of Congress Cataloging-in-Publication Data

Names: Lee, Su-Mi, editor. | Roehrig, Terence, 1955– editor.
Title: Negotiation dynamics to denuclearize North Korea : cohesion and
    disarray / edited by Su-Mi Lee and Terence Roehrig.
Description: Albany : State University of New York Press, 2023. | Includes
    bibliographical references and index.
Identifiers: LCCN 2022037677 | ISBN 9781438492940 (hardcover : alk. paper) |
    ISBN 9781438492957 (ebook) | ISBN 9781438492933 (pbk. : alk. paper)
Subjects: LCSH: Nuclear disarmament—Korea (North)—International
    cooperation. | Nuclear nonproliferation—Korea (North)—International
    cooperation.
Classification: LCC JZ6009.K7 N44 2023 | DDC 327.1/747095193—dc23/eng/20221202
LC record available at https://lccn.loc.gov/2022037677

10 9 8 7 6 5 4 3 2 1

Contents

Illustrations

Acknowledgments

We have many people to thank for making this book possible. First, we want to thank the Korea Foundation and its president, Lee Geun, for their generous support of this project. Thanks to their gracious assistance, we were able to gather an excellent group of authors and hold a public conference to share our findings with a wider audience. We also want to thank them for their flexibility as we navigated the challenges of the COVID-19 pandemic.

The strength of this book is the expert authors we were able to recruit for this project. Their research and analysis provide a comprehensive look at the goals, motivations, and negotiating strategies of the six countries involved in the many attempts to negotiate the denuclearization of North Korea. Thank you for all your hard work and insightful scholarship. We also want to thank Michael Rinella, our editor at SUNY Press, whose support and guidance for our project was invaluable. We have also benefited immensely from the feedback of the three anonymous reviewers. Your help is greatly appreciated and the volume is better thanks to your feedback.

Finally, we want to thank University of Hawai'i at Hilo Chancellor Bonnie Irwin and the Hawai'i County Mayor Mitch Roth for their support and encouragement of the project. We would also like to thank the people at the University of Hawai'i at Hilo in the Office of Research Services and the Research Corporation of the University of Hawai'i for all their outstanding work in administering the grant for this project and doing the logistics for our conference. All of their work was even more difficult given the upheavals of the pandemic and our need to make several scheduling changes. This project would not have been possible without your help and we are deeply grateful.

Introduction

Su-Mi Lee and Terence Roehrig

North Korea's interest in acquiring nuclear weapons began in the 1950s, but for three decades its nuclear ambitions received little attention from officials and analysts. By the mid-1980s, the evidence of a North Korean nuclear weapons program began to mount as did concern for the impact of this program on regional and international security. Since that time, the international community has employed various measures including diplomacy, incentives, and coercion to persuade North Korea to relinquish its goal of acquiring nuclear weapons. Negotiations with North Korea have been able to bring about notable bilateral and multilateral agreements that seemed to offer the possibility of progress including the North-South Joint Denuclearization Agreement (1992), the Agreed Framework (1994), the Six-Party Talks' disarmament principles (2005), the North Korea Denuclearization Action Plan (2007), and the Leap Day Deal (2012). The efforts by the Trump administration and the plethora of summit meetings in 2018 and 2019 also raised hopes for progress but little was forthcoming. Despite these many agreements and countless efforts to engage and coerce North Korea, the goal of achieving the denuclearization of North Korea is becoming an ever more distant possibility.

While many policy approaches have been used to address the complicated and challenging problem of North Korea, in this book we focus on the history of the negotiations between the six key players—North Korea, South Korea, the United States, China, Japan, and Russia—and seek to answer two fundamental questions: How did the unique nature of these multiparty negotiations affect the chance for a successful outcome to achieve denuclearization? and Was there ever a window of opportunity when the negotiations could have succeeded? To address these questions, we bring together country experts with negotiation specialists and utilize their different approaches in a complementary fashion to structure the analysis in this book.

From the perspective of negotiation scholars, talks on North Korea's nuclear weapons program are multiparty negotiations, but not multilateral. Multiparty and multilateral negotiations are different. Multiparty negotiation refers to dialogue involving more than two parties. However, a multiparty negotiation could be multilateral or bilateral. In multilateral multiparty negotiation, each party represents its own interests but they are not grouped together with similar goals. Bilateral multiparty negotiations imply that the parties are divided into two sides based on their overarching common goals and interests. In the case of North Korea nuclear negotiations, six parties participated but negotiations were largely bilateral, with North Korea on one side and the remaining five on the other. Thus, North Korea nuclear negotiation is an example of bilateral multiparty negotiation as it involved multiple parties that were divided into two camps with one camp seeking to denuclearize North Korea while the other had different goals.

Multiparty negotiations are difficult because there are simply too many interests and goals to satisfy and accommodate. Bilateral multiparty negotiations are particularly difficult because not only do each party's goals, motives, and strategies individually affect the negotiation process and outcome but also the dynamic and cohesion within each subgroup collectively can alter the course of negotiation. For example, in the case of North Korea, China and the United States had significant differences in their primary goals though both were on the same side in seeking denuclearization. The pursuit of divergent goals by individual members within one side of the negotiation would make it challenging to facilitate a zone of agreement with the other side that is acceptable to all the involved parties. Thus, in bilateral multiparty negotiations, parties need to prioritize their goals within their side before they can negotiate with the other side. Uncoordinated or underutilized strategies employed by individual members or subgroups might undermine the overall process of negotiation. The different factors that motivate individual members to become involved in the negotiation will dictate the extent of the concessions they are willing to make and their commitment to implement the agreement in the post-negotiation period. Without a cohesive action plan or voice from each side, it is highly unlikely that negotiation would be fruitful, sending mixed messages to the other side. Scrutinizing the differences of each party, this book seeks to highlight how the divergent goals, strategies, and motives of the six parties were coordinated/managed and affected the negotiation process and outcome in the case of North Korea nuclear negotiations.

For the second question—Was there ever a chance for success?—this book will apply the ripeness theory of William Zartman[1] to the case of North Korea to answer whether or not there was ever any window of opportunity for successful negotiation and, if there was, how the parties failed to grasp the opportunity to lead to a successful outcome. Has there ever been a ripe moment for success in the decades-long negotiations aiming to denuclearize North Korea? For a moment to be ripe, all parties must perceive: (1) a mutually hurting stalemate (MHS) where the parties do not see a chance of winning unilaterally, and (2) a way out (WO) where parties recognize a way to minimize their losses and reach an agreement through accommodation.[2] When the status quo is unbearable or costly, hurting both parties with no chance of winning unilaterally, parties are willing to choose to accept any negotiated outcome over the status quo. At the same time, for the ripeness of negotiation, they should also be optimistic about the prospect of an agreement, perceiving that it will lessen their losses.

In this book, the chapters of the country experts will provide a detailed assessment of the goals, motives, and strategies of the six parties along with contextual variables of each player such as political, economic, and social conditions while the negotiation scholars will collate and scrutinize the results of these key variables. Based on thorough descriptive contexts provided by the country experts, the negotiation scholars will examine at what point, if at all, cohesion among parties in terms of their goals, motives, and strategies was achieved and whether there was a moment that was ripe for a negotiated outcome.

In chapter 1 on negotiation theory, Su-Mi Lee and Pamela Aall introduce two approaches to negotiation—distributive and integrative negotiation—and discuss key components of negotiation that are applicable to the case of North Korea nuclear negotiations including actors in negotiation, issues under negotiation, motives and intention, power relationships and leverage, agenda setting and bargaining, strategy and tactics, agreement, ripeness, and party cohesion. By doing so, they situate the North Korea case in the framework of negotiation theory.

To set up the country chapters that follow, in chapter 2, Terence Roehrig reviews the history of the North Korean nuclear challenge with a specific emphasis on the several rounds of negotiations that sought denuclearization. Beginning with a brief overview of the start of North Korea's nuclear program, this chapter examines the first nuclear crisis in the early 1990s that led to the Agreed Framework followed by its collapse and the subsequent Six-Party Talks. The chapter will conclude with the Obama administration's efforts to reach out to North Korea, only to settle into "strategic patience," followed by the Trump administration's journey from "fire and fury" to summit diplomacy.

The next six chapters are the country case studies that address the goals their respective countries sought to achieve during the different periods of negotiation. In particular, was the complete denuclearization of North Korea the only acceptable goal, or were others possible? In North Korea's case, was denuclearization ever a possible goal or was it determined from the outset to acquire nuclear weapons? Each country chapter will also examine the motives and strategy used by their country along with the tools and leverage they chose to use over the years. Finally, these chapters will also assess the domestic and international conditions that affected their country's calculus on goals, motives, and strategy. These six chapters are the data set from which the negotiation scholars drew for their application of negotiation theory and deriving of lessons learned in chapter 9. We follow with a brief summary of each of these six chapters.

Analyzing three decades of North Korean statements and negotiation positions with the United States, Scott Snyder argues in chapter 3 that while the North Korean pursuit of nuclear development remained persistent and enduring throughout these phases of interaction with Washington, North Korean willingness to consider and negotiate alternative outcomes was influenced by the relative capabilities of its nuclear program. The failure of the United States and North Korea to successfully implement joint projects such as the Geneva Agreed Framework generated new obstacles to the establishment of mutual trust. These obstacles were further magnified by the failure of leadership-level summitry between Donald Trump and Kim Jong-un, leaving the Kim family regime with no attractive option other than nuclear development as the key to North Korea's absolute security.

In chapter 4, Uk Heo maintains that South Korea has used two types of strategies to achieve North Korea's denuclearization: (1) engagement; and (2) pressure. Progressive administrations (e.g., Kim Dae-jung, Roh Moo-hyn, Moon Jae-in) employed the engagement approach, seeking gradual changes in North Korea through economic aid and trade expansion while maintaining stability on the Korean peninsula. By contrast, conservative governments (e.g., Lee Myung-bak, Park Geun-hye) preferred pressure to force regime change or collapse, largely with economic sanctions to gradually undermine the power base of the Kim family and eventually collapse the regime. However, both of these negotiation strategies failed for three possible reasons. First, policymakers and security experts incorrectly assessed North Korea's willingness to abandon nuclear weapons in return for economic aid. Second, progressive administrations underestimated the risk embedded in providing economic aid to North Korea and, despite massive economic assistance, Pyongyang continued nuclear development and used the aid to support its nuclear programs, helping denuclearization efforts to fail. Finally, both Seoul and Washington underestimated the resilience of the Kim regime, despite extensive economic sanctions, and the North Korean regime turned out to be far more durable than expected. Negotiations require both sides to compromise and North Korea's behavior thus far suggests that it is determined to retain its nuclear weapons.

Why have several American presidents been unsuccessful in achieving North Korean denuclearization? In chapter 5, Paige Price Cone conducts a comparative analysis across seven U.S. administrations that have attempted to negotiate with the DPRK. In doing so, several patterns emerge that help provide an understanding of why the United States has hitherto been unsuccessful in its negotiation attempts. First, leaders come into office with prior beliefs about the importance of and means to deal with nonproliferation generally, and North Korea specifically, that influence their willingness to use sanctions or rewards. Second, each administration faced a combination of domestic and international constraints that specifically shaped how it dealt with North Korea. Finally, and perhaps most importantly, internal tensions between more hawkish and dovish administrations meant that hawkish presidents came into office with an "anything but [my predecessor]" policy that was detrimental to negotiations. Taken together, this analysis highlights why several U.S. administrations have been unsuccessful in dealing with North Korea and highlights a path forward for future administrations.

In chapter 6, Fei-Ling Wang argues that China's negotiation strategy has been driven by the Chinese Communist Party's political interest, rather than China's national interest, and Beijing has been walking a tightrope between opposing nuclear proliferation in Northeast Asia and seeking to resist, reduce, and replace American power in the region. China thus oscillates between supporting and sabotaging the course of peaceful denuclearization of North Korea. In hindsight, there was a small window of opportunity when the party's political interests overlapped with China's national interests, and essentially lined up with the interests of the United States and its allies. But that opening was conditional and transient. As the strategic rivalry between an assertive China and an alarmed United States unfolds and a new U.S.-led alliance network emerges in the Indo-Pacific, Beijing has jumped back to its North Korean comrades for its top strategic goal of regime survival. As long as the institutional and ideological incompatibility remains between the PRC-DPRK alliance and the USA-ROK/USA-Japan alliances, Beijing will talk the talk but not walk the walk, without much real effort employed for denuclearizing North Korea. Creative thinking and reframing actions are needed, therefore, to open any new window of opportunity.

We turn to Japan in chapter 7, written by Yuki Tatsumi. Over the last couple of decades, the Japanese government has shifted its North Korea policies as the North developed significant capacity to threaten Japan's national security. Initially pursing a policy of bilateral diplomatic normalization until the development of North Korea's nuclear and missile programs in the 1990s, current Japanese policy goals vis-à-vis the DPRK are a patchwork of goals meant to cover a wide swath of concerns, while adequately addressing none of them. Japan's broader goal of addressing its colonial legacy through normalization of relations is at odds with the dangers of North Korea's expanding weapons programs, and the Japanese persistence in prioritizing the abduction issue, aggravated by the politicization of this concern into a necessary precondition for any negotiation with North Korea, has effectively eliminated Japan's ability to engage directly with the DPRK on any other matters. This has also forced Japan to rely on the United States to reflect Japan's priorities in their policy platforms for North Korea. If Japan is to move forward in North Korea negotiations, it must adopt a more flexible position that allows for negotiation directly with the North Korean government while simultaneously exploring the entire diplomatic toolbox to establish a more effective incentive system of both carrots and sticks that can achieve Japan's policy objectives.

In chapter 8, Richard Weitz reviews Russia's main objectives regarding the North Korean nuclear program and argues that the Russian government does not want North Korea to have nuclear weapons due to the elevated war risks, Western countermeasures, economic obstacles, and other problems presented by DPRK nuclear efforts. Yet, Moscow has long joined China in opposing the vigorous sanctions and further coercive pressure to induce the DPRK to change its position. Russian officials argue that such measures are counterproductive because they increase North Korea's sense of insecurity. They also do not want to see regime change in North Korea that could remove a strategic buffer for the Russian Far East. Resolving the DPRK nuclear dispute might remove international sanctions that impede realization of Russian commercial objectives in Northeast Asia, but economic goals have always been of secondary importance in shaping the policies of the Russian government toward the DPRK nuclear weapons program. Other Russian objectives have included remaining a significant player on DPRK nuclear issue, exploiting the crisis to gain diplomatic leverage with other countries, and aspiring to broker any settlement through Moscow-led mediation.

Focusing on the two primary concepts of negotiation, party cohesion and ripeness, chapter 9 explores whether or not there was a window of opportunity in the North Korea nuclear negotiations. Lee and Aall show how a lack of cohesion within the group of the five parties on one side of the negotiations—South Korea, the United States, China, Japan, and Russia—in terms of goals, motives, and strategies prevented a window of opportunity from being created and that not all parties experienced a mutually hurting stalemate at the same time.

The book ends with some of the lessons from our study for future negotiation strategies and for effective ways to address future proliferation challenges.

Notes

1. William Zartman, "Ripeness: The Hurting Stalemate and Beyond," in *International Conflict Resolution after the Cold War*, ed. Daniel Druckman and Paul C. Stern (Washington, DC: The National Academies Press, 2000), 226.

2. Zartman, "Ripeness," 228.

Chapter 1

Negotiation

The Bedrock of Conflict Management

Su-Mi Lee and Pamela Aall

This book examines the strategies for and negotiations on prohibiting the development and use of nuclear weapons by North Korea. The primary aim of this review is to identify whether there have been moments—windows of opportunity—in which those objectives were achievable. As a first step in the process, we thought it useful to highlight some aspects of negotiation that are applicable across a wide variety of conflict situations. This firmer understanding of the dynamics and challenges of negotiation involved may help in recognizing windows of opportunity, both open and closed, and what might have aided in preserving an opportune moment for agreement. Given the nature of the North Korean negotiations, this section will also highlight the importance of party cohesion in creating and preserving this ripe moment.

Conflicts are inevitable in any domain of life and there is no uniform way such conflicts evolve or are terminated. Parties to the conflict might be able to resort to unilateral action and ultimately win and get their way. Some might realize after pursuing unilateral ways that they lack preponderant power to dictate the outcome of the conflict. Such realization may convince the parties to seek a political solution. Some parties, on the other hand, might reach out to their counterpart to resolve their differences at the outset. These parties might agree on a solution to the conflict right away, or, as more frequently happens, only after long discussion. This delicate situation necessitates negotiation between the parties.[1]

Negotiation is a process whereby parties seek to reach an agreement with their counterparts by exchanging and putting forward proposals that will advance their interests. Negotiation does not take place in a vacuum. When parties enter into negotiation, they are under certain situational constraints.[2] The number of parties to the negotiation has probably been determined prior to the negotiation, although pressure to include other voices might be a constant refrain. Whether a negotiation is between two parties or multiple parties affects each party's calculation about achieving its goals and its choice of strategies.[3] Each party enters the negotiation with a perception that their motives and goals are clear, although here again these perceptions may change during the course of the negotiation. All parties are aware of the issues that impel them to negotiate with each other but might not agree about the importance of those issues or even whether they should be on the agenda. The parties are also familiar with the internal dynamics within their own group—how supportive their members are of them and how much pressure they are under.[4] All these variables set the backdrop of the negotiations and influence the process (and ultimately the outcome), including the strategies negotiators employ, the way they interact with each other, the way they form an agreement, and the way they overcome obstacles.[5]

Iklé (1964) defines negotiation as "a process in which explicit proposals are put forward ostensibly for the purpose of reaching agreement on an exchange or on the realization of common interest where conflicting interests are present."[6] In other words, negotiations are recognition that parties share a common interest in resolving a problem or moving forward an agenda. The common interest might be in providing a multilateral platform for resolving conflict (Cambodia in the early 1990s)[7] or in settling a border dispute, as Ecuador and Peru did in 1998.[8] It could be in developing global mechanisms to combat climate change or address community issues that arise because of a pandemic. A common concern with an issue, however, does not necessarily lead to negotiations and certainly does not guarantee that negotiations will result in agreement. The long push and pull between India and Pakistan over Kashmir attest to this.

Even in those cases where parties have agreed to negotiate, they might start the process on quite different ground. In negotiations, for instance, between a sitting government and a rebel force, the government may have some tangible and intangible advantages: more financial and formal military resources, more experience in negotiation, greater ability to call on allies and to mobilize support for the state. The rebel group, on the other hand, may have better-trained fighters who are motivated by deep beliefs and ideology, or who feel an existential threat to their religious or ethnic group. What the rebel group lacks in resources it makes up for in determination. This negotiation would be asymmetrical by different measures: the state is strong in resources while the rebel group is strong in commitment.

A second important element of negotiation is its function as a communication device. In practically all negotiations, the parties have incomplete information about each other—what they are really concerned about and what they would agree to. The parties use negotiation both to increase communication on these important aspects and as a means to test each other's resolve and capabilities. In a transactional negotiation involving the sale of an item, this would take the form of bargaining over price and attempting to discover if there were nonfinancial aspects the other side cared about (e.g., an earlier delivery date) that could affect the price. In negotiations involving a border between two states—which might engage issues of power, security, and recognition as well as the actual dividing line—parties may test the other through a variety of tactics including threats, resolving proposals, and linkages.[9] While these propositions might not necessarily reveal their views on the final deal, they are a way to send messages to the other side which, through its reaction, sends messages back.

So far, we have been talking about negotiation as if there were only two parties engaged in the process. While that may be true in commercial negotiations or real estate transactions, it is rarely the case in the international sphere. Many current and recent peace processes in civil conflicts feature multiple parties. In Myanmar, for instance, the peace process that preceded the 2021 military coup involved more than twenty ethnic armed organizations, which engaged in negotiations with the government (itself split between military and civilian branches) both bilaterally and in groups. As we discuss later, party fragmentation introduces several layers of complexity. Some of these complexities will have a direct impact on the negotiation process itself. Parties will have different positions and interests as well as different goals. It is quite likely that the parties will also have a variety of BATNAs—an acronym for "best alternative to a negotiation agreement"[10]—which would make their willingness to walk away from the negotiation table quite variable.

However, the multiplicity of actors also may open up opportunities reaching agreement as well. In the 2015 Iran nuclear deal, the P-5+1 coalition of China, France, Germany, Russia, the United Kingdom and the United States (along with the European Union) provided the legitimacy and leverage needed to bring Iran to the table and eventually to the agreement.

Two Approaches to Negotiation

While it may be clear to parties that they share common interests (e.g., resolving the conflict), their approach to negotiation in pursuit of those interests may be quite different. The outcome of negotiation is contingent on not only your move but also your counterpart's move.[11] Thus, interaction between parties in negotiation is intentional and strategic in that each party takes into account the other party's interests and goals.[12] In this give-and-take, parties may choose from two patterns of strategic negotiation behavior: distributive or integrative bargaining.[13]

Some negotiators favor contending strategies that feature competitive tactics and value claiming. This is distributive negotiation, in which each party attempts to get the best deal for its side with no regard to what the other side gets. In a classic win-lose negotiation of this nature, there is a belief that your gain is your competitor's loss and vice versa. In distributive negotiation, parties duel.[14] Without accommodating the other party's position, dueling parties send a clear message to their counterpart that they will not make any concessions and can stay at a deadlock—costly as it may be—as long as it takes.[15] In such a situation involving a value-claiming process, parties are more occupied with their competing interests (dividing the "pie") than their shared interest (making the "pie" larger).[16]

Other negotiators employ an approach called integrative negotiation.[17] Parties using integrative techniques encourage each other to move toward a mutually beneficial agreement, exchanging concessions. They focus more on improving the agreement (making a "pie" larger) than on maintaining their position. Integrative negotiation takes the form of shared problem solving rather than the distribution of gains. Integrative negotiations attempt to achieve joint gains by sharing information and building relationships. This approach emphasizes the importance of setting aside negative attitudes about your negotiating counterparts and focusing instead on the issues. It also attempts to distinguish interests from positions, or in other words distinguishing underlying needs, values, and motivation from what parties say they want. If an agreement addresses one party's interests, that party might be willing to compromise on its position. The advantage of this approach in a negotiation is that it broadens the possible zone of agreement by providing a wider range of choices. Finally, the integrative approach to negotiation focuses on understanding the parties' BATNAs. A thorough understanding of your own BATNA will allow you as a negotiator to decide how far you are willing to go before withdrawing from the talks; understanding the other side's BATNA will allow you to anticipate their reaction to your proposals. In an integrative bargaining situation, a mutually beneficial agreement is possible thanks to values generated by cooperative strategies.[18]

Both approaches to negotiation have their place in the complex world of peacemaking, and, as we'll discuss later, parties will often mix both approaches in pursuit of their own ends.

Components of Negotiation

Negotiations are a complex interaction of a number of components, including the parties, their issues, motives, and power, and the way they choose to proceed with the negotiation. This next section examines these components.

THE PARTIES

Negotiations involve two parties (bilateral negotiation) or multiple parties (multiparty negotiation). Although the terms *multiparty* and *multilateral* seem exchangeable, *multiparty* simply implies there are multiple actors involved in negotiation while *multilateral* indicates there are multiple sides of the negotiation. All multilateral negotiations are multiparty; however, not all multiparty negotiations are multilateral, as some multiparty negotiations are bilateral if two coalitions form among the parties involved in negotiation.[19] North Korea nuclear negotiations are a great example of multiparty negotiations involving multiple actors—North Korea, South

Korea, the United States, China, Japan, and Russia—that are bilateral with two sides with one side of the six parties seeking to denuclearize the other side, North Korea.

The number of parties to negotiation indicates the extent of the complexity of negotiation.[20] As more parties join negotiation, naturally, there are more interests to accommodate, more interaction to take into account, more bargaining positions to study, more internal dynamics to figure out, and more strategies to devise.[21] Coalitions formed among parties may group the negotiating parties into two camps, transforming multilateral negotiation to bilateral negotiation and simplifying the dynamics among parties.[22] However, division within each side may complicate and derail the negotiations and ultimately jeopardize a potential agreement at the last minute.[23] Thus, it is particularly imperative in multiparty negotiations that all parties communicate with one another effectively as coherent information obtained via effective communication channels will dictate parties' next moves and help them identify a mutually acceptable solution within their side and with the other side.[24] For this reason, multiparty negotiators are expected to be equipped with broader skills than two-party negotiators.[25]

Cultural differences also augment the complexity of negotiation. Culture is not a simple variable to be considered in negotiation. Rather, it is a context where negotiation takes place. Cultural implications on a different spectrum—collectivism/individualism, hierarchy acceptance/egalitarianism, and courtesy/power demonstration[26]—dictate negotiators' concession-making and agenda-setting behavior, mannerisms, dominant strategies, and other factors that have consequential bearings on the process and outcome of negotiation.[27] Thus, unfamiliar cultural contexts and limited understanding of cultural characteristics might be a roadblock for negotiators to overcome to reach an agreement.[28]

ISSUES

Tangibles and Intangibles

Among a number of ways to categorize the disputing issues, the following three categorizations of the issues under negotiation are useful to examine how the disputing issues affect success or failure of negotiations. First, issue tangibility has significant bearing on the success rate of negotiation as well as negotiators' strategies and their satisfactions with the negotiated outcome. Tangible issues involve items that can be divided: wealth, land, access to resources, and prices. Intangible issues such as reputation, ideology, and religion are often indivisible and, thus, more difficult to resolve.[29] Indivisible issues make it challenging for each party to recognize a fair solution.[30] In negotiations over principle where some parties refuse to compromise, these issues are more difficult to resolve and negotiations are likely to fail. In reality, however, the division between tangibility and intangibility is not clear-cut. For example, territorial issues might be perceived as tangible and divisible; yet when a significant historical value is added to the land, it is no longer easily divided because of its emotional significance to the parties.[31]

The issue of nuclear proliferation is both tangible and intangible. On the surface, it is a tangible issue, as negotiation tends to center around whether or not to reduce or eliminate nuclear capabilities. Yet fundamentally it is also intangible because it concerns a sense of security, which cannot be reduced to a series of numbers. It is not at all clear that a 50 percent reduction of nuclear facilities provides a 50 percent greater sense of security to the other parties. To those who believe nuclear proliferation is an issue of principle, there is no room for negotiation or for concession making.[32] Thus, negotiation where each side is expected to make a series of concessions is not appropriate to an issue such as nuclear proliferation. Since concessions around nuclear proliferation would be off the table, negotiations involving nuclear issues might benefit from adding other items to the negotiation table. The added items could create opportunities for continued negotiation by allowing the party against nuclear proliferation to make concessions on the new items while making no concession on the issues pertaining to nuclear proliferation.

Number of Issues

The number of issues being negotiated expands the number of the options presented to negotiators. Although it might risk complicating the situation and negotiation, adding more issues to negotiation can diffuse tension over indivisible issues among parties and provide options whose valued interests vary across each party. By orchestrating shares of such options, negotiators may expand the zone of possible agreement (ZOPA).[33] Instead of negotiating over one sentimental photo of their parents, for example, adding two more sentimental objects to the negotiation table may ease tension among three siblings who negotiate over their parents' estate.

Given that three siblings feel a sentimental attachment to the three items at different levels, such an addition might present a creative way to resolve differences and help reach a beneficial solution to all three parties.

Intractability

Intractability of the issues complicates the process and outcome of negotiation. As the issues have been long-standing, the parties have become antagonized against each other for a long period of time and more issues might have been added to the initial set of the issues that triggered the first episode of clashes with each other. Intractability signals that the parties might not have been able to find a solution that satisfied both parties; or it suggests that the parties might have rejected a workable solution because they were not willing to or interested in settling the dispute.[34] In any case, it is challenging and difficult to resolve or manage intractable issues.

MOTIVES

Motives are difficult to pinpoint in a negotiation. Parties may not publicly express their motives for engaging in negotiation.[35] When they say yes to negotiation, they might sincerely wish to find a mutually beneficial agreement with the other party; or they may wish to gain more information about the others on their strengths and weaknesses, for example. It is also possible that they would want to be viewed as a member of the international community in good standing by engaging in a peaceful way to resolve conflict. At the outset, it is difficult to gauge what the other parties' motive to engage in negotiation is.[36] Nonetheless, the strength of the motives that bring parties into negotiation indicates how much they desire to reach an agreement with the other parties and thus how much they are willing to make concessions.[37]

POWER RELATIONSHIPS AND LEVERAGE

As mentioned above, many negotiations are asymmetrical with regard to tangible power resources such as military capacity and financial resources. Superiority in raw power, however, does not mean that the stronger party is willing or able to exercise that option. Democratic states are always constrained by domestic politics and even states with a strong autocratic bent such as Russia and China will choose the moment to play the power card carefully. Weaker states also have options to exercise their leverage. When the stronger entity truly wants the agreement, the weaker one can threaten to pull out if its conditions are not met, as happened in the negotiations between the Soviet Union and Afghanistan in the 1970s, and between the United States and the Taliban in 2020. Leverage can also arise from relationships—based on alliances or shared norms—that the parties can bring to the table. In the long negotiations between Sudan and South Sudan that culminated in the 2000s, Sudan vastly outstripped its opponent in terms of resources and populations. The South, on the other hand, had valuable supporters, including the United States and the European Union, that gave them power and standing at the negotiation table. In a multiparty negotiation, leverage also results from a strong cohesion of positions on one or both sides. When coalitions hang together, they project unity, commitment, and a willingness to back up their positions, all of which brings a sense of power to the coalition. However, leverage is an ephemeral attribute and can dissipate suddenly as conditions change. Recognizing when you have leverage and how to use it is a critical component of creating windows of opportunity in negotiation.

Processes

Agenda Setting and Bargaining

As we have noted, at the heart of negotiation are parties' common interests or zone of possible agreement (ZOPA).[38] However, each party will bring its own bargaining position when it enters negotiation. One end of the bargaining range can be labeled an aspiration point while the other end can be a reservation point.[39] Negotiators project that in the best scenario an agreement would be settled at their aspiration point while it would be at their reservation point in the worst scenario. They are not willing to sign an agreement that is located at a point beyond their reservation point.

When negotiation begins, parties will decide the ordering of the issues they will negotiate. They may want to bargain over the easier issues first to gain confidence in the negotiation process. Some might insist on discussing procedural matters first, while others prefer negotiating substantive matters before settling on procedural matters. The parties may also try to discuss the issues the other party considers crucial last to "impose time pressure."[40] Once the ordering of the agenda is set, the bargaining begins and parties will make their initial offers.

After learning about the others' offers, they will adjust their offer and present it to the other parties. When they do so, they will need to show their resolve, signaling that it is their most generous offer (which might be a misrepresentation) or they are willing to walk away (which might entail bluffing). By doing so, they hope to influence the others to make additional concessions. Should there be no agreement, bargaining continues with newly adjusted offers. As this step repeats, the party that is under the extreme time pressure might give in; or the party whose survival depends on securing an agreement might make more concessions, thereby moving the agreement toward its own reservation point.

In general, the bargaining process of multiparty negotiation is more complicated. Each party has more than one counterpart's bargaining range to take into consideration and accommodate. It is more challenging to find a mutually acceptable agreement and takes a long time to do so.

Strategy and Tactics

Parties select their strategies and tactics as a reflection in part of how they think the world works—they might think it is a realist environment in which every entity is out for themselves or, alternatively, they might view it as a cooperative environment in which problems are tackled and solved jointly. These worldviews are related to the two different approaches to negotiation we described earlier as distributive (realist environment) and integrative (cooperative environment). Tactics associated with distributive approaches include contending, inflexibility, stalling, and threatening to walk away from the negotiations, as has been a characteristic of both the North Korean and Iranian approaches to negotiations over their nuclear weapons programs. Tactics associated with integrative approaches include bargaining in a reciprocal fashion, suggesting confidence building measures (CBMs), sequencing, building coalitions, and using side channels or other unofficial talks to test ideas with the other side. In most negotiations, parties use a combination of these approaches, depending on what they think will work at the time.

Some Determinants of Success or Failure

When parties enter negotiation, they do so with their bargaining position defined. They know what they hope to achieve in negotiation and how they want the process to evolve. Yet the outcome of negotiation is not a function of one party's bargaining position. As noted above, once negotiation begins and parties exchange offers, they learn about the other parties' objectives and bargaining positions.[41] In some cases, the parties make adjustments to their offers to accommodate the other party and reach a mutually acceptable agreement, which might not be what they envisioned it to be at the outset. In other cases, parties fail to locate a zone of possible agreement and no agreement is reached. One may ask why some negotiations lead to an agreement and others do not. As with everything to do with negotiation, the answer is complex. Below we note several factors that help to determine success and failure, some of which arise from the parties' negotiating tactics and others from the larger context.

Negotiating Tactics

Flexibility

If parties want to reach an agreement at the end, they should be willing and ready to adjust their bargaining position. In the beginning of negotiation, parties tend to keep private information private; as negotiation progresses and moves toward the end, they share with the other party as much information as needed.[42] At the final stage of negotiation, parties are aware of each other's bargaining position, demands, objectives, and interests that are necessary to locate a zone of possible agreements. In such a moment, whether or not parties are ready to make concessions determines the outcome of negotiation. Only when they are willing to revise their bargaining position and objective can a mutually acceptable agreement form.[43]

Strong Motive and BATNA

Since parties carry out their initial assessment of negotiation without knowledge of the other party's bargaining position, concession making is expected and required for negotiation to be successful. The very motive that compelled parties to quit the status quo and seek negotiation is a good indicator of how much concession the parties are willing and ready to make as negotiation progresses. "The stronger a party's desire to escape the status quo, the more likely it is to make heavy concessions and accept an inferior settlement."[44] If both parties have a strong desire to change the status quo, they are willing to make any necessary adjustments to reach an agreement. In contrast, if either of the parties retains a strong BATNA, a compromised agreement would not be deemed worth concessions, and no agreement will be reached. However, BATNAs are not fixed and can change.[45] They are constantly reexamined by negotiators who face three options (joint agreement, breakdown, and giving in) at any moment throughout the course of negotiation.

Suboptimal Agreement

In an ideal world, parties enter into negotiation hoping to achieve an optimal agreement that reflects their own interests and satisfies the interests of the other side.[46] It should be also sufficiently durable that they will not resume fighting over the same issue in near future.[47] However, the final agreement often does not resemble what parties envisioned at the outset of negotiation. It is not a perfect or ideal document in any sense;[48] yet as long as the parties are willing to put their signature on it, the agreement is good enough. As negotiation progresses, negotiators' bargaining standard evolves. At the beginning of negotiation, they might look out for the best outcome that is close to their aspiration point; their criteria of an agreement at the end of negotiation may be any agreement that is acceptable to their constituents.[49] It is essential to note, though, that suboptimal agreements should not carry any negative connotation.[50] In a sense, any negotiated agreement may eliminate enormous pressure that is put on the shoulders of all the parties involved, settle their differences, and save any more resources required to continue with negotiation. However, there will always be a lingering question of whether the parties would have reached a better agreement that would have served both parties better had they continued with negotiations. It is possible that they would have. Yet in many cases due to constraints from a variety of factors, continuing with negotiation might not have been feasible.

Such constraints include deadlines. Time constraints would rush parties to settle on a good-enough agreement rather than exploring all alternatives available to them. Incomplete information also plays a role in tempting parties to settle on a suboptimal agreement. Although parties learn more about their counterparts' goals and bargaining positions as negotiation progresses, they still keep private information private until the end. Consequently, such private information is often not shared with parties' counterparts and therefore is not explored.

Larger Context: Ripeness, Cohesion, and an Enabling Environment

In addition to the parties' willingness to negotiate and compromise, we suggest that there are two elements internal to the negotiating process that are important in determining the success or failure of negotiations in intrastate or interstate conflict: ripeness and party cohesion. There are, however, factors out of the control of the negotiating parties that will also have an impact on the success or failure of the negotiation, particularly the role of domestic politics and the impact of global events. These last elements can provide an enabling environment for talks to succeed. Just as importantly, when they are not supportive of the process, they can scuttle even the best-planned negotiation.

Timing: Ripeness and Windows of Opportunity

In mediation literature, "ripeness" is a key concept, signifying the importance of the timing of negotiation. The tight bonds between mediation and negotiation suggest that the ripeness principle applies to negotiation as well as mediation. The ripeness theory suggests that two conditions are necessary (not sufficient) for negotiation to take place: a mutually hurting stalemate (MHS) and a way out (WO).[51] Negotiation should take place when both parties must perceive that they are in a state where they have no realistic chance of winning and are hurting themselves, and that there is an opportunity to escape the mutually hurting stalemate and reach a mutually beneficial agreement. Otherwise, a negotiated settlement is unlikely to be reached. Thus, mediators and negotiators must look out for a ripe moment and seize it when it is available.[52]

Identifying such a ripe moment may be "a matter of feel and instinct."[53] Attentive negotiators recognize signs of ripeness and, if it is in their power, use that moment to initiate or advance negotiations.[54] In his effort to resolve the conflict in Kenya over the 2007 elections, Kofi Annan recognized a moment of ripeness. He was aware, however, that the moment could fade if an agreement was not reached. To avoid this outcome, he announced to the parties that he was available for just over five weeks—if they were not able to resolve their differences in this time, he would be obliged to withdraw as mediator. In light of his prestige and legitimacy, the Kenyan political parties were anxious that he remain engaged and stick to his timetable. In this instance, Annan created a forcing event through his use of the calendar and this sustained the ripe moment throughout the negotiations.

The absence of ripeness does not imply that no action taken by parties will be fruitful.[55] If a ripe moment does not occur naturally, it might be created by third parties.[56] In the situation where objective indicators of ripeness exist but negotiators fail to perceive it, third parties might help the negotiators perceive MHS and WO. If no objective indicator of ripeness is found, third parties might incentivize parties to engage in negotiation by creating a mutually enticing opportunity (MEO).[57]

As a contextual variable, ripeness indicates when negotiation may take place. In the course of negotiation, another discussion around a ripe moment occurs. The difference between the concept at the different phases of negotiation is that a ripe moment for closure is not determined by the external, contextual variables, as ripeness for initiation is; rather, it is internally engineered as negotiation evolves.[58] Based on their thorough introspection of the state of the negotiation process, parties would decide whether they sign an agreement, walk away from the table, or continue to negotiate.[59] Facing those three options, they would ask themselves how the current status of the negotiation is compared to a better alternative to a negotiated agreement (BATNA). At a ripe moment, negotiators believe all their cards (e.g., interest, bargaining positions) are put on the table and opt for the first two options.[60] When they perceive that an agreement that is less favorable than their original position is still good enough, there will be an agreement; if it is not good enough, there will not be an agreement.[61] When a moment is not ripe yet, they will continue with negotiation.[62]

Party Cohesion

Negotiation between two people is on one level quite simple. Each person represents a single point of view and the positions are clear. In a more complex scenario involving multiple players—for instance, a group or a country—negotiators will likely encounter diverse perspectives on their own side. These different voices can add to the depth of commitment and varieties of options to resolve the issues at hand. Just as often, however, these differing perspectives can hamper the development of a unified position on the issues and can trip up negotiations, if in fact they even manage to start under these circumstances. In order to succeed, participants in multilateral negotiations need to build coalitions of interests around common positions.[63] As it is likely that each participant will feel strongly about its particular interests, building a coalition will require leadership of a person or entity willing to bear the costs of organizing the group.[64] It will also necessitate using deliberate tactics to keep the group together: ambiguous formulations, risk sharing, limiting of liability through incremental approaches to settling issues.[65] The costs of maintaining party cohesion might be high, but the rewards may be even higher if the outcome is a sustainable agreement, as was the case with the Cambodian settlement in the Paris Agreement of 1991. The Iran nuclear deal of 2015 (JCPOA) also seemed to be a good example of the power of party cohesion until the United States pulled out in May 2018. It is now a good example of the difficulty of maintaining party cohesion over time.

Domestic Politics

A number of domestic factors play a significant role in altering the process and outcome of negotiation. One of them is the domestic audience. In negotiation, each party aims to resolve differences with their counterpart and reach an agreement that pleases both sides. However, for negotiation to be successful, the agreement should be acceptable to their constituents; if it is not, the agreement is invalid. Either parties need to return to the negotiation table or their difference remains the same. Thus, negotiators are under pressure not only to resolve differences and reach an agreement with their counterpart but also coordinate their actions and demands with their constituents as the final outcome must satisfy them.[66] As a domestic political consideration, regime types matter. In a democracy, there are more constituents to please, such as outspoken opposition parties, general public, and interest groups.[67] This entails more parties for negotiators to coordinate with during the negotiation. A decision-making process is more complex in a democracy due to institutional restraints such as checks and balances. Lastly, electoral cycles also influence the negotiation process and outcome. The election date might be perceived as the deadline for the negotiation. It could push the parties to settle on an agreement as quickly as they can; or they may want to hold off reaching any agreement, anticipating a new leader to be in office.[68]

Global Events

As we have learned in this era of the COVID-19 pandemic, global events can have an effect on many aspects of interstate, intrastate, intergroup, and interpersonal relations, including negotiations. The pandemic inspired the

UN Secretary General to call for a global ceasefire in 2020 and a number of conflict parties complied.[69] The effect on negotiations, however, has been more muted and the level of violence—even in some countries that signed up to the ceasefire—has not abated.[70] While the impact of global events, from financial troubles to changes in norms, might be indirect and only discernible over time, they will affect how people, societies, and states frame their issues and proceed with talks.

Conclusion

As the foregoing section makes clear, there is no single set of variables that shapes the process and outcome of negotiation. A variety of factors influence how negotiation proceeds and how it ends. In this chapter, we examined some of those variables. Contextual variables such as the nature of issue, the number of parties, their goals, interest, motives and intentions, and timing condition the environment where negotiation takes place.

Issues that are intangible and pertaining to principle are associated with unsuccessful negotiation. The number of issues being negotiated has mixed effects on the negotiation outcome. Parties' common interests compel them to negotiate with one another over their competing interests. Parties' motives serve as an indicator of the amount of concession they are willing to make.

Ripeness as a contextual variable is a necessary component for any successful negotiation to occur. Factors at work during the negotiation play a significant role in shaping the course of negotiation. Parties bring into negotiation their bargaining position, whose range moves from a reservation point to an aspiration point. As parties exchange their offers, they revise their bargaining positions. Only when there is a zone of possible agreement (ZOPA), an overlapping section of parties' bargaining zones, is there a chance of reaching an agreement. To move the final agreement closer in the ZOPA and move away from their reservation point, parties employ strategies such as dueling and driving. In a bargaining situation concerning distributive zero-sum issues, parties tend to duel with each other, sending a message that they will not make concessions; driving is a strategy parties prefer when their goal is to improve the final agreement in an integrative bargaining situation. Ripeness during the negotiation occurs when, after reviewing the entire negotiation course, parties realize they have acquired all the information needed to decide whether to sign an agreement, walk away from the table, or continue with negotiation.

Why some negotiations lead to an agreement and other do not was briefly discussed. Concessions are required for any negotiation to be fruitful. When there is a small ZOPA, heavy concessions will make or break the negotiation. If parties are not willing to do so, negotiation is not likely to lead to an agreement. How many concessions a party is willing and ready to make depends on the strength of the motive that impelled parties to engage in negotiation. The party might have a strong motivation for entering negotiation because a BATNA is bleak or weak and it is likely to make as much concession as it could make to reach an agreement. Parties' willingness to accept a suboptimal agreement that is far different from what they envisioned at the outset of negotiation increases the likelihood of an agreement at the end of negotiation. Under time pressures such as deadlines, parties are more likely to be ready to take any agreement that would be acceptable to their constituents. In a different circumstance, parties might sign the suboptimal agreement without knowing that there is a better agreement that would benefit both of them more.

In multiparty negotiations, the work of negotiation becomes more complicated. There are more interactions and offers to consider, bargaining ranges to examine, more issue linkages to discover, and possible agreements to review. It is difficult to figure out why some parties succeed in reaching an agreement and others fail to do so. Nonetheless, in international relations, many negotiations involve multiple parties. They are not all multilateral negotiations, in a sense that some multiparty negotiations have two primary camps. However, bilateral multiparty negotiations are not as simple as two-party negotiations, as one needs to consider the internal dynamic within each camp in addition to the interaction between the two camps.

In the following chapters, this book will look closely at the negotiations to prevent North Korea's acquisition of nuclear weapons. In chapter 2, Terence Roehrig gives an overview of the history of North Korea denuclearization negotiations. In chapters 3–8, six eminent experts examine the motives and tactics of the countries engaged in nuclear nonproliferation talks in Northeast Asia over the past forty years.

As discussed in the following chapters, each of these countries—China, Japan, North Korea, South Korea, Russia, and the United States—has employed a combination of fixed and changeable strategies to achieve their ends, whether it was nonproliferation, improved regional relationships, increased recognition and legitimacy, or global stability and security. This has been a highly complex series of negotiations, at once bilateral, multilateral, biparty, and multiparty. The concluding chapter tries to pull some lessons from this complex history, lessons we hope will be of value to future negotiators brave enough to take on the task of negotiating nuclear nonproliferation on the Korean peninsula.

Notes

1. Ho-Won Jeong, *International Negotiation: Process and Strategies* (Cambridge: Cambridge University Press, 2016), 3.
2. Daniel Druckman, "Linking Micro and Macro-Level Processes: Interaction Analysis in Context," *The International Journal of Conflict Management* 14, no. 3/4 (2003): 177.
3. Jeong, *International Negotiation*, 4.
4. Ariane Tabatabai and Camille Pease, "The Iranian Nuclear Negotiations," in *How Negotiations End*, ed. I. William Zartman (Cambridge: Cambridge University Press, 2019), 44.
5. Druckman, "Linking Micro and Macro-Level Processes," 177.
6. Fred Iklé, *How Nations Negotiate* (New York: Harper and Row, 1964), 3–4.
7. The 1991 Paris Peace Agreement that ended the two-decades-long protracted conflict and internal strife in Cambodia was the first major multilateral peace accord in the post–Cold War era and involved nineteen different state actors.
8. Chester A. Crocker, Fen Osler Hampson, and Pamela R. Aall, eds, *Herding Cats: Multiparty Mediation in a Complex World* (Washington, DC: U.S. Institute of Peace Press, 1999).
9. Parties negotiate over multiple issues, whose importance to them may vary. Thus, linking issues (e.g., making resolving one issue contingent upon resolving another one) might help facilitate negotiations that otherwise would stall at the crossroads.
10. Roger Fisher, William Ury, and Bruce Patton, *Getting to Yes: Negotiating Agreement Without Giving In*, 2nd ed. (New York: Penguin Books, 1991).
11. Oran R. Young, *Bargaining: Formal Theories of Negotiation* (Urbana: University of Illinois Press, 1975), 5.
12. Leszek Buszynski, *Negotiating with North Korea: The Six Party Talks and the Nuclear Issue* (Abingdon, UK: Routledge, 2013), 9.
13. I. William Zartman, "Lessons for Theory," in *How Negotiations End*, ed. I. William Zartman (Cambridge: Cambridge University Press, 2019), 289.
14. Niki Kitzantonis and Liz Alderman, "Greece Defers Payment," *New York Times*, June 5, 2015.

15. I. William Zartman, "Introduction," in *How Negotiations End*, ed. I. William Zartman (Cambridge: Cambridge University Press, 2019), 7.

16. Jeong, *International Negotiation*, 8.

17. Zartman, "Introduction," 9.

18. Richard E. Walton and Robert B. McKersie, *A Behavioral Theory of Labor Negotiations* (New York: McGraw-Hill, 1965); John S. Odell, *Negotiating the World Economy* (Ithaca: Cornell University Press, 2000).

19. Larry Crump and A. Ian Glendon, "Towards a Paradigm of Multiparty Negotiation," *International Negotiation* 8, no. 2 (2003): 199.

20. Jeong, *International Negotiation*, 7.

21. Buszynski, *Negotiating with North Korea*, 13.

22. Jeong, *International Negotiation*, 7.

23. Jeong, *International Negotiation*, 15.

24. Jeong, *International Negotiation*, 15; Crump and Glendon, "Towards a Paradigm of Multiparty Negotiation," 208.

25. Larry Crump, "Multiparty Negotiation: What Is It?" *ADR Bulletin* 8, no. 7 (2006): 6.

26. In many negotiation cases, these opposite tendencies represent the East-West dichotomy, with collectivism, hierarchy acceptance, and courtesy representing cultural values in the East and the rest representing cultural values in the West. For instance, one party subscribing to collectivism would expect the other party to make concessions to achieve a greater good for the group; yet, the other party accustomed to individualism might focus on advancing its own position. This mismatching expectation would likely lead to stalemate as they expect different behaviors/demands from the other parties.

27. Anne Marie Bülow and Rajesh Kumar, "Culture and Negotiation," *International Negotiations* 16 (2011): 349–59.

28. Kevin Groves, Ann Feyerherm, and Minhua Gu, "Examining Cultural Intelligence and Cross-Cultural Negotiation Effectiveness," *Journal of Management Education* 39, no. 2 (2015): 209–43.

29. Thomas C. Schelling, *The Strategy of Conflict* (Cambridge: Harvard University Press, 1960); Dean G. Pruitt, *Negotiation Behavior* (New York: Academic Press, 1981); Jeffrey Z. Rubin and Bert Brown, *The Social Psychology of Bargaining and Negotiation* (New York: Academic Press, 1975); James D. Fearon, "Rationalist Explanations for War," *International Organization* 49, no. 3 (1995): 379–414; Steven Brams and Jeffrey M. Togman, "Camp David: Was the Agreement Fair?" *Conflict Management and Peace Science* 15, no. 1 (1996): 99–112.

30. Fearon, "Rationalist Explanations for War."

31. Ron E. Hassner, "To Halve and To Hold: Conflicts Over Sacred Space and the Problem of Indivisibility," *Security Studies* 12, no. 4 (2003): 1–33.

32. Buszynski, *Negotiating with North Korea*, 11.

33. Jeong, *International Negotiation*, 7.

34. Chester A. Crocker, Fen Osler Hampson, and Pamela R. Aall, *Taming Intractable Conflicts: Mediation in the Hardest Cases* (Washington, DC: U.S. Institute of Peace Press, 2004), 9.

35. Buszynski, *Negotiating with North Korea*, 7.

36. I. William Zartman, "Ripeness: The Hurting Stalemate and Beyond," in *International Conflict Resolution after the Cold War*, ed. Daniel Druckman and Paul C. Stern (Washington, DC: The National Academies Press, 2000), 226.

37. Dean G. Pruitt, "When Is 'Enough' Enough? Approach-Avoidance," in *How Negotiations End*, ed. I. William Zartman (Cambridge: Cambridge University Press, 2019), 263.

38. Jeong, *International Negotiation*, 6; Zartman, "Lessons for Theory," 294.

39. Jeong, *International Negotiation*, 9.

40. Barry O'Neill, "International Negotiation: Some Conceptual Developments," *Annual Review of Political Science* 21 (2018): 528.

41. Tabatabai and Pease, "The Iranian Nuclear Negotiations," 45.

42. Zartman, "Introduction," 21.

43. Zartman, "Lessons for Theory," 291.

44. Pruitt, "When Is 'Enough' Enough? Approach-Avoidance," 264.

45. Zartman, "Lessons for Theory," 292.

46. Hopmann, "When Is 'Enough' Enough?" Settling for Suboptimal Agreement," in *How Negotiations End*, ed. I. William Zartman (Cambridge: Cambridge University Press, 2019), 265.

47. Hopmann, "When Is 'Enough' Enough? Settling for Suboptimal Agreement," 285.

48. Tabatabai and Pease, "The Iranian Nuclear Negotiations," 45.

49. Zartman, "Introduction," 21.

50. Hopmann, "When Is 'Enough' Enough? Settling for Suboptimal Agreement," 266.

51. Zartman, "Ripeness," 228.

52. Zartman, "Ripeness," 232.

53. Chester A. Crocker, *High Noon in South Africa: Making Peace in a Rough Neighborhood* (New York: W. W. Norton, 1992), 481.

54. Zartman, "Ripeness," 235.

55. Crocker, *High Noon in South Africa*, 471.

56. Zartman, "Ripeness," 229.

57. Zartman, "Ripeness," 244.

58. Zartman, "Introduction," 18.

59. Iklé, *How Nations Negotiate*; Zartman, "Introduction," 3.

60. Zartman, "Introduction," 1.

61. Zartman, "Introduction," 4.

62. Zartman, "Introduction," 1.

63. Fen Osler Hampson with Michael Hart, *Multilateral Negotiations: Lessons from Arms Control, Trade, and the Environment* (Baltimore and London: The Johns Hopkins University Press, 1999).

64. Mancur Olson, *The Logic of Collective Action: Public Goods and the Theory of Groups* (Cambridge: Harvard University Press, 1971).

65. Fen Osler Hampson, "The Risks of Peace: Implications for International Mediation," *Negotiation Journal* 22, no. 1 (2006): 15; Hampson summarizes a few tactics that mediators could use to manage parties' perceptions of risk. Mediators could intentionally make proposals ambiguous so that they could be "re-interpreted or manipulated as circumstances change," construct a situation where risks are shared equally among the parties in case a negotiation fails, and "limit liability by separating assets and "taking an incremental approach toward negotiations." In the case of multiparty negotiations, by manipulating parties' perceptions of risks, these tactics might help build a coalition.

66. Robert D. Putnam, "Diplomacy and Domestic Politics: The Logic of Two-level Games," *International Organization* 42, no. 3 (1988): 427–60.

67. Hopmann, "When Is 'Enough' Enough? Settling for Suboptimal Agreement," 278.

68. Chester A. Crocker, "Lessons for Practice," in *How Negotiations End*, ed. I. William Zartman (Cambridge: Cambridge University Press, 2019, 295.

69. According to an Associated Press report [Edith M. Lederer, Associated Press, April 3, 2020, https://abcnews.go.com/US/wireStory/chief-cease-fire-appeal-backed-parties-11-nations-69961494, accessed 5/3/21], Guterres named eleven countries, including Cameroon, the Central African Republic, Colombia, Libya, Myanmar, the Philippines, South Sudan, Sudan, Syria, Ukraine, and Yemen. The need for pandemic response has emboldened leaders to crack down on protests (see for instance Bangladesh [https://www.hrw.org/news/2021/01/13/bangladesh-pandemic-pretext-authoritarian-crackdown]), stifling civil society voices in what can be seen as a national negotiation on significant issues.

70. Richard Gowan, "COVID-19 and Conflict," *Sustainable Goals*, October, 23, 2020, https://www.sustainablegoals.org.uk/covid-19-and-conflict/.

Chapter 2

The History of North Korea Denuclearization Negotiations

Terence Roehrig[1]

Introduction

Efforts to maintain a nuclear-free Korean Peninsula have been going on for decades, yet success has continued to elude all who have tried. The negotiations have included bilateral and trilateral forums along with the multilateral Six-Party Talks. There have been times when the talks held out promise for reaching a solution and other times when the negotiations appeared deadlocked beyond repair with a Gordian knot of epic proportions. Thus, was there ever a time that the goals of all the parties aligned and the process was ripe for a solution? Views of the chances these efforts had for success differ. While some have argued that North Korea never intended to give up its nuclear weapons ambition, others maintain there were opportunities but problems of mistrust, misperception, and tentative agreements that were poorly implemented all undercut the chances to reach a final agreement on North Korea ending its nuclear program.

Before proceeding to the chapters that assess the goals and negotiation strategies of the six major players in this diplomatic puzzle, we begin here with a chapter that provides an overview of the more than forty years of negotiations that sought to achieve a nuclear-free North

Korea.[2] Addressing the complexities as well as the multiple interpreta-
tions of these events would be a challenging task for a volume devoted
solely to that endeavor and that is not the goal here. Instead, this chapter
will help to provide a broad historical framework to better understand
and assess the positions of the individual countries and their impact on
negotiations.

Origins of the North Korean Nuclear Weapons Program

Kim Il-sung's interest in nuclear weapons began early in his rule of North
Korea. He was well aware of the destruction of the atomic bombs that
forced a quick Japanese surrender. During the Korean War, he witnessed
firsthand the devastation of conventional bombing and U.S. threats to use
nuclear weapons on three different occasions during the conflict.[3]

After the Korean War, Kim approached the Russians for help. and in
1956 they signed an important cooperation agreement that led to DPRK
scientists and personnel receiving training in the Soviet Union. In 1959,
North Korea built, with Soviet help, the Yongbyon complex that became
the hub of its program, and, later, Moscow gave North Korea a small
research reactor. However, despite the early assistance, the Soviets were
reluctant to support North Korea's nuclear weapon ambitions and did
not fulfill all of the North's requests, largely for fear that the technology
would end up in China.[4]

Though the evidence is thin, Kim seems to have made the decision
to use the energy program as a gateway to nuclear weapons sometime in
the early 1960s. North Korea had lived for years under the U.S. nuclear
threat, and starting in 1958, U.S. tactical nuclear weapons were deployed
in Korea.[5] According to historian James Person, the Cuban Missile Crisis
may have been the turning point. When Khrushchev backed down from
U.S. pressure in the standoff over missiles in Cuba, Kim feared he could no
longer count on the Soviet Union and its nuclear umbrella.[6] After China
tested its first nuclear weapon in October 1964, Kim approached Mao for
help in building a bomb, but Mao showed no interest. Using the help it
obtained from the Soviets, North Korea slowly built a largely indigenous
program that remained relatively obscure for the next two decades.

By the mid-1980s, evidence of North Korean progress became more
visible. The facility at Yongbyon had expanded with a five megawatt (MW)
reactor along with another fifty MW reactor under construction, as well

as a fuel rod fabrication facility, a plutonium reprocessing plant, and evidence of an active testing program for components. Moreover, these facilities began showing up on U.S. satellite images. Concerns that the North could pull off such a technological feat had been relatively low but these pictures set off alarms that North Korea had advanced farther than most thought possible.[7]

If North Korea were indeed making these advancements, it became paramount that Pyongyang sign onto the Nuclear non-Proliferation Treaty (NPT) as a non-nuclear weapons state to ensure it would forgo a weapons option. At the urging of Washington, Moscow pressured North Korea to sign the NPT as a condition to satisfy a DPRK request for four light-water reactors (LWR). In December 1985, North Korea joined the NPT, allaying many of the concerns for its nuclear weapons ambitions. Subsequently, the Soviets balked at providing the promised LWRs, much to Kim Il-sung's dismay. North Korea likely did not fully appreciate the problems and pressure that would come its way as a result of signing the NPT.[8]

As a member of the NPT, North Korea was required to provide a declaration of all its nuclear material and open its nuclear facilities to inspections by the UN's International Atomic Energy Agency (IAEA) to verify that North Korea was not producing nuclear weapons. To finalize the safeguards agreement and set up the inspections process, the IAEA sent forms to North Korea with a standard eighteen month deadline for their return. As the deadline approached, IAEA officials realized North Korea had been sent the wrong documents. After furnishing the correct forms, North Korea received another eighteen months for their return, giving Pyongyang three years before any inspections were to take place.[9] When the deadline finally arrived in December 1988, North Korea balked at fulfilling the inspection obligations.

While efforts continued to obtain Pyongyang's compliance with inspections, North and South Korea pursued talks that raised hopes for improved relations as well as moving North Korea to comply with its NPT obligations. On December 13, 1991, Pyongyang and Seoul signed an agreement pledging reconciliation and nonaggression[10] and on January 20, 1992, signed the Joint Declaration of the Korean Peninsula where both pledged to "not test, manufacture, produce, receive, possess, store, deploy or use nuclear weapons," and prohibited construction of any facilities for reprocessing nuclear materials and uranium enrichment.[11] However, little in either agreement was ever implemented though these remain important markers for North-South relations and denuclearization.

First Nuclear Crisis: 1992–94

After several delays where North Korea appeared to be stalling, in 1992, IAEA inspections finally occurred.¹² The IAEA requested follow-on inspections and after several more delays, on March 12, 1993, Pyongyang announced that it would leave the NPT. The treaty has a provision for withdrawal based on "extraordinary events" that have "jeopardized the supreme interests of its country," and takes effect after giving three-months' notice.¹³ The next weeks saw a flurry of diplomatic activity to keep North Korea in the NPT, and to the surprise of many, Pyongyang acquiesced and announced it was suspending its withdrawal, one day before the three-month deadline expired.

Despite Pyongyang's reversal, there was little progress on inspections. Some visits took place in March 1994, but eventually the United States again threatened to impose sanctions and conduct airstrikes should North Korean noncompliance continue. Pyongyang did allow limited additional inspections but not to all the sites the IAEA sought to examine. Soon after, North Korea unloaded eight thousand fuel rods from its reactor for reprocessing into weapons-grade material, and in the months that followed tensions rose to unprecedented levels. Washington and Pyongyang broke off talks, and the United States followed with more threats to impose sanctions, while U.S.-ROK forces went on a heightened state of alert. The Clinton administration also sent a letter to South Korean president Kim Young-sam assuring him of the U.S. commitment to defend South Korea if it was attacked. Though the United States also offered incentives such as resuming talks, suspending the Team Spirit military exercises, and the possibility of economic aid, the administration was also considering airstrikes on DPRK nuclear facilities. North Korea responded that U.S. sanctions would be an act of war accompanied by the threat that "Seoul will turn into a sea of fire."¹⁴ War in Korea appeared to be a distinct possibility.

The Agreed Framework

With storm clouds gathering, conflict was averted from an unexpected source. In June 1994, former president Jimmy Carter traveled to Pyongyang to meet with Kim Il-sung and convinced the North Korean leader to suspend his nuclear program in return for high-level talks and concessions from the United States.¹⁵ Follow-on meetings were delayed by the death of Kim Il-sung on July 8, 1994, and the final agreement, the Agreed Framework, was signed on October 21, 1994, in Geneva.

The Agreed Framework had four central provisions.[16] First, North Korea agreed to freeze and eventually dismantle its nuclear program, including the 5 MW reactor that was in operation along with the 50 and 200 megawatt reactors and the reprocessing plant that were under construction. North Korea's fissile material would be stored and later shipped to a third party. Pyongyang would remain a party to the NPT and be in full compliance with its NPT obligations, including IAEA inspections.

Second, North Korea would receive two 1,000 MW LWRs. To facilitate the construction of the two LWRs, the United States organized the Korean Peninsula Energy Development Organization (KEDO), a consortium consisting of South Korea, Japan, and the European Union. Despite not participating in Agreed Framework negotiations, South Korea was asked to provide 70 percent of the funding for KEDO to supervise and finance the construction of the LWRs.

During the Agreed Framework talks, U.S. negotiators tried to convince North Korea to accept conventional power reactors rather than LWRs but North Korea refused. Negotiators relented, believing that the LWRs were less of a proliferation risk than what Pyongyang currently had, and North Korea did not possess the requisite technology for reprocessing spent fuel. Moreover, many U.S. leaders believed that North Korea was in a precarious economic position so that it would not be long before North Korea collapsed as had many of the communist regimes, resulting in reunification under South Korean rule. Once this occurred, the reactors would be in the hands of a responsible Korean government and no longer a proliferation concern.

Third, while the LWRs were under construction and to offset the lost energy from the reactor freeze, the United States committed to providing an annual delivery of five hundred thousand tons of heavy fuel oil (HFO).

Finally, the agreement also contained several measures to improve diplomatic and economic relations between the United States and North Korea. These provisions included reducing trade and investment restrictions and opening a liaison office in each country's respective capital that would eventually be upgraded to a full embassy. The United States also agreed to provide formal assurances that it would not threaten or use nuclear weapons against North Korea.

From the outset, the Agreed Framework was a struggle to implement. Critics in the United States were quick to slam the agreement, maintaining that Washington had succumbed to blackmail. Senator Frank

Murkowski (R-AK) complained, "It is a bad agreement because it carries the scent of appeasement,"[17] and Senator John McCain (R-AZ) complained that the Clinton administration "extended carrot after carrot, concession after concession, and pursued a policy of appeasement based . . . on the ill-founded belief that North Korea really just wants to be part of the community of nations."[18] In November 1994, U.S. congressional elections brought in a Republican majority to the House of Representatives that was equally skeptical of the agreement and now controlled the purse strings. As a result, the Congress was often slow to authorize the funding for the heavy fuel oil deliveries. The Clinton administration was also tardy providing the security assurances concerning nuclear weapons, removing economic sanctions, and starting the process of normalizing relations. North Korea believed these problems, along with delays in building the LWRs, were deliberate efforts to stall the project.

North Korea also played a role in the implementation difficulties. Pyongyang often frustrated negotiations with provocative rhetoric and the use of brinksmanship to push its agenda. Several times, North Korea threatened to restart its nuclear program to compensate for the slow LWR construction and lost electricity. Implementation was delayed by North Korea's 1996 and 1998 submarine intrusions along the South Korean coast and the 1998 ballistic missile test that traveled over Japanese airspace. North Korea was also disagreeable over wages that were paid to its workers at the LWR site. Though North Korea carried a significant share of the responsibility for smooth implementation, Pyongyang laid most of the blame on others.[19]

The August 1998 ballistic missile test shook Japan and demonstrated that North Korea had made more progress on its missile program than many had thought. The test ramped up tensions, particularly when it became clear that North Korea was preparing for another test soon after.[20] In the wake of this missile launch, Clinton commissioned former secretary of defense William Perry to gather a team of experts to review U.S. policy. The Perry Process, as it was later called, produced a set of recommendations that called for the suspension of North Korean missile tests and dismantling its nuclear weapon and missile programs in return for measures to address the North's security concerns and for the two countries to establish normal diplomatic relations.[21] North Korea responded favorably, and in September 1999 the United States and North Korea concluded a deal where Pyongyang agreed to a one-year moratorium on further missile tests in return for the lifting of some U.S. sanctions, a provision that had been part of the Agreed Framework but never implemented. The agreement was viewed as an interim step for a longer-term testing moratorium.

Efforts to engage North Korea received another boost in 1997 when Kim Dae-jung won South Korea's presidential election, his fourth try to win the office. The centerpiece of his foreign policy was the "sunshine policy," an approach that sought to improve relations and grow economic and political ties between the North and South.[22] In June 2000, Kim Dae-jung traveled to Pyongyang and met North Korean leader Kim Jong-il for several days of meetings. Few of the difficult security and political issues between the two countries were solved, and later it was revealed that South Korea had paid Pyongyang $500 million for the summit. Yet, the visit generated a great deal of momentum for better relations and reenergized Clinton administration efforts to continue negotiations. In October 2000, North Korean General Jo Myong-rok traveled to Washington for talks on limiting the North's ballistic missile program, and Secretary of State Madeline Albright journeyed to Pyongyang the following month for further talks on a comprehensive missile deal. Though important issues remained after Albright's visit, North Korea reassured Washington that these details on a testing moratorium could be worked out if President Clinton were to travel to North Korea, not only to conclude a missile agreement but also to further improve U.S.-DPRK relations. In the end, Clinton decided not to go, citing a lack of time before the new U.S. president George W. Bush took office. With the new Bush administration, DPRK-U.S. relations took a different turn.

The End of the Agreed Framework

Early in the Bush Administration, it became clear that U.S. policy and Washington's willingness to negotiate with North Korea were likely to change. Soon after his inauguration, Bush suspended further dialogue with Pyongyang and ordered a full review of U.S. policy for North Korea. In March 2001, Bush and Kim Dae-jung met at the White House, exchanging views on North Korea and the South's "sunshine policy." Though the meeting was cordial, Bush expressed his displeasure with the prospects of continued engagement with the North.[23] Bush indicated he was not opposed to dialogue, but was concerned with verification of an agreement since he had little confidence that North Korea could be trusted to keep any commitment it signed.

The Bush administration completed its policy review in June 2001, and talks between North Korea and the United States resumed through the New York channel with North Korea's representative to the United Nations. Later in August, Kim Jong-il met with Russian president Vladimir Putin and pledged to maintain the moratorium on ballistic missile tests for another two years. However, little else occurred for the remainder of the year.

The following year was an odd mix of progress in negotiations and implementing the Agreed Framework along with other signs of the difficulty that lay ahead. In January 2002, President Bush delivered his first State of the Union address, labeling Iraq, Iran, and North Korea as part of an "axis of evil." Bush criticized North Korea for being a "regime arming with missiles and weapons of mass destruction, while starving its citizens."[24] Though the administration maintained it was open to resuming talks, the atmosphere for dialogue worsened. In April 2002, the Bush administration concluded that North Korea was not complying with its Agreed Framework obligations and a July meeting was canceled in the wake of a West Sea naval clash between North and South Korea along the Northern Limit Line.[25] Yet Secretary of State Colin Powell met his North Korean counterpart Paek Nam-sun in July on the sidelines of an Association of Southeast Asian Nations meeting and in August the concrete was poured at Yongbyon for the foundation of the first LWR. The United States imposed sanctions on North Korea for the transfer of missile technology to Yemen and criticized Pyongyang for not complying with IAEA safeguard provisions. North Korea followed with threats to leave the Agreed Framework but in a meeting with Japanese prime minister Koizumi Junichiro, Kim Jong-il declared an indefinite extension of its missile testing moratorium. But there was another shoe to drop that would ultimately seal the fate of the Agreed Framework, and the shoe hit with a thud.

At some point in the late 1990s, North Korea began work on a clandestine nuclear program based on highly enriched uranium, which was a different path from the plutonium program frozen under the Agreed Framework. These efforts were aided in large part by cooperation with Pakistan and AQ Khan where Pakistan supplied highly enriched uranium (HEU) technology in return for North Korea's assistance on missile technology. The Clinton administration discovered indications of the program sometime in 1998 or 1999 and in July 2002, a CIA report confirmed that North Korea had moved from a research program to one that was intent on building weapons, an assessment that was confirmed by other sources.[26]

The motives for embarking on this path are unclear. Some argue that North Korea started its HEU program in response to U.S. hesitation in complying with its side of the agreement including the often slow delivery of heavy fuel oil and the delays in building the LWRs. These holdups during the Clinton years were followed by the George W. Bush administration's deep skepticism of the agreement that was evident in the 2002 Bush National Security Strategy and the 2002 Nuclear Posture Review that included references to using nuclear weapons against North Korea. As Jonathan Pollack noted, "It is difficult to imagine action and policies more certain to reinforce North Korea's abiding suspicion of US strategy."[27] Others maintain the HEU program is evidence that North Korea never had any intention of abandoning its nuclear weapons ambitions and was a further signal that North Korea could not be trusted to keep to any agreement it signed.

In early October 2002 after a lengthy hiatus in US-DPRK contact, James Kelly, assistant secretary of state for East Asian and Pacific Affairs, traveled to North Korea for three days of talks with DPRK officials. On October 4, the second day of the meetings, Kelly confronted his counterparts with the evidence of a clandestine HEU nuclear program. Kelly noted these actions were a violation of the Agreed Framework, the 1992 Joint North-South denuclearization agreement, and the NPT. North Korean officials initially denied Kelly's accusation but the next day admitted to the program and indicated they had more powerful weapons. They also offered to end the program if the United States vowed not to attack the DPRK, to conclude a formal peace treaty ending the Korean War, and to acknowledge North Korean sovereignty.[28] However, Washington was not interested.

The Bush administration viewed this in simple terms—North Korea had violated existing agreements and there would be no further negotiations until Pyongyang was back in compliance with these deals. In November 2002, Washington convinced KEDO to suspend the HFO deliveries and a year later, halted LWR construction. North Korea responded in December by removing the IAEA seals and surveillance equipment at the Yongbyon facility and restarting operations, including reloading the 5 MW reactor with new fuel rods, accessing the spent fuel that was scheduled for removal under the Agreed Framework, and restarting the reprocessing facility. Pyongyang ordered the departure of IAEA inspectors, and the last one left on December 31, 2002. An IAEA spokesperson lamented, "Now we virtually have no possibility to monitor North Korea's nuclear activities nor to provide any assurances to the international community that they are not producing a nuclear weapon."[29] The North Korean ambassador to Russia, Pak Ui-chun explained: "North Korea is not currently able to meet its commitments under the Treaty on the Nonproliferation of Nuclear Weapons—this is the fault of the United States."[30] Ten days later, North Korea followed through on an earlier threat and announced its withdrawal from the NPT on January 10, effective the following day. Though a ninety-day period is required from announcement to formal withdrawal, North Korea maintained the clock had already started in 1993 and its decision to suspend its departure with one day remaining meant only one additional day was required in 2003 to finalize its exit, making North Korea the only member ever to leave the NPT. For all intents and purposes, the Agreed Framework was dead.

In the wake of the Agreed Framework's demise, the Bush administration softened its position somewhat by offering the possibility of talks and authorizing an informal visit by New Mexico governor Bill Richardson, who was the U.S. representative to the UN during the Clinton administration and had maintained a good working relationship with North Korea. Hardliners in the administration were vehemently opposed to this approach believing the only sound policy was increased pressure and isolation to coerce DPRK compliance. Yet, while being open to dialogue, the policy continued to require North Korea to relinquish its nuclear program first in return for economic aid, energy assistance, and a formal security guarantee. For North Korea, this was a non-starter that meant surrendering all of its leverage before receiving any of the benefits. The DPRK Foreign Ministry maintained: "in essence, there is no change in the U.S. conditional stand that it would have dialogue with the D.P.R.K. only after it scraps its 'nuclear program.' It is clear that the U.S. talk about dialogue is nothing but a deceptive drama to mislead the world public opinion."[31]

The Bush administration was also pushed by other leaders to soften the U.S. position. In December 2002, ROK voters elected Roh Moo-hyun to succeed Kim Dae-jung. Roh was also a proponent of engagement and continuing Kim's "sunshine policy." As president-elect, Roh was adamant on the need for dialogue and argued, "We cannot face or embrace war with North Korea. It is such a catastrophic result that I cannot even imagine. We have to handle the North-South relations in such a way that we do not have to face such a situation."[32]

Chinese leaders were also concerned about ratcheting up pressure on North Korea. While Beijing strongly supported the goal of denuclearization and was often frustrated with Pyongyang's intransigence, it feared increased pressure might provoke North Korea to lash out, or worse yet, would collapse the regime. Instability in North Korea raised a host of dangerous possibilities, and China believed diplomacy was the best course of action.[33] Thus, pressure from both Seoul and Beijing pushed Washington to soften its policy and as a result, another major diplomatic initiative was on the horizon to seek the denuclearization of North Korea.

Six-Party Talks (2003–07)

As calls for dialogue increased, a debate ensued over the format of these efforts—should the meetings be bilateral talks or broader multilateral venues that involved others? In particular, North Korea was insistent that the central issues were largely between Washington and Pyongyang and needed to be settled in bilateral meetings. However, the United States maintained that the North's nuclear weapons program was a regional security concern and that reaching a solution, particularly ensuring that others had a stake in North Korea's compliance and reducing the likelihood of North Korea reneging on any agreement, required a multilateral forum.[34] In April 2003, North Korea agreed to a hybrid event where U.S. and North Korean negotiators met in Beijing with China acting as a mediator. Eventually, Pyongyang relented to calls for a multilateral forum and on August 27, 2003, less than a year since the United States had leveled accusations of an enriched uranium program, the first formal gathering of what became known as the Six-Party Talks commenced in Beijing. The six participants included South Korea, North Korea, the United States, China, Japan, and Russia.

At the start of the first meeting, North Korea offered a detailed, incremental proposal for the United States to normalize relations with the North, provide a formal nonaggression treaty, finish construction of the LWRs and restart HFO deliveries as specified in the Agreed Framework, provide increased food aid, and stop efforts to restrict DPRK economic cooperation with other countries. In return, North Korea pledged to dismantle its nuclear facility and halt the testing and export of ballistic missiles. North Korea also denied that it had a uranium enrichment program but threatened to test a nuclear weapon. After the meeting, North Korea made it clear that if their "reasonable proposal is turned aside, we will judge that the U.S. does not intend to give up its attempt to stifle the D.P.R.K. by force. In this case the D.P.R.K. cannot dismantle its nuclear deterrent force but will have no option but to increase it."[35] However, the United States held to its position that no political or economic benefits would be forthcoming until North Korea ended its nuclear program.

The meeting concluded without a consensus joint document but China released a statement that noted several points of agreement, including a commitment to address the issue through dialogue, obtain a nuclear-free Korean Peninsula while recognizing North Korea's security needs, including an understanding to avoid any actions that would worsen matters. Most importantly, all parties agreed to meet again for another round of talks.

The second round began on February 25, 2004, and lasted for four days. At the outset, Chinese and Russian negotiators announced that North Korea had indicated to them that it was willing to give up its nuclear weapon ambitions but insisted on retaining a civilian nuclear energy program, a position both Beijing and Moscow supported.[36] However, the United States, Japan, and South Korea opposed this option and insisted that all elements of North Korea's nuclear program must be eliminated. In particular, they were skeptical that North Korea could effectively utilize nuclear reactors for power generation given the decrepit condition of its power grid and that this program would simply provide North Korea with cover for continuing its weapons program. Without complete abandonment of its nuclear program, North Korea would retain the infrastructure for a nuclear breakout sometime in the future. This was particularly worrisome since Pyongyang continued to deny the existence of its enriched uranium facilities. South Korea proposed as an alternative an interim agreement whereby North Korea would freeze and promise to dismantle its nuclear program in return for energy assistance, but there was no consensus on the proposal. In the end, the talks concluded with little progress but all parties agreed to meet again for another round that would include dividing into smaller working groups to address different issues.

A third round began June 23, 2004, with a new proposal initiated by South Korea and modified in consultation with Washington. The plan contained a detailed set of provisions tied to a timeline. First, North

Korea must commit to dismantling its nuclear program and within three months of this commitment, provide a complete disclosure of all of its nuclear materials and facilities, halt all operations at these facilities, seal the buildings, and allow access to international inspectors to verify these measures. When North Korea commits to this plan, South Korea, China, Japan, and Russia will resume HFO shipments, and the United States will furnish a provisional security guarantee to not invade the North or seek to remove the Kim Jong-il regime from power. Washington would also begin talks with Pyongyang to lift economic sanctions, conclude long-term agreements for energy assistance, and initiate programs to retrain North Korean nuclear scientists for other fields.[37] All of these concessions would be contingent on North Korea meeting the specified deadlines.

The U.S. willingness to provide concessions before complete and verifiable denuclearization was a significant shift from its previous position, and was, in part, a result of pressure it received from China, South Korea, and Japan. China had expressed concerns that the rigid U.S. position was the chief obstacle to progress in the talks,[38] and South Korea and Japan had also indicated that they believed North Korea might be ready to bargain if an appealing deal were on the table.[39] In addition, China, Japan, and South Korea appeared to be pressing ahead with their own proposals with the possibility that Washington might be left behind as they concluded separate deals with Pyongyang. Finally, though hardliners in the Bush administration opposed concessions, they did see these circumstances as an opportunity to test North Korean intent. As they saw it, when Pyongyang would give its expected rejection of the proposal, their position would be vindicated and the United States would be well placed to press others to follow their lead. As one Bush administration official noted, "Our allies have been telling us that they think Kim Jong Il is ready for a test of his intentions. So we are prepared to offer them a strategic choice."[40]

North Korea responded that it would freeze its program in return for concessions but as an interim step toward denuclearization if the concessions were received. DPRK negotiators indicated the proposal would be considered further, and the talks ended with little substantive progress. However, all sides agreed that any process going forward would need to be incremental and reciprocal with "words for words" and "action for action."[41]

A month later, North Korea changed its mind and rejected the proposal. During a seminar in Washington, D.C., North Korea's UN ambassador, Pak Gil Yon, maintained that the United States was to blame for the lack of progress. North Korea "will give up its nuclear program if conditions are met through ending the USA's hostile policy against it. Mistrust and misunderstandings are the biggest obstacles" to DPRK-U.S. relations.[42] Pak indicated that the proposal had some merit but "we also found a lot of regrettable elements in it. We concluded it was a roadmap to disarm [North Korea] step by step."[43] Further dialogue came to a stand-still until the outcome of the November 2004 U.S. presidential election.

George W. Bush won a second term, defeating John Kerry, but the Six-Party Talks were slow to resume, in part because North Korea waited to see if a second-term Bush administration might change its approach. The early signs from Washington were not encouraging for Pyongyang. In her Senate confirmation hearings in January 2005 for secretary of state, Condoleezza Rice included North Korea in her list of six countries that were "outposts of tyranny" and maintained, "We must remain united in insisting that Iran and North Korea abandon their nuclear weapons."[44] North Korea followed with an announcement that it had produced nuclear weapons and that it would no longer be bound by its 2000 missile testing moratorium. In spring 2005, North Korea announced that it had unloaded the eight thousand fuel rods from the Yongbyon reactor and, a few weeks later, added that it had begun to reprocess the fuel rods and had reloaded the reactor with new fuel rods. Pyongyang also indicated it had little interest in returning to the Six-Party Talks.

As tensions were growing and Washington feared North Korea might soon test a nuclear weapon, on July 9, 2005, Christopher Hill, U.S. Assistant Secretary of State for East Asian and Pacific Affairs, and Kim Gye Gwan, DPRK vice foreign minister, met in Beijing. During the meeting, Hill indicated that the United States would be willing to acknowledge North Korea's sovereignty and pledge that the United States had no intention to invade the North. Pyongyang was impressed by the changes in U.S. policy along with the softening of U.S. rhetoric in recent months and by Hill's willingness to reach out to North Korea.[45] As a result, Pyongyang indicated it would be willing to return to the Six-Party Talks.

The Fourth Round began on July 26, 2005, and after brief opening statements, the deliberations broke off into smaller working groups in what former U.S. negotiator Jack Pritchard called "actual negotiations," where Hill was allowed more freedom of maneuver by the administration.[46] After several weeks of talks, negotiators adjourned and agreed to reconvene in September. The Fourth Round restarted on September 13, and in a few days negotiators achieved a breakthrough.

On September 19, the group announced the conclusion of the Joint Statement outlining a detailed plan for North Korea to relinquish its nuclear weapons program in return for a series of concessions.[47] The opening clause noted that the goal was "the verifiable denuclearization of the Korean Peninsula in a peaceful manner" and that "the DPRK committed to abandoning all nuclear weapons and existing nuclear programs and returning, at an early date, to the Treaty on the Non-Proliferation of Nuclear Weapons and to IAEA safeguards." In return, the United States stated it had no intention to attack or invade North Korea, and Washington and Seoul agreed not to deploy nuclear weapons on the peninsula. North Korea maintained its right to use peaceful nuclear energy, and the other signatories agreed to discuss providing LWRs "at an appropriate time." The United States and Japan consented to work toward normal relations with North Korea, and in the case of Japan, to settle past issues of concern, in particular the abductee issue. All agreed to promote energy cooperation and provide North Korea with energy assistance. Finally, the parties agreed to work for regional peace and stability and, later, to seek a peace regime on the Korean Peninsula. The agreement concluded with a pledge to implement the deal consistent with the principle of "commitment for commitment, action for action," and to meet again in early November.

The September deal was a major development that laid out a feasible, step-by-step plan that had a chance to reach the goal of denuclearizing the Korean Peninsula. However, obstacles were already in play that would scuttle the agreement. First, during the September meetings, the U.S. Treasury Department announced its designation of Banco Delta Asia in Macau as a "primary money laundering concern" under the USA Patriot Act for the services it provided to North Korean entities involved in illegal activities and the circulation of counterfeit U.S. currency.[48] The measure froze $25 million in North Korean funds and Pyongyang later threatened to void the September agreement if the sanctions were not lifted.

A second issue involved the LWR provision. North Korea maintained that the agreement provided assurances that the LWRs would be provided and were, in fact, part of the deal. The United States countered that the LWRs were not guaranteed and that their delivery was contingent on North Korea following through on its commitments and only after the dismantling of its nuclear program.

Delegates met as scheduled in November for a fifth round of talks with a focus on implementing the September agreement, but the meetings were contentious. On the first day, North Korea was quick to condemn the Banco Delta sanctions, accusing the United States of "spoiling the atmosphere" and that U.S. negotiators rejected the North's offer to freeze its program in return for aid.[49] The meeting adjourned two days later without further progress.

Negotiations remained on hold for several months and were compounded by other ominous events that raised serious doubts about the possibility of further dialogue, placing the entire September agreement in jeopardy. In July 2006, North Korea launched several missiles, including short-range SCUD missiles, medium-range Nodong missiles, and a long-range Taepodong-2 that blew up shortly after launch. Then, on October 9, 2006, North Korea joined the nuclear club with its first nuclear weapon test. A few days later, the UN Security Council passed Resolution 1718 that condemned the North's actions, called on Pyongyang to rejoin the Six-Party Talks, and imposed sanctions on the import of luxury goods and trade for military equipment, including materials and technology for nuclear weapons and ballistic missiles.

The spate of missile tests and North Korea's first nuclear weapon test added an increased sense of urgency; if implementation of the 2005 agreement had any chance, the process had to be put back on track soon. Six-Party Talks resumed on February 8, 2007, for another session of the Fifth Round. The meeting appeared to make progress in delineating steps in an "Initial Action Plan" for implementation. In the plan, North Korea committed to closing and sealing its nuclear facilities at Yongbyon and developing a declaration of all its nuclear materials and facilities. Washington and Tokyo committed to resuming bilateral talks with Pyongyang on outstanding issues of concern. The United States agreed to start a process to remove North Korea from the State Department list of states that sponsor terrorism, and end the sanctions under the Trading with the Enemy Act. The parties agreed to provide the North with an initial fifty thousand tons of HFO and an additional 950,000 tons upon delivery of North Korea's fissile material and facilities declaration. Members also agreed to form five working groups to address a variety of remaining issues. These measures were given a sixty day deadline to complete, and talks would resume for a sixth round on March 19, 2007.

The dialogue resumed as scheduled but broke up after a few days with North Korea angry over the delayed release of the $25 million held in Banco Delta Asia. In April, Washington agreed to release the money, and North Korea confirmed receipt of the funds in June. The five working groups met again in July but little was accomplished.

The group convened once more on September 27, 2007, and, over the next few days, made progress in drafting a second action plan for implementing the 2005 agreement. On October 3, the parties issued a joint statement where North Korea committed to dismantling all of its nuclear facilities at Yongbyon and providing a "complete and correct declaration of all its nuclear programs—including clarification regarding the uranium issue."[50] North Korea had until December 31, 2007, to provide this information. Pyongyang also agreed to not transfer nuclear technology or material to any third parties. In return, the other participants pledged to provide the remaining 950,000 tons of HFO promised in the February agreement. The United States also renewed its pledge to remove North Korea from the terrorism list and Trading with the Enemy Act sanctions.[51]

North Korea did not meet the December 31 deadline, and the United States was slow to remove the North from the State Department terrorism list. Much of 2008 was spent in negotiations over what should be in the North Korean declaration of nuclear facilities and material. Another contentious issue was the verification protocols to ensure North Korean compliance. Eventually, Pyongyang agreed on a draft verification agreement but that also soon started to unravel over the details.

The death knell for the Six-Party Process came in Spring 2009. In February, reports began to surface that North Korea was preparing for another launch of a Taepodong-2 missile. Pyongyang maintained the purpose of the launch was to place a communications satellite in orbit. Washington, Seoul, and Tokyo warned North Korea in no uncertain terms to not follow through with the launch, maintaining it was simply cover for what would be a long-range missile test. Despite these objections, North Korea launched the missile on April 5, and though it claimed the endeavor was a success, the U.S. military confirmed that the launched had failed.[52]

Soon after, the UN Security Council issued a presidential statement condemning the launch as a violation of UNSC 1718 and called for expanding the sanctions in that resolution.[53] The next day, North Korea announced that it would no longer participate in the Six-Party Talks and would not be bound by any of its previous agreements. North Korea also expelled IAEA inspectors from Yongbyon. To make matters worse, on May 25, 2009, North Korea conducted its second nuclear weapons test.

Though there have been subsequent calls to restart the Six-Party process, no further talks have taken place.

Leap Day Agreement

The Six-Party talks came to an end in the early years of the Obama administration, yet Obama entered the White House with a willingness to reach out to North Korea. In his inauguration, he offered troublesome regimes a willingness to "extend a hand if you are willing to unclench your fist."[54] However, North Korea's response was more testing, and, in 2010, made it even more difficult to restart engagement with the sinking of the ROK warship *Cheonan* and the shelling of the South Korean island of Yeonpyeong.

In July 2011, with prodding from Seoul, the United States and North Korea held a round of bilateral meetings to restart the denuclear- ization process. Another round of talks occurred in October and after a brief hiatus caused by the death of Kim Jong-il on December 17, 2011, and subsequent succession of Kim Jong-un, restarted again in February 2012. On February 29, the United States and North Korea announced in separate statements the details of an agreement dubbed the "Leap Day Deal."[55] In the pact, North Korea committed to a moratorium on nuclear weapon and ballistic missile testing, shutting down the Yongbyon facility, and allowing the return of inspectors. In return, the United States would provide 240,000 tons of food aid.

The Leap Day Deal was a positive start and it was viewed by many as an indication that perhaps Kim Jong-un might be more amenable to returning to a negotiated denuclearization process. However, it was not long before a serious complication arose with the arrangement. While the United States intended the missile moratorium to apply to all missiles, North Korea maintained that space launch vehicles were not included in the ban. U.S. negotiators made it clear that a satellite launch was tan- tamount to a ballistic missile test and would nullify the deal. During negotiations, Washington pressed this issue but Pyongyang would not agree and each side opted for a separate statement with different language. The United States gambled that North Korea would not follow through, but that was not to be the case.[56] In March, North Korea announced its intention to conduct the satellite launch on April 13, 2012, a Unha-3 missile carrying a weather satellite to commemorate the one hundredth anniversary of Kim Il-sung's birthday. The launch was a failure, with the missile blowing up shortly after takeoff, and the United States cancelled the deal, as expected. The UN Security Council condemned the launch and dialogue again looked like a remote possibility.

Having reached out to North Korea, and concluded a deal that had considerable risk, only to be burned in the end, Obama was reluctant to use any further political capital attempting to engage North Korea. Instead, the Obama administration settled in on a policy that has been called "strategic patience." As Obama's national security advisor Susan Rice noted: "We are prepared for negotiations, provided that they are authentic and credible, get at the entirety of the North's nuclear program, and result in concrete and irreversible steps toward denuclearization. Pyongyang's attempts to engage in dialogue while keeping critical elements of its weapons programs running are unacceptable, and they will not succeed."[57] The United States remained willing to dialogue but would hold North Korea to any agreements it had previously signed and maintain economic sanctions and diplomatic pressure until North Korea was ready to return to the table. The policy was a recognition of the difficulty in finding a solution and the need for patience. But to South Korea, strategic patience demonstrated that North Korea was no longer a top U.S. priority. The Obama administration came to an end with little progress on denuclearization but with significant advancements in North Korea's nuclear and missile programs.[58]

The Trump Administration and the Revival of Diplomacy

In an election that defied many of the pollsters, Donald Trump defeated Hillary Clinton in the 2016 presidential election bringing a unique style to the White House and a president who had no experience in foreign affairs. When Obama met with Trump in the closing days of his administration, he told the president-elect that North Korea would be the most difficult problem he would have to contend with.[59] During the first year of the Trump administration, North Korea lived up to this prediction with more than twenty missile tests and a nuclear weapons test that was possibly a hydrogen bomb. Throughout the year, invective flew back and forth between Washington and Pyongyang with Trump threatening "little rocket man" with "fire and fury" and Kim Jong-un calling Trump a "dot-ard." It is not an overstatement to say that war on the Korean Peninsula appeared to be a distinct possibility and negotiations a distant memory.

The surprise and welcome reversal came on January 1, 2018. After a year of rising tensions, Kim Jong-un appeared to offer an olive branch in his New Year Address.[60] Kim repeated an earlier declaration that North Korea's nuclear deterrent was complete but also included an offer of talks with the South. With the 2018 Pyeongchang Winter Olympics approaching, Kim also held out the possibility of North Korean attendance. After these many months of rising tensions, this was the opening South Korean president Moon Jae-in was hoping for, and he moved quickly to capitalize on the opportunity. In rapid succession, a North Korean delegation led by Kim Yo-jong and Kim Yong-nam attended the Olympics and met with Moon for talks. Soon after, a South Korean delegation led by then-National Security Advisor Chung Eui-yong and Director of National Intelligence Suh Hoon traveled to Pyongyang to continue the dialogue with Kim Jong-un. At this March meeting, it was agreed that the two Korean leaders would meet for a summit meeting in April, and Kim indicated he would refrain from further missile and nuclear weapons testing. In addition, Kim gave the South Korea delegation a verbal invitation to deliver to President Trump for a summit sometime in spring.

A few days later, the South Korean delegates traveled to Washington to provide an update to the Trump administration and deliver Kim Jong-un's offer. Trump quickly accepted the invitation to meet Kim, much to the surprise of his advisors who would have urged caution to carefully consider the implications.[61] Later in the evening on March 8, the South Korean delegation made the formal announcement in front of the White House that Trump had accepted the invitation and would meet Kim sometime before May.[62]

The announcements of the South Korean and U.S. summits with North Korea opened the floodgates for a plethora of other meetings. Chinese president Xi Jinping and Kim Jong-un had yet to meet since Kim had come to power, a significant anomaly in Sino-DPRK relations. Once the U.S. and ROK summits were announced, Kim traveled to China and met Xi in March, prior to his meeting with Moon in April, and again in May before his second meeting with Moon that month.

Kim and Moon held their historic summit meeting at the Joint Security Area of Panmunjom on April 27 and produced the Panmunjom Declaration, wherein they pledged to improve inter-Korean relations and reduce military tensions. They also agreed to "cooperate to build a permanent and stable peace regime on the Korean peninsula" and "to make active efforts to seek the support and cooperation of the international community for the denuclearization of the Korean peninsula."[63]

The long awaited U.S.-North Korea summit finally took place in Singapore on June 12, 2018. For a short time, there were doubts the meeting would occur at all after the United States abruptly cancelled on May 24 in response to a harshly worded statement by Vice-Foreign Minister Choi Son-hui. However, two days later, Moon held another meeting with Kim and through his intercession, was able to get the meeting back on track. On June 1, Kim Yong-chol, North Korea's nuclear negotiator, delivered a letter from Kim Jong-un to the White House and the meeting was back on.[64]

Trump and Kim met in Singapore for two days of talks, the first meeting of a sitting U.S. president with a North Korean leader. The meeting concluded with a joint statement that contained four chief points: the United States and North Korea would work to "establish a new U.S.-DPRK relationship"; they would "seek to build a lasting and stable peace regime on the Korean Peninsula"; North Korea "commits to work toward complete denuclearization of the Korean Peninsula"; and both countries would cooperate to recover POW/MIA remains; and commit to hold follow-on talks at the earliest possible date.[65]

The meeting was historic and many lauded the progress toward peace and stability in Korea after several tumultuous years. Some, however, questioned the efficacy of the meeting. A Trump-Kim meeting put North Korea on the same stage as the United States which was in itself a huge U.S. concession and received little in return. Others argued that the order in which the summit occurred in a typical diplomatic process was backward. Usually, lower-level officials who are the policy and issue experts first hold multiple working-level meetings to hammer out the details. The leaders arrive at the end of the process to address any concluding points and formally sign the agreement. The Singapore summit reversed this order.

Others hailed the summit as an important effort to break a logjam that had been in place for several years and it was worth the risk along with any political costs for the leaders to meet face to face early. Moreover, though the meeting did not produce a detailed plan for moving forward, it was a start to laying the groundwork for further dialogue and developing concrete steps to achieve denuclearization. Shortly after the meeting, Trump exclaimed in two tweets that his meeting was successful and, "There is no longer a Nuclear Threat from North Korea. Meeting with Kim Jong Un was an interesting and very positive experience . . . sleep well tonight!"[66] However, a great deal of work remained for such an optimistic assessment, and it was not long afterward that reports of North Korea's growing nuclear program undercut this hopeful appraisal.[67]

After Singapore, Kim traveled the next week to Beijing for another meeting with Xi Jinping to brief him on the summit. In mid-September, Kim and Moon met again, this time in Pyongyang, and, simultaneously, North and South Korean defense officials concluded the Comprehensive Measures Agreement that sought to reduce military tensions and implement concrete confidence-building measures, particularly along the demilitarized zone.[68]

Despite the expectations in the wake of Singapore, the months that followed showed few signs of progress, and did not produce a detailed roadmap for next steps. On September 11, 2018, the White House announced that plans were underway for a second summit between Kim and Trump, and later, the United States confirmed that the meeting would take place on February 27–28, 2019 in Hanoi, Vietnam. Hopes were high that Trump and Kim would be able to add some detail to the scant framework that came from Singapore and produce a detailed plan for reaching denuclearization that might be part of a "small deal" to advance the process in an incremental fashion.

When the meetings began, it became clear that both sides came to Hanoi with ambitious goals that would be difficult to achieve.[69] During an early session, Trump passed Kim a note that asked him to relinquish all of his nuclear weapons and material up front to be followed by economic and political concessions, a proposal akin to the "Libya model" where Qaddafi gave up his nuclear program early in the process.[70] On many occasions in the past Pyongyang had indicated that this proposal was a non-starter and Kim's answer was no different now. North Korea countered that it would be willing to close and dismantle its facilities at Yongbyon, a move that would essentially end its plutonium path to nuclear weapons, and U.S. inspectors could observe and verify these measures. Kim would also be willing to codify his nuclear and missile testing moratorium. In return, Kim asked for the lifting of economic sanctions imposed in 2016 and 2017.

After the summit, Trump characterized Kim's request as lifting all economic sanctions, but Kim was asking only for relief from the five most recent UN sanctions measures of the eleven that had been enacted. However, these were the measures having the greatest impact on the North's economy. Trump asked Kim if he could possibly add more to his offer, perhaps agree to a partial reduction in the sanctions relief he was requesting but Kim would not agree. If Kim had altered his initial offer, it was possible Trump may have been willing to make a deal.[71] With no apparent room for further negotiation, the United States abruptly terminated the summit and cancelled the luncheon that was to conclude the meetings. DPRK Foreign Minister Ri Yong-ho declared: "This proposal was the biggest denuclearization measure we can take at the present stage in relation to the current level of confidence between the DPRK and the United States," but Trump later remarked at his press conference before departing Hanoi, that "sometimes you have to walk. This was one of those times."[72]

Instead of either a big deal or small deal, the result was no deal. Many were very disappointed that there had not been even minimal progress while others expressed relief that President Trump had not leapt into a bad deal that offered far too many concessions with little in return from the North. Though the possibility of a third meeting had not been foreclosed, it was clear that another summit without any certainty of success, regardless of how each side defined that differently, was a risky proposition for both leaders.

In June 2019, Kim and Trump exchanged letters that spoke highly of the relationship they had developed and left the door open for further talks. Later in June, Trump was in Tokyo to attend the G-20 meeting and tweeted a message intended for Kim that "I would meet him at the Border/DMZ just to shake his hand and say Hello(?)!"[73] The next day, June 30, Trump, Kim, and Moon met for an impromptu meeting at Panmunjom. Though the meeting accomplished nothing of substance, it did help sustain whatever momentum remained after Hanoi.

A round of working-level meetings took place in Stockholm, Sweden, in October 2019, but this time it was North Korea's turn to end the meeting abruptly, with chief negotiator Kim Myong Gil complaining: "It is entirely because the U.S. has not discarded its old stance and attitude that the negotiation failed this time. The U.S. came to the negotiations empty-handed and this shows after all it is not willing to solve the issue."[74] North Korea continued to slam the U.S. position but refrained from criticizing Trump directly and remained positive regarding the relationship Kim had with Trump. U.S. officials disagreed with the North's assessment of the meeting; U.S. negotiators had brought new ideas to the talks, and the discussions were productive, adding: "The United States and the DPRK will not overcome a legacy of 70 years of war and hostility on the Korean peninsula through the course of a single Saturday. These are weighty issues, and they require a strong commitment by both countries."[75]

There was one more possibility the following year, though a long shot, for diplomacy between Washington and Pyongyang. With the 2020 U.S. presidential election approaching in November, some began to suggest the preceding summer of the possibility of an "October surprise" where Trump might meet Kim for another meeting, in large part to boost his reelection fortunes. Arranging a summit during the COVID pandemic in the middle of the campaign was a daunting proposition from the outset and most assessments maintained this was unlikely. In the end, the summit did not happen and negotiations have remained on hold during the Biden administration, despite several efforts to reach out the North Korea.

Conclusion

For more than forty years, the players have sought to maintain a nuclear-free Korean Peninsula. Despite multiple efforts to convince or coerce North Korea to relinquish its nuclear ambitions using a variety of forums and approaches, negotiations have been unable to achieve lasting results. Why was success so elusive? Was there ever an opportunity for success? Did the players miss an opportunity because they were intent on concluding a comprehensive agreement? Were the interests, goals, and strategies of the individual players insufficiently aligned for success to occur? This chapter provided an overview of the history to help set the stage for finding answers to these questions. The next six chapters will provide detailed assessments from the perspective of the six major players—North Korea, South Korea, the United States, China, Japan, and Russia.

Notes

1. The views expressed in this report are the author's alone and do not represent the official position of the Department of the Navy, the Department of Defense, or the U.S. government.

2. This chapter benefited from four detailed chronologies of North Korea's nuclear weapons program: Arms Control Association, "Chronology of U.S.-North

Korean Nuclear and Missile Diplomacy," July 2020, https://www.armscontrol.org/factsheets/dprkchron; "North Korea—Nuclear," Nuclear Threat Initiative, October 2018, https://www.nti.org/learn/countries/north-korea/nuclear/; Eleanor Albert, "North Korean Nuclear Negotiations (1985–2019)," Council on Foreign Relations, July 2, 2019, https://www.cfr.org/timeline/north-korean-nuclear-negotiations; and "Nuclear Negotiations with North Korea," CRS Reports, R45033, May 4, 2021, https://crsreports.congress.gov/product/pdf/R/R45033.

3. Roger Dingman, "Atomic Diplomacy During the Korean War," *International Security* 13, no. 3 (Winter 1988–89): 50–91, and Rosemary Foote, "Nuclear Coercion and the Ending of the Korean Conflict," *International Security* 13, no. 3 (Winter 1988–89): 92–112.

4. Jonathan D. Pollack, *No Exit: North Korea, Nuclear Weapons, and International Security* (New York: Routledge, 2011), 56.

5. Terence Roehrig, *Japan, South Korea, and the United States Nuclear Umbrella: Deterrence after the Cold War* (New York: Columbia University Press, 2017): 56–62.

6. James Person and William Stueck, "Unfinished War, Unfinished Questions: A Historical Perspective on the Korean War," Korea Economic Institute of America, June 24, 2020, https://www.youtube.com/watch?v=ogiv1bU_IDU.

7. Michael J. Mazarr, *North Korea and the Bomb: A Case Study in Nonproliferation* (New York: St. Martin's Press, 1995), 35–54.

8. Don Oberdorfer, *The Two Koreas: A Contemporary History*, 2nd ed. (New York: Basic Books, 1997), 254.

9. Oberdorfer, 254.

10. "Agreement on Reconciliation, Non-aggression and Exchanges and Cooperation between the South and the North," December 13, 1991, available at NCNK, https://www.ncnk.org/sites/default/files/content/resources/publications/North_South_1991_Agreement.pdf.

11. "Joint Declaration of South and North Korea on the Denuclearization of the Korean Peninsula," February 19, 1992, available at Nuclear Threat Initiative, https://media.nti.org/documents/korea_denuclearization.pdf.

12. For a detailed examination of the events of this nuclear crisis, see Joel S. Wit, Daniel B. Poneman, and Robert L. Gallucci, *Going Critical: The First North Korean Nuclear Crisis* (Washington, D.C.: Brookings, 2004).

13. United Nations, "Treaty on the Non-Proliferation of Nuclear Weapons (NPT)," July 1, 1968, https://www.un.org/disarmament/wmd/nuclear/npt/text.

14. Michael R. Gordon, "U.S. Will Urge U.N. to Plan Sanctions for North Korea," *New York Times*, March 20, 1994.

15. Leon V. Segal, *Disarming Strangers: Nuclear Diplomacy with North Korea* (Princeton: Princeton University Press, 1998), 150–62.

16. Full text available at: "Agreed Framework between the United States of America and the Democratic People's Republic of Korea," US Department of State, October 21, 1994, https://2001-2009.state.gov/t/ac/rls/or/2004/31009.htm.

17. Pat Towell, "Senators Grudgingly Accept Nuclear Agreement," *Congressional Quarterly*, January 28, 1995, 294.

18. Nancy Mathis, "U.S.-N. Korea Must Comply before Aid Is Considered," *Houston Chronicle*, June 13, 1994, A9.

19. Jeffrey Lewis, "Revisiting the Agreed Framework," *38 North*, May 15, 2015, https://www.38north.org/2015/05/jlewis051415/.

20. Sheila Smith, *Japan Rearmed: The Politics of Military Power* (Cambridge: Harvard University Press, 2019), 100–13.

21. William J. Perry, "Review of United States Policy toward North Korea: Findings and Recommendations," U.S. Department of State, October 12, 1999, https://1997-2001.state.gov/regions/eap/991012_northkorea_rpt.html.

22. Uk Heo and Terence Roehrig, *South Korea's Rise: Economic Development, Power, and Foreign Policy* (Cambridge: Cambridge University Press, 2014), 37–44.

23. David E. Sanger, "Bush Tells Seoul Talks with North Won't Resume Now," *New York Times*, March 8, 2001, https://www.nytimes.com/2001/03/08/world/bush-tells-seoul-talks-with-north-won-t-resume-now.html.

24. George W. Bush, "State of the Union Address," January 29, 2002, https://georgewbush-whitehouse.archives.gov/news/releases/2002/01/20020129-11.html.

25. Terence Roehrig, "Korean Dispute over the Northern Limit Line: Security, Economics, or International Law?," Maryland Series in Contemporary Asian Studies 2008, no. 3, Article 1, https://digitalcommons.law.umaryland.edu/mscas/vol2008/iss3/1.

26. Mary Beth Nikitin, "North Korea's Nuclear Weapons: Technical Issues," Congressional Research Service, April 3, 2013, 10–12, https://fas.org/sgp/crs/nuke/RL34256.pdf.

27. Jonathan D. Pollack, *No Exit: North Korea, Nuclear Weapons, and International Security* (Abington: Routledge, 2011), 132.

28. Doug Struck, "Nuclear Program Not Negotiable, U.S. Told N. Korea," *Washington Post*, October 20, 2002, A18.

29. James Brooke, "South Opposes Pressuring North Korea, Which Hints It Will Scrap Nuclear Pact," *New York Times*, January 1, 2003, https://www.nytimes.com/2003/01/01/world/threats-responses-weapons-south-opposes-pressuring-north-korea-which-hints-it.html.

30. Brooke, "South Opposes Pressuring North Korea."

31. Howard W. French, "2 Koreas Agree to Resume Talks on Nuclear Crisis," *New York Times*, January 16, 2003, https://www.nytimes.com/2003/01/16/world/threats-responses-korean-peninsula-2-koreas-agree-resume-talks-nuclear-crisis.html.

32. Howard W. French, "South Korea's President-Elect Rejects Use of Force against North Korea," *New York Times*, January 17, 2003, https://www.nytimes.com/2003/01/17/world/threats-responses-korean-peninsula-south-korea-s-president-elect-rejects-use.html.

33. Lyle J. Goldstein, *Meeting China Halfway: How to Defuse the Emerging US-China Rivalry* (Washington, D.C.: Georgetown University Press, 2015), 191–223.

34. Charles L. Pritchard, *Failed Diplomacy: The Tragic Story of How North Korea Got the Bomb* (Washington, D.C.: Brookings, 2007), 84–106.

35. Joseph Kahn, "Korea Arms Talks Close with Plans for a New Round," *New York Times*, August 30, 2003, https://www.nytimes.com/2003/08/30/world/korea-arms-talks-close-with-plans-for-a-new-round.html.

36. Joseph Kahn, "U.S. and North Korea Agree to More Talks," *New York Times*, February 29, 2004, https://www.nytimes.com/2004/02/29/world/us-and-north-korea-agree-to-more-talks.html.

37. Terence Roehrig, *From Deterrence to Engagement: the US Defense Commitment to South Korea* (Lanham, MD: Lexington 2006), 221.

38. Joseph Kahn and Susan Chira, "Chinese Official Challenges U.S. Stance on North Korea," *New York Times*, June 9, 2004, https://www.nytimes.com/2004/06/09/world/chinese-official-challenges-us-stance-on-north-korea.html.

39. David E. Sanger, "About-Face on North Korea: Allies Helped," *New York Times*, June 23, 2004, https://www.nytimes.com/2004/06/24/world/the-reach-of-war-about-face-on-north-korea-allies-helped.html.

40. David E. Sanger, "U.S. to Offer North Korea Incentives in Nuclear Talks," *New York Times*, June 23, 2004, https://www.nytimes.com/2004/06/23/world/us-to-offer-north-korea-incentives-in-nuclear-talks.html.

41. *Xinhua News Agency*, "Chairman's Statement of Third Round of Six-Party Talks," June 26, 2004, http://www.china.org.cn/english/3rd/99447.htm.

42. Glenn Kessler, "North Korean U.N. Envoy Visits Capitol Hill," *Washington Post*, July 21, 2004, A15.

43. Kessler, "North Korean U.N. Envoy Visits Capitol Hill."

44. "Rice Names 'Outposts of Tyranny,'" *BBC*, January 19, 2005, http://news.bbc.co.uk/2/hi/americas/4186241.stm.

45. Charles L. Pritchard, "Six Party Talks Update: False Start or a Case for Optimism?" Working Paper, December 1, 2005, https://www.brookings.edu/wp-content/uploads/2016/07/20051201presentation.pdf.

46. Pritchard, "Six Party Talks Update."

47. U.S. Department of State, "Joint Statement of the Fourth Round of the Six-Party Talks," September 19, 2005, https://2001-2009.state.gov/r/pa/prs/ps/2005/53490.htm.

48. U.S. Department of the Treasury, "Treasury Designates Banco Delta Asia as Primary Money Laundering Concern under USA PATRIOT Act," September 15, 2005, https://www.treasury.gov/press-center/press-releases/pages/js2720.aspx.

49. Joseph Kahn, "North Korea and U.S. Spar, Causing Talks to Stall," *New York Times*, November 12, 2005, https://www.nytimes.com/2005/11/12/world/europe/north-korea-and-us-spar-causing-talks-to-stall.html?searchResultPosition=4.

50. U.S. Department of State, "Six Parties October 3, 2007 Agreement on 'Second-Phase Actions for the Implementation of the Joint Statement,'" https://2001-2009.state.gov/r/pa/prs/ps/2007/oct/93223.htm.

51. Terence Roehrig, "North Korea and the US State Sponsors of Terrorism List," *Pacific Focus* 24:1 (April 2009): 82–106.

52. William J. Broad, "North Korean Missile Launch Was a Failure, Experts Say," *New York Times*, April 5, 2009, https://www.nytimes.com/2009/04/06/world/asia/06korea.html.

53. UN Security Council, "Statement by the President of the Security Council," April 13, 2009, http://www.securitycouncilreport.org/atf/cf/%7B65BFCF9B-6D27-4E9C-8CD3-CF6E4FF96FF9%7D/NKorea%20SPRST%2020097.pdf.

54. Barak Obama, "Inaugural Address," *New York Times*, January 20, 2009, https://www.nytimes.com/2009/01/20/us/politics/20text-obama.html.

55. Daniel Wertz and Chelsea Gannon, "A History of U.S.-DPRK Relations," National Committee on North Korea, November 2017, 7, https://www.ncnk.org/sites/default/files/US_DPRK_Relations_November2015.pdf.

56. Joel S. Wit, "The Leap Day Deal: A Cautionary Tale for the Trump Administration," 38 North, March 7, 2019, https://www.38north.org/2019/03/editor030719/.

57. White House Press Secretary, "Remarks as Prepared for Delivery by National Security Advisor Susan E. Rice," November 21, 2013, https://obamawhitehouse.archives.gov/the-press-office/2013/11/21/remarks-prepared-delivery-national-security-advisor-susan-e-rice.

58. Katharine H. S. Moon, "Caught in the Middle: How the North Korean Threat Is Ultimately Seoul's Problem," Brookings Institution, September 21, 2017, https://www.brookings.edu/blog/order-from-chaos/2017/09/21/caught-in-the-middle-how-the-north-korean-threat-is-ultimately-seouls-problem/.

59. Gerald F. Seib, Jay Solomon, and Carol E. Lee, "Barack Obama Warns Donald Trump on North Korea Threat," *Wall Street Journal*, November 22, 2016, https://www.wsj.com/articles/trump-faces-north-korean-challenge-1479855286.

60. Kim Jong-un, "New Year's Address," January 1, 2018, https://www.ncnk.org/node/1427.

61. Bob Woodward, *Rage* (New York: Simon and Schuster, 2020), 90–92.

62. Peter Baker and Choe Sang-hun, "With Snap 'Yes' in Oval Office, Trump Gambles on North Korea," *New York Times*, March 10, 2018, https://www.nytimes.com/2018/03/10/world/asia/trump-north-korea.html.

63. ROK Ministry of Foreign Affairs, "Panmunjom Declaration for Peace, Prosperity, and Unification of the Korean Peninsula," April 27, 2018, https://www.reuters.com/article/uk-northkorea-southkorea-summit-statemen/panmunjom-declaration-for-peace-prosperity-and-unification-of-the-korean-peninsula-idUKKBN1HY193.

64. Scott Horsley, "President Trump: Summit with Kim Jong Un Is On for June 12," *NPR*, June 1, 2018, https://www.npr.org/2018/06/01/616175971/top-north-korean-official-visits-president-trump-at-white-house.

65. "Joint Statement of President Donald J. Trump of the United States of America and Chairman Kim Jong Un of the Democratic People's Republic of Korea at the Singapore Summit," CNN, June 12, 2018, https://www.cnn.com/2018/06/12/politics/read-full-text-of-trump-kim-signed-statement/index.html.

66. "Trump Claims N. Korea No Longer Nuclear Threat, Tells Americans to 'Sleep Well,'" CBS News, June 13, 2018, https://www.cbsnews.com/news/trump-claims-end-to-nuclear-threat-from-n-korea-tells-u-s-to-sleep-well/.

67. David E. Sanger, "North Korea's Trump-Era Strategy: Keep Making A-Bombs, but Quietly," *New York Times*, September 16, 2018, https://www.nytimes.com/2018/09/16/world/asia/trump-north-korea-nuclear.html.

68. "Agreement on the Implementation of the Historic Panmunjom Declaration in the Military Domain," ROK Ministry of National Defense, September 19, 2018, https://ncnk.org/resources/publications/agreement-implementation-historic-panmunjom-declaration-military-domain.pdf.

69. Ankit Panda and Vipin Narang, "The Hanoi Summit Was Doomed from the Start," *Foreign Affairs*, March 5, 2019, https://www.foreignaffairs.com/articles/north-korea/2019-03-05/hanoi-summit-was-doomed-start.

70. John Bolton, *The Room Where It Happened: A White House Memoir* (New York: Simon and Schuster, 2020), 326–32.

71. Bolton, *The Room Where It Happened*, 326–32.

72. Shashank Bengali, Eli Stokols, Victoria Kim, "Trump Says He Still Trusts Kim, but Needed to 'Walk away' from a Bad Nuclear Deal," *Los Angeles Times*, February 29, 2018, https://www.latimes.com/world/la-fg-trump-kim-vietnam-summit-20190228-story.html.

73. David Nakamura, "In a Tweet, Trump Appears to Invite Kim Jong Un to Meet Him at the Korean Demilitarized Zone," *Washington Post*, June 29, 2019, https://www.washingtonpost.com/politics/in-a-tweet-trump-appears-to-invite-kim-jong-un-to-meet-him-at-the-korean-demilitarized-zone/2019/06/28/0e9fc900-99f9-11e9-830a-21b9b36b64ad_story.html.

74. William Gallo, "After North Korea Walks Away from Talks, Experts See Familiar Tactic," *Voice of America*, October 6, 2019, https://www.voanews.com/east-asia-pacific/after-north-korea-walks-away-talks-experts-see-familiar-tactic.

75. Gallo, "After North Korea Walks Away."

Chapter 3

North Korean Strategies and Responses

Scott A. Snyder

Following three decades of U.S. failure to achieve its objective of negotiated denuclearization with North Korea, it is reasonable to ask whether this objective was ever feasible. Under what conditions was North Korea's denuclearization possible and, if so, when did it become impossible? These questions have often arisen as part of the partisan political debate within the United States over who has come the closest to having effective policies toward North Korea. But the framing of debates over the relative merits of successive administration policies toward North Korea neglects to consider the question of whether North Korea's strategies, goals, and intentions have evolved based on its relative capabilities and fluctuations in threat perceptions, or whether North Korea's strategic goals have remained fixed on objectives that ultimately make it impossible to dissuade the country from its nuclear pursuits.

This chapter will consider both possibilities by reviewing more than three decades of efforts to persuade North Korea to pursue denuclearization. An assessment of North Korea's mindset, objectives, and strategies by way of both official and unofficial statements will set the stage for examining how North Korea has approached negotiations with the United States and clarify the role of nuclear weapons in North Korea's strategic plan to achieve its objectives. The paper will then review four periods of North Korean diplomatic engagement with the United States to gauge the evolution of North Korean statements and actions: the Geneva Agreed Framework (1993–94), the Six-Party Talks (2005–08), the Leap Day Agreement (2011–12), and the summitry between U.S. president Donald Trump and North Korean leader Kim Jong-un (2018–19).

The paper will further analyze three transition periods to identify changes influencing North Korean perceptions and behavior in negotiations with the United States: the period of KEDO (Korean Peninsula Energy Development Organization) implementation (1995–2002), North Korean nuclear and missile tests and provocations against South Korea (2009–11), and North Korean establishment of its *byungjin* policy, intensification of missile testing, and "fire and fury" (2013–17). The paper will conclude with a discussion of whether there were missed opportunities for denuclearization of North Korea, how North Korea views its relationship with the United States in relation to the issue of denuclearization, whether North Korean strategic objectives have evolved as a result of changes in capabilities, and the extent to which U.S. negotiating strategies have kept up with evolving North Korean objectives.

Factors Shaping North Korea's Worldview and Strategies

North Korea's objectives, self-perceptions, and behavior in the international community tie closely into the metanarrative surrounding its founder, Kim Il-sung. This narrative rests on the extensive hagiography around the establishment of Kim Il-sung's cult of personality and his inculcation within North Korean society as both a father figure and the brain center for North Korea. Kim's lifelong pursuit of the revolutionary objective of unifying the Korean people under his rule made the attainment of Korean unification on North Korean terms a strategic objective for the Democratic People's Republic of Korea (DPRK).

The central elements of North Korea's founding myth under Kim Il-sung include his use of a guerrilla mindset to offset advantages held by stronger opponents, distrust of outside influence due to risks of betrayal, self-reliance as a vehicle for encouraging xenophobia, and the value of making oneself the subject, or motive force, of historical narratives, rather than the object or victim of such narratives.[1] This combination of attributes and North Korea's peripheral position in the international community have contributed to a sense of North Korean exceptionalism and defiance of international norms, leading North Korea to seek nuclear capabilities as an equalizer in the face of its relative weakness and to attain self-reliance over dependence on potentially unreliable external patrons. It also made direct negotiations with the United States on an equal footing a powerful symbol of prestige and validation that could be portrayed domestically as a leadership accomplishment.

North Korea's leadership has seen the acquisition of nuclear capabilities as a solution to a number of problems. Certainly, the transformative power of nuclear weapons on international relations was embedded in Kim Il-sung's consciousness from the moment he saw his long-standing foes in the Japanese imperial army vanquished by the atomic weapons dropped on Hiroshima and Nagasaki at the end of World War II. The effectiveness of the threat of nuclear use was further impressed upon Kim by periodic U.S. threats to again brandish nuclear arms during the Korean War.

Kim saw early on that nuclear weapons development would reinforce North Korea's asymmetric capabilities to respond to aggression by more powerful neighbors, strengthening self-reliance and enhancing deterrence against nuclear adversaries. Second, nuclear weapons would give North Korea an asymmetric advantage over South Korea that might be used to thwart South Korea and negate its economic advantages, neutralize South Korean conventional superiority, and potentially extort South Korean economic payments to North Korea. Third, nuclear capability in combination with the development of a missile capability would provide North Korea with the capacity to employ mutual nuclear deterrence against the United States and to potentially neutralize U.S. support for the defense of South Korea.

But North Korea's attainment of nuclear capabilities has not been easy, or guaranteed. It has been a decades-long project that began in the 1950s and arguably came to fruition in 2006, when North Korea conducted its first nuclear test.[2] Even then, the United States redoubled its efforts to change North Korea's strategic calculus regarding the development of a nuclear arsenal both by imposing sustained costs and by providing alternative security pathways for North Korea. Such efforts may have slowed North Korea's pursuit of nuclear weapons, so to understand whether a deal might have been possible and to explore the conditions under which North Korea became irreversibly committed to a nuclear deterrence–based security-first policy, it is necessary to assess North Korea's approach to diplomacy with the United States.

Geneva Agreed Framework

The Geneva Agreed Framework, signed between chief U.S. negotiator Robert L. Gallucci and head of the North Korean delegation Kang Seok-ju on October 21, 1994, marked the end of a nearly two-year crisis, the details of which are described elsewhere in this volume. The negotiations began in June 1993, on the eve of the deadline for North Korea to execute its withdrawal from the Nuclear Non-Proliferation Treaty (NPT), and concluded with the signing of the U.S.-DPRK Agreed Framework on October 21, 1994, in Geneva.[3]

Negotiations to establish the Geneva Agreed Framework occurred in the context of the end of the Cold War, through which North Korea had lost its two primary patrons, the Soviet Union and the People's Republic of China. In response to the decision of those countries to normalize relations with South Korea, North Korea threatened to both Soviet foreign minister Eduard Schevardnadze and Chinese foreign minister Qian Qichen that it would pursue an independent pathway for securing North Korea's defense, implying a redoubling of North Korean efforts to attain nuclear weapons.[4] The end of the Cold War catalyzed a number of diplomatic initiatives, including the signing of the inter-Korean Agreement on Reconciliation, Nonaggression, Exchanges, and Cooperation (known as the Basic Agreement).[5] North Korea also expressed interest in better relations with the United States in an unprecedented U.S.-DPRK meeting in January 1992 between U.S. undersecretary of state Arnold Kanter and Korean Workers' Party International Department chairman Kim Yong-sun. North Korea joined the IAEA on January 30, 1992, agreeing to allow inspections of its nuclear facilities.[6] North Korean diplomatic outreach to South Korea, the United States, and the IAEA came in the context of dramatic political stresses on North Korea's leadership resulting from its loss of patronage from China and the collapse of the Soviet Union.[7] At the same time, following decades of investment in nuclear development, North Korea had completed a graphite-moderated plutonium-based reactor and had irradiated fuel rods containing a few kilograms of plutonium, possibly enough fissile material to build one to two nuclear weapons.[8] Moreover, waves of economic distress were hitting North Korea due to dramatic drops in the supply of food and energy from the Soviet Union and China.[9]

In joining the IAEA, North Korea apparently sought to allow pro forma inspections of its facilities to receive a good housekeeping seal of approval while continuing covert development of its nuclear program. North Korea did not realize that IAEA inspectors would retrieve samples from a glove box that provided information on the history of the program, including the prior removal and reloading of irradiated fuel rods that produced weapons-grade plutonium.[10] The subsequent crisis led to North Korea's declaration of withdrawal from the NPT and a UN call on the United States to engage in unprecedented direct negotiations with North Korea.[11] At two rounds of bilateral negotiations in June and July 1993, North Korea put forward its need to obtain additional energy resources, including the possible acquisition of a light water nuclear reactor for civilian energy production and its desire to improve relations with the United States.[12] Both objectives might have seemed even more important in light of the cutoff of support from North Korea's former allies.

As the first North Korean nuclear crisis was heating up, Kim Il-sung gave an interview to foreign journalists in Pyongyang in April 1994, asserting that "North Korea has neither the capability nor the desire to build up a nuclear arsenal. The world is now calling on North Korea to show a nuclear weapon we don't have." Kim also pointed to the absence of a missile system, which would have been necessary to deploy nuclear weapons against more distant targets.[13] At this stage, it was feasible to structure a negotiated settlement around denuclearization in part because North Korea still had limited capabilities or confidence that the country could attain nuclear capabilities.

The Geneva Agreed Framework provided a politically guaranteed economic transaction backed by a letter of assurance from the U.S. president pledging to provide North Korea with alternative nuclear energy sources to replace the North's ostensible need for nuclear energy. The agreement was accompanied by a political transaction involving the expectation of establishing liaison offices and normalizing political and economic relations between the United States and North Korea. The dual aim of the agreement suggests that North Korea's negotiation of the Agreed Framework hinged on a mix of economic, energy, and political objectives. North Korea's economic distress precluded serious progress in building a nuclear capability and its participation in the agreement reduced the risk of hostility from the United States as North Korea attempted to recover from that distress. The Agreed Framework bought time for North Korea to pursue that recovery and opened a small stream of income through trade and aid from the United States. It also partially offset losses from Chinese and Soviet assistance and forestalled the mounting economic crisis that ravaged North Korea and compounded the effects of a severe famine in the mid-1990s. The dual structure of the Agreed Framework suggests that North Korea was leaving its options open by seeking security through a transformed relationship with the United States, while hedging its bets with a suspended and latent nuclear development program until it could assess the costs and benefits of adhering to the Agreed Framework.

Transitional Developments: Agreed Framework Implementation, KEDO, and the Perry Process

Implementation of the Agreed Framework proved a complex undertaking, mostly due to obstacles on the U.S. side. The United States faced difficulties in raising money from the Japanese and South Korean governments to fund the construction of light water reactors in North Korea and faced resistance from North Korea to the selection of a South Korean reactor design and firm as the primary contractor. But the timetable for constructing light water reactors lagged and congressional threats not to authorize HFO funding cast doubts on whether the administration could count on Congress to ratify the nuclear cooperation agreement with North Korea necessary to complete reactor construction.[14]

Moreover, implementation of pledges to normalize relations between the United States and North Korea faced obstacles. North Korea harbored suspicions that a U.S. liaison office in Pyongyang might be used for spying and North Korea denied U.S. requests to allow diplomatic pouches to be conveyed across the Demilitarized Zone (DMZ) dividing the two Koreas, while North Korean site surveys in Washington, D.C., ground to a halt over the exorbitant expenses associated with establishing a North Korean diplomatic presence there. Meanwhile, South Koreans complained that North Korea was pursuing a *tongmi bongnam* (through the United States, marginalizing South Korea) strategy to cut out South Korea and balked at making improvements in inter-Korean relations.[15] The United States navigated these difficulties as it established an international consortium known as the Korean Peninsula Energy Development Organization (KEDO), including the United States, Japan, South Korea, and the European Union, to build a South Korean–model light water reactor, overcoming North Korean objections to South Korea's central involvement in the project.

These delays might have led to North Korean skepticism that the Agreed Framework would ever be fully implemented and to doubts that the U.S.-DPRK relationship would be fully normalized. Or, North Korea might have always intended to cooperate just enough to satisfy U.S. suspicions about its nuclear intentions while buying time to overcome economic difficulties and covertly restart its nuclear acquisition efforts by pursuing a uranium-based route to nuclear weapons development. North Koreans may have reasoned that if caught they could always put their covert uranium enrichment efforts up for sale by negotiating a second agreed framework in which the North Koreans would pledge to halt the manufacture and reprocessing of uranium in exchange for additional political and economic benefits from the United States. It is not clear exactly when the North Koreans decided to hedge their bets on the implementation of the Agreed Framework by resuming nuclear development through uranium enrichment. However, it seems that doubts were circulating regarding North Korea's adherence to the Agreed Framework as early as 1998, when the Bill Clinton administration authorized annual HFO provision on national security grounds rather than on the basis of assurances that North Korea was faithfully implementing the agreement.[16]

Republican skepticism about the Agreed Framework and intelligence community suspicions that North Korea had established a covert site at Keumchang-ri for the purpose of covertly continuing its nuclear development in breach of its pledges made the Agreed Framework an object of ongoing political contention between the Clinton administration and Republican congressional leaders. In an effort to dispel these criticisms, the Clinton administration negotiated an inspection of the site (which found no evidence of North Korean cheating) and initiated a review of U.S. policy led by former secretary of defense William Perry. The review, which came to be known as the Perry Process, included a series of high-level consultations with South Korean and Japanese allies and a team sent to Pyongyang as a presidential envoy to ascertain North Korean intentions vis-à-vis the Agreed Framework. The Perry report evaluated U.S. policy toward North Korea and concluded that the United States must "deal with the North Korean government as it is, not as we might wish it to be." The report recommended that the United States take a "comprehensive and integrated approach" to North Korea's nuclear and missile programs by strengthening coordination within the U.S. government and with Japan and South Korea through the Trilateral Coordination and

Oversight Group (TCOG), enhance bipartisan support for North Korea policy, and strengthen planning for North Korea–related contingencies.[17]

A historic inter-Korean summit and accompanying unprecedented exchange of high-level visitors between the United States and North Korea took place in 2000. The famine in North Korea had peaked in the late 1990s and the country was gradually recovering, but North Korea's willingness to engage diplomatically at a summit level was unprecedented in inter-Korean relations. However, the summitry and exchange of visits occurred on the assumption that North Korea was in compliance with the Agreed Framework, as news regarding North Korea's clandestine nuclear development efforts had not yet surfaced. Moreover, the remarkable accomplishment of the historic first ever inter-Korean summit between South Korean president Kim Dae-jung and North Korean leader and son of Kim Il-sung, Kim Jong-il, was subsequently tarnished by the revelation that South Korea's Hyundai corporation had transferred $300–500 million to make it happen.[18] North Korea's financial motives were affirmed when it emerged that the summit was delayed by a day due to North Korea's late confirmation that the money had in fact been transferred prior to Kim Dae-jung's arrival.[19]

Nonetheless, the inter-Korean summit and subsequent exchange of visits by North Korea's special envoy General Cho Myung-rok and U.S. secretary of state Madeleine Albright seemed to shape a path toward improvements in both inter-Korean and U.S.-DPRK relations.[20] Cash for access appears to have provided the fuel for growing the inter-Korean relationship, with levels of inter-Korean trade and investment in tourism at Mount Gumgang and the Kaesong Industrial Complex gradually growing after the inter-Korean summit, along with the emergence of a wide range of inter-Korean cultural and sports exchanges.[21] However, the improvement of inter-Korean relations was confined to the political and economic spheres, and did not reach the security relationship. On the U.S. side, a U.S.-DPRK joint memorandum on combating terrorism marked a high point in the relationship even without the realization of a prospective Bill Clinton visit to Pyongyang following the protracted George W. Bush–Al Gore election debacle in 2000.[22]

The Bush administration came into office with a skeptical attitude toward cooperation with North Korea, which ultimately led to the scuttling of the Agreed Framework, the shuttering of the KEDO project, and North Korea's breakout from constraints it faced under the Agreed Framework. Most significantly, the development of a consensus within the U.S. intelligence community during the summer of 2002 that North Korea was covertly pursuing a uranium enrichment program and the Bush administration's October 2002 confrontation with North Korea over its covert uranium enrichment activities led to the suspension of HFO deliveries and provided North Korea with a pretext to walk away from the Agreed Framework and free itself from constraints imposed on North Korea's nuclear development.[23] With the Agreed Framework scuttled and international inspectors kicked out, North Korea accessed the twenty-five to thirty kilograms of reprocessed plutonium that under the agreement had been safely stored in cans at Yongbyon, and began preparations to conduct its first nuclear test in September 2006.[24]

Six-Party Talks

By the resumption of U.S.-DPRK negotiations under the framework of the Six-Party Talks in 2004, North Korea's circumstances, threat perception, and objectives had changed considerably. North Korea had broken out of the constraints of the Agreed Framework and secured for the first time a plutonium stock sufficient to test a nuclear device and have additional plutonium left over.[25] The North Korean leadership had survived the cutoff of assistance from its socialist patrons and had weathered a severe famine. And North Korea was closer than ever to harnessing a nuclear capability.

With the breakdown of the Geneva Agreed Framework, North Korea signaled that it would advance its nuclear development efforts. The North Koreans might have envisioned a future resumption of bilateral talks with the United States in which there would be an opportunity to resell an expanded nuclear program at a higher price, but the Bush administration opted to engage with North Korea through a multilateral framework on the premise that a multilateral approach would isolate and bring greater pressure to bear on North Korea. In addition, the breakdown of the Geneva Agreed Framework played out against the backdrop of the U.S. invasion of Iraq in 2003. By that time, a President Bush who had professed skepticism about Kim Jong-il's intentions and horror at the regime's human rights abuses had coined the term "Axis of Evil" to refer to rogue outliers Iran, Iraq, and North Korea.[26] As the United States invaded Iraq, tensions also increased in North Korea, as rumors swirled that following an easy victory in Iraq, North Korea would be the next priority on the U.S. attack list. Following North Korea's interception of a

U.S. RC-135 intelligence plane on March 2, 2003, Kim Jong-il was quoted in the North Korean state media as saying, "Should a war break out on the Korean peninsula due to the U.S. imperialists, it will escalate into a nuclear war." Shortly thereafter, North Korean interlocutors told U.S. officials that their main lesson from Iraq was that the invasion was possible because Iraq had not acquired nuclear weapons. They then threatened to reprocess spent fuel rods from the Yongbyon reactor to "create a nuclear deterrent so you cannot invade us."[27]

Following an initial three-party meeting held in Beijing in April 2003, the North Koreans agreed to a Beijing-based six-party negotiating framework, the first meeting of which was held in 2004. As part of preparations for the Six-Party Talks, the Bush administration honed the messaging on its objective, settling on the formula of "Comprehensive, Verifiable, Irreversible Dismantlement."[28] In its initial phase, the Six-Party Talks were hindered in the ability of the U.S. chief negotiator James Kelly to interact with his North Korean counterparts. North Korean willingness to address denuclearization in a multilateral forum was hampered by its desire for direct interaction with the United States, suggesting that the North Korean side still tied denuclearization to improvements in U.S.-DPRK relations.

Following a shift in personnel at the start of the second Bush administration, talks were further hampered by offense taken by North Korea to comments by U.S. secretary of state-designate Condoleezza Rice in her confirmation hearing, where she referred to North Korea as an "outpost of tyranny."[29] Following a bilateral meeting with newly appointed assistant secretary for East Asia Christopher Hill in Beijing, the North Koreans announced their return to Six-Party Talks in a statement that emphasized that the United States had "clarified that it would recognize the DPRK as a sovereign state, not to invade it and hold bilateral talks within the framework of the six-party talks, and the DPRK interpreted it as a retraction of its remark designating the former as an 'outpost of tyranny' and decided to return to Six Party Talks."[30]

In its approach to the Six-Party Talks, North Korea sought to reframe the purpose of the negotiation from denuclearization to mutual arms reduction, while consistently defending North Korea's right to peaceful use of nuclear energy and framing the discussions with reference to ongoing mutual distrust between North Korea and the United States. North Korean delegation leader Kim Kye-gwan's public statements to CNN during negotiation sessions of the Six-Party Talks reflected these views:

The denuclearization of the Korean Peninsula is the legacy of our President Kim Il-sung and it is the firm conviction of our supreme leadership. According to this we have been maintaining our principal position to resolve the nuclear issue through dialogue and negotiations. . . . The denuclearization of the Korean Peninsula does not mean that this should be done by the DPRK (Democratic People's Republic of Korea) side only but this should be a job to be done by the United States as well as South Korea. And at this round we have made a strategic decision to denuclearize the Korean Peninsula. However, we find that South Korea and the United States are not yet ready and prepared for that.[31]

Renewed diplomatic negotiations under the Six-Party umbrella in Beijing yielded progress toward the negotiation of a Joint Statement of Principles during the summer of 2005 that was finally adopted in September, with China playing a central role in drafting and closing the gaps between the United States and North Korea.[32] The multilateral framework created pressure and competition between the United States and North Korea, as each sought to use the multilateral framework to isolate the other, while North Korea continued to seek bilateral talks with the United States as the main vehicle for achieving progress under the Six-Party Framework.

During the talks, Kim Kye-gwan reportedly cited Pakistan as a model for North Korea's nuclear development, suggesting that the North Koreans saw a pathway to develop a nuclear weapon, weather U.S. sanctions, and earn international acceptance as a nuclear state.[33] The only major difference between Pakistan and North Korea was that North Korea had at one time been a signatory to the NPT, while Pakistan and India had always stood outside the NPT. The North Koreans might have miscalculated the extent to which the United States saw this distinction as important to upholding the credibility of the NPT.

The September 19, 2005, Six-Party Joint Statement, carefully brokered and drafted by Chinese hosts, offered a pathway that linked denuclearization and peace building in a step-by-step process, but almost immediately upon the conclusion of the Joint Statement, the U.S. Treasury action under the Patriot Act brought further Six-Party Talks to a halt. After the breakdown, North Korean foreign minister Kim Kye-gwan issued a statement that "if the U.S. tries to pressure us, we will only take

stronger measures. We will employ our traditional tactic of direct confrontation. There is nothing wrong with delaying the resumption of the
six-party talks. In the meantime, we can make more deterrents."[34]

Following a period of stalemate, North Korea held its first nuclear
test on October 9, 2006. The action was a firm expression of North Korea's
intent to secure a nuclear deterrent and achieve status as a nuclear state.
The test was accompanied by the following statement, framing North
Korea's nuclear test within the context of U.S.-DPRK relations: "The ultimate goal of the DPRK is not 'denuclearization' to be followed by its unilateral disarmament but one aimed at settling the hostile relations between
the DPRK and the US and removing the very source of all nuclear threats
from the Korean Peninsula and its vicinity."[35]

The test also constituted a unilateral step toward shifting the terms
of dialogue from denuclearization to arms control, as North Korea had
foreshadowed in its February 2005 statement. However, the United States
pushed for a renewal of Six-Party Talks under Chinese leadership and,
with Chinese mediation, Hill announced the resumption of talks within
a month of North Korea's nuclear test.

Following a Six-Party meeting in Beijing the following December
at which no progress was made, the U.S. and North Korean negotiating
teams agreed to meet bilaterally in Berlin for an additional session, at
which they brokered the outlines of an implementing agreement laying
out next steps.[36] Notably, despite the multilateral veneer, North Korea
still perceived bilateral negotiations with the United States as the most
consequential vehicle by which to establish agreements, even within the
framework of Six-Party Talks. Both the United States and North Korea
returned to Beijing within weeks to announce an implementing agreement
in February 2007 involving limited steps by North Korea in the direction
of denuclearization, including the high profile destruction of a cooling
tower at Yongbyon the following summer.[37] At the same time, the North
Koreans successfully narrowed the scope of negotiations to facilities at
Yongbyon involving plutonium reprocessing only, while excluding negotiations over enriched uranium.[38] The delimited and partial scope of North
Korean willingness to implement steps toward denuclearization suggests
North Korea's continued intent to retain a nuclear capability.

Even more worrisome signs came with the inability of the United
States and North Korea to agree on steps related to North Korea's declaration of nuclear facilities and accompanying verification measures. Efforts
to close the gap between the United States and North Korea ultimately

foundered on these issues, with North Korea taking an increasingly rigid stance despite efforts by Hill to move negotiations forward through talks in Pyongyang in the fall of 2008 and at the final Six-Party meeting in December 2008. While North Korea's rigidity on these issues might be attributed to efforts to take advantage of the U.S. political transition from the Bush to the Obama administration, a more dramatic indicator came in the form of Kim Jong-il's absence from a significant national commemorative event in Pyongyang in September 2008 and swirling rumors that he had suffered a stroke.[39] North Korea's position hardened during Kim's incapacitation in the fall of 2008 and recovery in early 2009.

Transitional Developments: North Korean Nuclear/ Missile Testing and Provocations toward South Korea

In conjunction with a disappointing end to the Six-Party Talks over issues of verification in December 2008, the North Koreans pursued a strategy designed to: challenge a new U.S. leadership through active missile and nuclear testing while retrenching in anticipation of a possible North Korean leadership transition; pursue additional testing necessary to break out of the Six-Party framework that had determined denuclearization as the objective of implementation; gain the upper hand in any future U.S.-DPRK talks by unambiguously establishing North Korea's nuclear capabilities; and test the U.S. leadership under the incoming Obama administration.

North Korean determination to return to missile and nuclear testing appears to have been an intentional and nonnegotiable part of its strategy. Though the Obama campaign signaled willingness to engage in negotiations with North Korea, the North was set on employing confrontational unilateral provocations. The decision to pursue additional missile and nuclear tests appears to have been made during the months following Kim Jong-il's stroke but prior to his recovery and return to public life. Unofficial delegations including former U.S. ambassador to South Korea Stephen Bosworth, who subsequently became the Obama administration's part-time special representative for North Korea, tested North Korea's openness for diplomatic engagement in February 2009. North Korea brushed off such overtures as well as public warnings and continued to prepare to test a missile, which it provocatively launched on the same day that President Obama gave a speech in Europe outlining his support for nuclear arms reductions. The Obama administration led a campaign at the UN to condemn North Korea for the launch, to which the North responded by declaring its withdrawal from the Six-Party Talks and asserting that it would "no longer be bound" by any of its prior agreements.[40] North Korea subsequently conducted its second nuclear test in May 2009. The success of this test as judged by the size and yield of the explosion erased any doubts about whether North Korea had crossed the nuclear threshold following its initial less definitive October 2006 test. After the second test, the Obama administration's focus shifted from diplomacy to sanctions as a punishment for North Korea's provocative actions. In response to the Obama administration's push for UN Security Council Resolution 1874 that condemned North Korea's nuclear test, the North Korean Ministry of Foreign Affairs declared in June 2009 that "it has become an absolutely impossible option for the DPRK to even think about giving up its nuclear weapons."[41]

North Korea's use of provocations as an early test of new U.S. leadership soon became a familiar component of North Korean strategy. Through a series of unilateral nuclear demonstrations in May 2009 following Obama's inauguration and in January 2013, immediately prior to the political transition in South Korea to the Park Geun-hye administration in February 2013, and the political transition in China to the Xi Jinping administration in March 2013, North Korea sought to assert that it must be dealt with as a de facto nuclear weapons state. But these demonstrations dampened prospects for diplomacy and pushed all parties toward punishment strategies involving the strengthening of North Korea–focused sanctions at the United Nations. Following each North Korean nuclear or missile test, a consensus grew among UN member states, including China and Russia, in support of ever more restrictive economic sanctions measures toward North Korea. But UN sanctions could not deny the message in the nuclear testing—North Korea had indeed already become a de facto nuclear weapons state.

North Korea's return to a strategy of provocations was shaped in part by Kim Jong-il's illness, recovery, and subsequent focus on the grooming of his son, Kim Jong-un, as his successor. Kim was publicly named as Kim Jong-il's successor in 2009, under the ostensible guidance and protection of his uncle Chang Song-taek and North Korean general Ri Yong-gil. As part of succession preparations, the North Korean Reconnaissance General Bureau was assigned to undertake provocative actions toward South Korea, including the sinking of South Korea's warship *Cheonan* in March

2009 and the shelling of Yeonpyong Island the following November. These military actions, subsequently attributed to Kim Jong-un, were intended to burnish his credentials as a strategist and military leader. However, they also raised the level of inter-Korean tensions, and South Korean president Lee Myung-bak responded by imposing economic sanctions on inter-Korean trade following an international investigation that identified a North Korean torpedo as the cause of the sunken vessel.

Leap Day Understanding

Following delays resulting from the impact of North Korean provocations and the U.S.-led adoption of UN sanctions resolutions in response, the Obama administration finally reengaged with North Korea in 2011. North Korea accepted U.S. feelers and engaged in bilateral discussions without evidence of hesitation. The unadvertised series of bilateral meetings yielded limited pledges to pursue in parallel unilateral self-restraint and small confidence-building gestures to build trust.[42] In anticipation of those talks, North Korean media outlet KCNA reasserted publicly and privately that North Korea had a right to launch satellites and pursue a space program for "peaceful purposes," suggesting that the North considered peaceful satellite launches to be justifiable separate from any moratorium on ballistic missile testing.[43] The final round of negotiations was scheduled for the third week of December 2011 in Beijing, but talks were suspended due to Kim Jong-il's death. Negotiators went home, but left open the possibility of an early reengagement while Kim Jong-un was in the process of consolidating domestic support and securing his rule.

Amid uncertainty resulting from North Korea's leadership transition, the Obama administration received a positive response from North Korean counterparts to reinitiate diplomatic talks, and forged a limited agreement announced on Leap Day, February 29, 2012, in the form of parallel statements from the United States and North Korea, the specifics of which are discussed elsewhere in this volume.

In mid-March 2012, within two weeks of the signing of the agreement as part of Kim Jong-un's drive to establish his leadership credentials around the hundredth anniversary of his grandfather Kim Il-sung's birth, the North Koreans announced plans to conduct a satellite launch, which the United States regarded as a violation of the Leap Day Declaration. In perhaps the most rapid failure of a U.S.-DPRK accord on record, the

North Koreans carried out a failed satellite launch on April 12, 2012, only sixteen days after the announcement of the agreement.[44] Kim Jong-un credited his father and grandfather as the authors of North Korea's nuclear development and moved to insert North Korea's status as a nuclear state into the preamble of the revised North Korean constitution.[45] Thus, Kim Jong-un used North Korea's nuclear accomplishments as an instrument and foundation for legitimating his rule, tying his legitimacy as a ruler to North Korea's nuclear development.

The rapid failure of the Leap Day Declaration underscored the gap between the U.S. desire for North Korea to pursue denuclearization and Kim Jong-un's use of the nuclear program as a foundation for the legitimacy of his rule. The failed declaration served to affirm the absence of a window of opportunity to pursue North Korea's denuclearization and was a profound disappointment to those in the Obama administration involved with negotiations with North Korea. Despite assertions offered privately by North Korea's chief negotiator Ri Yong-ho that the advent of new leadership in North Korea might bring an opportunity to put aside the difficult past between the United States and North Korea, Kim Jong-un's use of the nuclear program as a source of domestic legitimation indicated that the U.S. goal of denuclearization was becoming increasingly distant, if not impossible.[46]

Obama administration efforts to negotiate with North Korea so early in the transition of leadership to Kim Jong-un might have been motivated by the idea that an open channel of negotiations could provide an opportunity to turn a new page in the relationship by dissuading Kim from continuing down a nuclear path, just as Ambassador Ri hinted privately during March 2012 talks in New York. If so, the effort may have been warranted. But Kim's main motive was clearly regime consolidation, and the U.S.-DPRK negotiations proved ill-timed and unsuccessful. The failure of the agreement and Kim's efforts to frame his legitimacy on the basis of his family's nuclear accomplishments underscore the deepening gap between the United States and North Korea over the question of denuclearization.

Transitional Developments: Adoption of *Byungjin*, Intensified Missile Testing, and Fire and Fury

Kim Jong-un's consolidation of power was accompanied by his development of a two-pronged strategy, referred to as *byungjin* and backed by the

Korean Workers' Party, to simultaneously promote economic and military development. Kim saw consolidation of power and national self-strengthening as requiring both a strong military and a strong economy. But Kim prioritized military development as the precondition for economic growth, and nuclear advancement became the instrument by which Kim sought to secure a peaceful environment for economic development. Kim saw the pursuit of economic and military development as mutually intertwined prerequisites for his goal of becoming a "strong and powerful state."[47]

The United States responded to North Korea's nuclear development by seeking to economically isolate the nation through comprehensive sanctioning, with the goal of forcing Kim Jong-un to view his nuclear aspirations as an obstacle to his economic prosperity objectives. The United States ratcheted up the economic pressure at the end of the Obama administration both through a series of executive orders and through compliance with the 2016 North Korea Sanctions and Policy Enforcement Act.[48] These measures laid the foundation for the Trump administration's "maximum pressure" strategy in 2017.[49] Meanwhile, Kim Jong-un authorized establishment of special economic zones, pursued sanctions evasion, and sought to embed North Korean procurement in shadowy Chinese-based supply chains to circumvent the U.S. pressure campaign.[50]

As part of the *byungjin* strategy of self-strengthening, Kim ramped up missile testing dramatically in early 2017, relying once more on unilateral provocations to assert North Korea's capabilities during a period of leadership transition in the United States from the Obama to the Trump administration. In addition to strengthening North Korean capabilities and demonstrating his own leadership domestically, Kim's missile testing challenged the U.S.-South Korea alliance as well as the tolerance of an unproven U.S. president and his "America first" agenda. Kim's 2017 New Year's address signaled his intent to test an intercontinental ballistic missile, and through intensified frequency of testing North Korea sought to shape the strategic environment such that the United States felt that time was not on its side. North Korea might have anticipated a conventional U.S. response consisting of cautious strategies designed to limit risks of crisis escalation, enhancing the likelihood that the United States would finally acquiesce to North Korea as a nuclear state.

The escalation of tensions and Trump's response to North Korean missile tests in 2017 challenged conventional North Korean assumptions that the United States was risk adverse and therefore would avoid challenging incremental North Korean steps to build a nuclear capability. Trump's threat of "fire and fury" and that he would wipe North Korea off the face of the earth in a September 2017 speech to the UN General Assembly introduced doubt that the United States would avoid a confrontation with North Korea.[51] Kim Jong-un himself appeared to have been caught off guard by Trump's response to North Korea's continued missile testing. The premise underlying Kim's acquisition of nuclear weapons was that it would deter military conflict, yet Trump's escalation of tensions pointed to the possibility that the nuclear deterrent itself could trigger military conflict.

Trump's UN General Assembly speech induced a direct public statement from Kim Jong-un, who spoke of his surprise at Trump's rhetoric. Kim stated that Trump "is surely a rogue and a gangster fond of playing with fire, rather than a politician" and that Trump's "straightforward expression of his will have convinced me, rather than frightening or stopping me, that the path I chose is correct and that it is the one I have to follow to the last."[52] An interesting question is whether Kim's response indicates a realization that the stakes and burdens accompanying nuclear acquisition were greater than he had anticipated. Kim's response reveals the possibility that his nuclear acquisitions and missile development were actually risking North Korea's security rather than preserving it. While Kim's statement sought to establish that he was in control of the situation, Trump's speech might have contributed to Kim's turn away from missile testing and toward diplomacy only weeks later.

Trump-Kim Summitry

The crisis and the stakes involved led both Trump and Kim Jong-un to seek ways to tamp down U.S.-DPRK tensions. Following a November 2017 test of North Korea's largest missile to date, the Hwasong-15, Kim declared North Korea's nuclear development complete. By claiming that he had established North Korean missile capabilities as part of North Korea's deterrence against external threats, Kim could argue that he was approaching diplomacy with the outside world from a position of strength. This apparent accomplishment helped set the stage for Kim to pivot to a diplomatic charm offensive around the Pyeongchang Winter Olympics planned for the following February in South Korea. In December 2017, Trump invited North Korea to open a dialogue with the United States through the visit of senior UN official Jeffery Feltman to Pyongyang.[53] South Korea's Moon administration proved a persistent and supportive interlocutor, seeking opportunities to establish dialogue between the United States and North Korea during the opening and closing ceremonies of the Olympics, and even sent a special envoy to Pyongyang and then to Washington following the Olympics in an effort to enable a Trump-Kim summit meeting.[54]

For the United States, direct summitry represented the last untested hypothesis around the question of whether negotiated denuclearization with North Korea could succeed because, for the first time, the United States was negotiating with the decision maker himself—Kim Jong-un. In a positive sign, Kim reiterated to both Moon and Trump his willingness to pursue "complete denuclearization" at Panmunjom and Singapore.[55] But the conditions under which Kim might pursue complete denuclearization remained untested and the term "complete denuclearization" undefined. North Korean unwillingness to discuss details of denuclearization at working level talks became an insurmountable obstacle to defining "complete denuclearization" or to taking steps in that direction.

By necessity, the defining of denuclearization conditions was left to subordinates. But North Korea referred to U.S. secretary of state Mike Pompeo's follow-on proposals during a July 2018 visit to Pyongyang as "gangster-like."[56] Newly appointed U.S. special representative for North Korea Stephen Biegun's efforts to define specific mechanisms for continuing talks on denuclearization also failed to gain traction as working talks faced regular delays.[57] Momentum appeared to gather when Kim Yong-chul, director of North Korea's United Front Department, visited Washington in January 2019 to make arrangements for a second Trump-Kim summit in Hanoi.[58] However, working-level negotiations in preparation for the Hanoi summit held in Pyongyang in early February made progress on every issue but denuclearization, ostensibly because lower-level negotiators were not authorized to discuss the topic.[59] Biegun reached out to Kim Yong-chul following the arrival of delegations in Hanoi for the summit meeting, but received no response. As a result, all issues related to progress on denuclearization were left for Trump and Kim to discuss directly. Trump and Kim exchanged proposals on the scope and conditions for progress on allowing inspectors at Yongbyon and corresponding measures, but could not reach an agreement before Trump decided to walk out on the talks.[60] Neither did working-level negotiators to remain in Hanoi to hammer out any agreement on outstanding issues from the summit. So long as subordinates were not authorized to discuss denuclearization at working-level talks, no progress could be made. But

Trump and Kim themselves likely lacked the patience or command of technical details necessary to actually forge a meaningful agreement on how to implement complete denuclearization.

The difficulties associated with the establishment of working-level diplomacy revealed dysfunctions between the leaders and their respective bureaucracies in both countries. The failure of the Hanoi summit generated skepticism that Kim Jong-un was ever serious about moving toward denuclearization or that North Korea's denuclearization would ever be possible. North Korean negotiators complained in a post-Hanoi press conference about U.S. unwillingness to meet North Korean demands to lift five sanctions resolutions passed during 2016 and 2017. Ri Yong-ho claimed that North Korea had offered to dismantle its main nuclear facility at Yongbyon and formally pledge to end all nuclear and long-range missile tests.[61] At the same time, there remained ambiguity around the extent of access North Korea would offer to its nuclear-related sites at Yongbyon or in other parts of the country. North Korea's first vice minister Choe Sun-hee stated that the United States had missed a "once-in-a-lifetime opportunity," while U.S. national security advisor John Bolton expressed relief that Trump walked away rather than make a bad deal with North Korea.[62]

An unintended consequence of Trump's bold decision to engage in summitry with Kim Jong-un involved the Chinese response and its impact on China's relationship with North Korea. North Korea's intense testing of missile and nuclear tests involving ever-increasing ranges and yields in 2017 had pushed China into greater alignment with the United States than ever before in opposition to North Korean nuclear activities, as evidenced by the increasingly stringent sanctions on North Korea's ability to export coal, minerals, and seafood products to China. In addition, China undertook unilateral sanctions that led to a significant drop in Sino–North Korean bilateral trade in 2017. But Trump's decision to meet with Kim had ramifications for China's strategic interests, leading to a Chinese reversal in strategy and policy toward North Korea. After having shunned Kim Jong-un during his first five years as president due in part to objections to Kim's nuclear development, Xi Jinping reversed course and met with Kim prior to and following each of Kim's major summits with Moon Jae-in and Donald Trump. The renewed embrace of a strategic relationship at the leader-to-leader level and growing tensions in Sino-U.S. relations had a material impact on China's implementation of sanctions toward North Korea, with China abandoning sanctions enforcement and calling for sanctions relaxation following the failure of Trump-Kim summitry in February 2019. To the extent that Xi had promoted denuclearization alongside stability during 2013–17, growing Sino-U.S. strategic mistrust and the renewal of Sino–North Korean leadership ties as a result of Kim's 2018 turn toward summitry revived the traditional Sino–North Korean strategic relationship, with North Korean stability firmly entrenched as China's main strategic objective over denuclearization.

In light of the Hanoi summit failure and North Korea's unwillingness to return to negotiations, the primary public yardstick for assessing Kim's seriousness of intent regarding willingness to denuclearize lies in the declarations it made together with South Korea in the September 2018 Pyongyang Declaration.[63] It is striking that inter-Korean negotiations touched on denuclearization issues, which normally were reserved for discussion with the United States. In the Pyongyang Declaration, North Korea showed a willingness to allow limited inspections of Yongbyon in return for corresponding measures by the United States, subsequently revealed as the lifting of the five latest UN sanctions resolutions. The outstanding question, therefore, is whether this agreement would have put North Korea on a path to complete denuclearization or whether Kim Jong-un hoped to trade partial denuclearization for sanctions relief while retaining his nation's nuclear capabilities in the long-term.

The Trump-Kim meeting at Panmunjom on June 30, 2019, attempted to jumpstart working-level talks to no avail. The *Chosun Sinbo*, a North Korean newspaper published in Japan, stated that "for 'complete denuclearization' the United States must do its own thing, such as removing the threat of nuclear war against [North] Korea. The transition is a process of withdrawing hostile policies against Korea and changing the US itself."[64] This statement suggests that Kim Jong-un had walked away from negotiations and adopted a new approach toward the United States that cast negotiations as acceptable only to achieve the objectives of détente between nuclear powers or mutual denuclearization.

Kim Jong-un's review of progress at the Korean Workers' Party Eighth Party Congress further reinforces his new approach and provides an authoritative North Korean inventory of its own intent around negotiations with the United States. At the Eighth Workers' Party Congress in January 2021, Kim candidly admitted to economic failures while emphasizing defense and military accomplishments to cope with what he described as an unchangeable U.S. hostile policy. Kim's military priorities for development included "ultra-modern tactical nuclear weapons," "hypersonic gliding flight warheads," "multi-warhead missiles, reconnaissance satellites, a nuclear-powered submarine, and solid-fuel, land- and submarine-launched, and intercontinental ballistic missile."[65]

The report pointed to research accomplishments on multi-warhead rocket guidance technology, hypersonic gliding flight warheads for new ballistic rockets, the modernization of a medium-sized nuclear-powered submarine, design of new electronic weapons, unmanned striking equipment, and research on reconnaissance and detection capabilities and military reconnaissance satellites. The Korean People's Army's contributions to both national defense and socialist construction were publicly recognized, and the Party Central Committee was credited with "upraising the country to the position of a world nuclear power and military power in both name and reality and putting an end once and for all to the era in which big powers attempted to make bargains with the interests of our state and nation."[66]

In foreign relations, the report argued that North Korea had "created a trend toward peace and atmosphere of dialogue" and that these activities had elevated North Korea's international prestige, citing progress in relations with fellow socialist countries China, Russia, Cuba, and Vietnam. The report argued that the Party Central Committee "brought about a dramatic turn in the balance of power" between the United States and North Korea, stated that the realization of summit talks with the United States "demonstrated to the world the strategic position of the DPRK," and pointed to the adoption of the joint declaration "that assured the establishment of new DPRK-US relations." But the report ignored other elements of the Singapore Declaration, including the establishment of a permanent peace and the task of working toward complete denuclearization.

The assessment provided at the Eighth Party Congress, in combination with North Korean actions following the Singapore Declaration, suggest that Kim Jong-un was primarily interested in the prestige and normalization benefits that North Korea would gain from the optics of a summit with Trump, but that North Korea's pledge of "complete denuclearization" probably required a very long time frame for implementation, if it would even be possible. In essence, Kim Jong-un sought détente, not denuclearization, while the United States sought denuclearization in exchange for détente. In the end, Trump-Kim summitry delivered neither détente nor denuclearization. North Korea concluded that U.S. hostility toward North Korea would be durable, while U.S. suspicions regarding

Kim's intentions to denuclearize and its resolve not to accept North Korea as a legitimate nuclear weapons state have deepened.

Kim Jong-un's decision to use summitry to engage with the United States and willingness to pledge North Korea's complete denuclearization was risky. He had to balance external messaging allowing for the possibility of North Korea's denuclearization with internal messaging centered around the nuclear program as a foundation for guaranteeing regime security and a source of legitimation for Kim family rule. Kim risked the loss of his international credibility as a leader, while the United States tried with limited success to use sanctions and other leverage to bind Kim to a denuclearization path. But in reality, Kim was too far out of the mainstream of the international community for such efforts to have much effect, and in practice it was hard to maintain sanctions intended to prevent North Korea from accessing normal international exchanges while judging Kim for not meeting the standards of credibility necessary to gain greater acceptance internationally.

Conclusion

The above review of North Korean motives and objectives around four stages of denuclearization negotiations with the United States spanning three decades suggests the following conclusions:

First, the North Korean intent to develop nuclear weapons was persistent and enduring. North Korean geopolitical circumstances, worldview, and desires to preserve autonomy in service of the regime's survival and self-defense made it unlikely that the goal of becoming a nuclear state would be willingly abandoned. In light of North Korean persistence, U.S. efforts to use diplomacy in combination with an array of sanctions and incentives packages designed to dissuade North Korea from continued nuclear development were never sufficiently robust to achieve that objective.

Second, the level of North Korean nuclear capabilities influenced the North's responses to U.S. diplomatic efforts to block its nuclear development. North Korean motives and intentions may have remained focused on the goal of becoming a nuclear state, but North Korea's relative capabilities decisively impacted the country's actions and responses to international pressure. The United States had some success in dissuading North Korea from nuclear development prior to its first nuclear test in October

2006. U.S. diplomacy around denuclearization conducted between October 2006 and the end of 2008 also yielded modest progress in restraining North Korea's program, as the 2006 test delivered ambiguous results that did not fully establish North Korea's nuclear status. However, North Korean pragmatism based on its modest capabilities appears to have faded with North Korea's unilateral decision to end participation in the Six-Party Talks and definitive achievement of a nuclear weapons production and delivery capability at the beginning of the Obama administration in 2009. Subsequent efforts to pursue diplomatic channels for neutralizing and reversing North Korea's nuclear capabilities have failed.

Third, failures in the implementation of the Geneva Agreed Framework and North Korean progress in improving its nuclear capabilities following the agreement's breakdown made it increasingly difficult for North Korea to plausibly consider U.S. security guarantees or a transformation of U.S. policy toward North Korea to be an adequate assurance of regime security compared to the pathway of nuclear development. Nor was the United States able to raise the costs of North Korean nuclear development sufficiently to dissuade North Korea from continuing its program. In fact, although economic sanctions may indeed have slowed and raised the costs of North Korea's nuclear development, they may also have been interpreted by North Korea as evidence of external hostile intent that served to redouble its resolve to pursue nuclear development. Moreover, the history of reversal and relinquishment of nuclear capabilities shows regime change as a prominent factor accompanying nuclear abandonment, making North Korea all the more unlikely to see regime security guarantees and normalized relations as a sufficient incentive to take risks that might be accompanied by a decrease in regime security.

Finally, despite the low probability for success of negotiated denuclearization, there remained a plausible logic associated with leader-to-leader dialogue as a path forward, despite perceived costs of indirectly providing prestige gains and legitimation signals to Kim Jong-un. Only the failure of a diplomatic test involving the decision maker himself could allow negotiators to conclude that prospects for diplomacy as an instrument by which to pursue denuclearization have been exhausted. In other words, summitry was ultimately necessary to remove the possibility of missing a final diplomatic opportunity for denuclearization.

But the failure of summitry generates an even more challenging problem, and that is whether to abandon the objective of denuclearization of North Korea, with all the contingent implications for the international nonproliferation regime, peninsular security balance, and security of the United States and U.S. allies in Northeast Asia. Even if there might have been a chance to prevent North Korea from advancing its nuclear program through a more robust period of engagement and confidence building in the 1990s, it is still hard to imagine that a regime so vulnerable, isolated, and singleminded could ever rely on external assurances from a "hostile" international community as a basis upon which to attain security. Instead, the twin needs of legitimation and regime survival could probably never be fully guaranteed by the United States or any other external actor, leaving the Kim family regime with no attractive option other than a nuclear development as the key to absolute security.

Notes

1. Adrian Buzo, *The Guerilla Dynasty: Politics and Leadership in North Korea* (New South Wales, Australia: Allen and Unwin, 1999); Kim Il Sung, *With the Century* (Pyongyang: Foreign Languages Publishing House, 1992).

2. James Clay Moltz and Alexandre Y. Mansourov, eds., *The North Korean Nuclear Program: Security, Strategy, and New Perspectives from Russia* (New York: Routledge, 1999).

3. Kelsey Davenport, "The U.S.-North Korean Agreed Framework at a Glance," Arms Control Association, last reviewed July 2018, https://www.arms-control.org/factsheets/agreedframework.

4. Sergey Radchenko, "Russia's Policy in the Run-Up to the First North Korean Nuclear Crisis 1991–1993," Woodrow Wilson International Center for Scholars Nuclear Proliferation International History Project, February 2015, https://www.wilsoncenter.org/sites/default/files/media/documents/publication/wp4_radchenko-russia_north_korea_nuclear_-_ver_2.pdf; Xiaoxiong Yi, "China's Korea Policy: From 'One Korea' to 'Two Koreas,'" *Asian Affairs: An American Review* 22, no. 2 (Summer 1995): 128–31.

5. Paul Blustein, "Two Koreas Pledge to End Aggression," *Washington Post*, December 13, 1991, https://www.washingtonpost.com/archive/politics/1991/12/13/two-koreas-pledge-to-end-aggression/d104ab96-1a85-4024-8b61-bf9e43d779eb/.

6. Marion Creekmore Jr., *A Moment of Crisis: Jimmy Carter, The Power of a Peacemaker, and North Korea's Nuclear Ambitions* (New York: Public Affairs, 2006), 4–6.

7. Don Oberdorfer and Robert Carlin, *The Two Koreas: A Contemporary History*, 3rd ed. (New York: Basic Books, 2013); Joel S. Wit, Daniel B. Poneman,

and Robert L. Gallucci, *Going Critical* (Washington, DC: Brookings Institution Press, 2004), 10–16.

8. Daniel Wertz, Matthew McGrath, and Scott LaFoy, "North Korea's Nuclear Weapons Program," NCNK, last updated April 2018, https://www.ncnk.org/resources/publications/DPRK-Nuclear-Weapons-Issue-Brief.pdf.

9. Nicholas Eberstadt, "North Korea's Interlocked Economic Crises: Some Indications from 'Mirror Statistics,'" *Asian Survey* 38, no. 3 (March 1998): 223–25.

10. Wit, Poneman, and Gallucci, *Going Critical*, 13–21.

11. Kongdan Oh and Ralph C. Hassig, "North Korea: A Rogue State outside the NPT Fold," Brookings Institution, March 1, 2005, https://www.brookings.edu/articles/north-korea-a-rogue-state-outside-the-npt-fold/.

12. Wit, Poneman, and Gallucci, *Going Critical*, 51–78.

13. "North Korean Leader Insists He has No Nuclear Weapons President Kim Il Sung Tells Journalists Invited for a Rare Visit that His Country Wants Peace," *Associated Press*, April 17, 1994.

14. Wit, Poneman, and Gallucci, *Going Critical*, 331–70.

15. Richard Fontaine and Micah Springut, "Coordinating North Korea Policy—An American View," in *The US-ROK alliance in the 21ˢᵗ Century*, ed. Jungho Bae and Abraham Denmark (Seoul, South Korea: Korea Institute for National Unification, 2009), 136.

16. "President Clinton Approves a Plan to Give Aid to North Koreans," *New York Times*, October 19, 1994, https://www.nytimes.com/1994/10/19/world/clinton-approves-a-plan-to-give-aid-to-north-koreans.html.

17. William J. Perry, "Review of United States Policy toward North Korea: Findings and Recommendations," October 12, 1999, https://1997-2001.state.gov/regions/eap/991012_northkorea_rpt.html.

18. "Special Prosecutor's Office Confirms '500 Million dollar' was transferred to North Korea," *SBS News*, May 12, 2003, https://news.sbs.co.kr/news/endPage.do?news_id=N0311420022&plink=SEARCH&cooper=SBSNEWSSEARCH.

19. "Independent Counsel Announces Outcome of Probe into Money Transfer," *Dong-a Ilbo*, June 25, 2003, https://www.donga.com/en/article/all/20030625/229526/1/Independent-Counsel-Announces-Outcome-of-Probe-into-Money-Transfer.

20. "Secretary of State Madeleine K. Albright Remarks on the Occasion of the Visit of His Excellency Vice Marshall Jo Myong Rok," U.S. State Department National Archive, October 10, 2000, https://1997-2001.state.gov/statements/2000/001010.html; "Interview with Madeline Albright," *PBS*, March 27, 2003, https://www.pbs.org/wgbh/pages/frontline/shows/kim/interviews/albright.html.

21. "October of the Korean Peninsula Expects Favorable Wind," *Munhwa Ilbo*, October 1, 2001, http://www.munhwa.com/news/view.html?no=2002100101030523005003.

22. "US-DPRK Joint Communique," U.S. State Department, October 12, 2000, https://1997-2001.state.gov/regions/eap/001012_usdprk_jointcom.html.

23. "North Korea: A Chronology of Events, October 2002–December 2004," CRS Report, January 24, 2005.

24. Siegfried S. Hecker, "The Nuclear Crisis in North Korea," *Engineering and Foreign Policy* 34, no. 2 (June 1, 2004).

25. "North Korea's Nuclear Weapons Development and Diplomacy," CRS Report, January 5, 2010.

26. "President Delivers State of the Union Address," White House Archives, January 29, 2002, https://georgewbush-whitehouse.archives.gov/news/releases/2002/01/20020129-11.html.

27. Mike Chinoy, *Meltdown: The Inside Story of the North Korean Nuclear Crisis* (New York: St. Martin's Press, 2010), 164, 166.

28. Chinoy, *Meltdown*, 169–74.

29. "Rice Targets 6 Outposts of Tyranny," *Washington Times*, January 19, 2005, https://www.washingtontimes.com/news/2005/jan/19/20050119-120236-9054r/.

30. Chinoy, *Meltdown*, 240.

31. Mike Chinoy, "Transcript of Interview with Kim Kye Gwan," *CNN*, August 14, 2005, http://edition.cnn.com/2005/WORLD/asiapcf/08/14/gwan.transcript/index.html.

32. "Six-Party Talks, Beijing, China," U.S. State Department Archive, September 19, 2005, https://2009-2017.state.gov/p/eap/regional/c15455.htm.

33. "North Korea's Nuclear Weapons Program," CRS Issue Brief for Congress, May 25, 2006.

34. Chinoy, *Meltdown*, 273.

35. "DPRK Foreign Minister Clarifies Stand on New Measures to Bolster War Deterrent," *Korean Central News Agency*, October 3, 2006.

36. Christopher Hill, *Outpost* (New York: Simon and Schuster, 2014), 245–62.

37. "Senate Hearing 110-665: The North Korean Six-Party Talks and Implementation Activities," U.S. Government Publishing Office, July 31, 2008,
https://www.govinfo.gov/content/pkg/CHRG-110shrg46091/html/CHRG-110shrg46091.htm.

38. "North Korea's Nuclear Weapons: Technical Issues," CRS Report, April 3, 2013.

39. "North Korea Leader's Absence Spurs Stroke Rumors," *NPR*, September 9, 2008, https://www.npr.org/templates/story/story.php?storyId=94428411.

40. Kelsey Davenport, "Chronology of U.S.-North Korean Nuclear and Missile Diplomacy," *Arms Control Association*, last reviewed July 2020, https://www.armscontrol.org/factsheets/dprkchron.

41. "DPRK Foreign Ministry Declares Strong Counter-measures against UNSC's Resolution 1874," *Korean Central News Agency*, June 13, 2009.

42. Emma Chanlett-Avery and Ian E. Rinehart, "North Korea: U.S. Relations, Nuclear Diplomacy, and Internal Situation," Congressional Research

Service, January 13, 2013, https://www.everycrsreport.com/files/20130104_R41259_cbc240893487398872d8ba7a47ecc42ff940d093.pdf.

43. Scott Bruce, "Space is a Common Wealth: North Korea, China, and the Peaceful Development of Outer Space," *Sino NK*, February 8, 2012, https://sinonk.com/2012/02/08/space-is-a-common-wealth-north-korea-china-and-the-peaceful-development-of-outer-space/, in which Bruce references a DPRK White Paper entitled "Space Is a Common Wealth," November 29, 2011.

44. "NORAD and USNORTHCOM Acknowledge Missile Launch," *NORAD News*, April 12, 2012, https://www.northcom.mil/Newsroom/News-Stories/Article/Article/563715/norad-and-usnorthcom-acknowledge-missile-launch/.

45. K.J. Kwon, "North Korea Proclaims Itself a Nuclear State in New Constitution," *CNN*, May 31, 2012, https://www.cnn.com/2012/05/31/world/asia/north-korea-nuclear-constitution.

46. Author observations based on participation in meetings with Ri Yong-ho in New York in March 2012.

47. Alexander Vorontsov, "North Korea 2012, Grandson Greets Grandfather: Celebration by Satellite Salute," *Brookings Institution*, April 26, 2012, https://www.brookings.edu/opinions/north-korea-2012-grandson-greets-grandfather-celebration-by-satellite-salute/; Cheon Seong-whun, "The Kim Jong-un Regime's 'Byungjin' (Parallel Development) Policy of Economy and Nuclear Weapons and the 'April 1st Nuclearization Law,'" *Korea Institute for National Unification*, Online series CO 13-11, accessed at https://repo.kinu.or.kr/bitstream/2015.oak/2227/1/0001458456.pdf.

48. "Executive Order 13722: Blocking Property of the Government of North Korea and the Workers' Party of Korea, and Prohibiting Certain Transactions with Respect to North Korea," National Archives and Records Administration, March 18, 2016, https://home.treasury.gov/system/files/126/nk_eo_20160316.pdf.

49. Mark E. Manyin and Mary Beth D. Nikitin, "North Korea: A Chronology of Events from 2016 to 2020," *Congressional Research Service*, May 5, 2020, https://www.everycrsreport.com/files/20200505_R46349_6307d94932ea867fd-6c287e740681164c6f83bd3.pdf.

50. "Senate Hearing 115-50: Secondary Sanctions Against Chinese Institutions: Assessing Their Utility for Constraining North Korea: Examining How Chinese Banks, Businesses, and Persons Provide North Korea with Direct and Indirect Access to Financial Markets and Resources, Allowing Pyongyang to Evade or Mitigate International Sanctions," U.S. Government Publishing Office, May 10, 2017, https://www.govinfo.gov/content/pkg/CHRG-115shrg26242/html/CHRG-115shrg26242.htm.

51. "Would Trump Attack North Korea? Here's What We Learned from His 'Rocket Man' Speech at the UN," *Washington Post*, September 20, 2017, https://www.washingtonpost.com/news/monkey-cage/wp/2017/09/20/would-trump-attack-north-korea-heres-what-we-learned-from-his-rocket-man-speech-at-the-u-n/.

52. "Statement of Chairman of State Affairs Commission of the DPRK," *Korean Central News Agency*, September 22, 2017.

53. Philip Sherwell, "Donald Trump Opened Back Channel to Kim Jong Un," *Times*, February 21, 2021, https://www.thetimes.co.uk/article/donald-trump-opened-back-channel-to-kim-jong-un-pftp2kw9b.

54. Felicia Schwartz and Michael R. Gordon, "U.S. Meets with South Koreans Bearing a 'Message' from Pyongyang," *Wall Street Journal*, March 8, 2018, https://www.wsj.com/articles/u-s-meets-with-south-koreans-bearing-a-message-from-pyongyang-1520545394.

55. Jonathan Cheng and Andrew Jeong, "Kim Reaffirms Korean Denuclearization Push, Looks Forward to Trump Meeting, Moon Says," *Wall Street Journal*, May 27, 2018, https://www.wsj.com/articles/kim-jong-un-south-koreas-moon-meet-amid-uncertainty-over-u-s-summit-1527334020; Choe Sang-hun, "Kim Jong-un Says He Wants Denuclearization in Trump's Current Term," *New York Times*, September 6, 2018, https://www.nytimes.com/2018/09/06/world/asia/kim-jong-un-donald-trump-denuclearize.html.

56. Gardiner Harris and Choe Sang-hun, "North Korea Criticizes 'Gangster-Like' U.S. Attitude after Talks with Mike Pompeo," *New York Times*, July 7, 2018, https://www.nytimes.com/2018/07/07/world/asia/mike-pompeo-north-korea-pyongyang.html.

57. Bruce Klingner, "Congressional Testimony: Stalled Denuclearization Talks: Waiting for the Phone to Ring or the Other Shoe to Drop," February 25, 2020, https://www.foreign.senate.gov/imo/media/doc/022520_Klingner_Testimony.pdf.

58. Hwang Joon-bum, Kim Oi-hyun, and Kim Ji-eun, "Kim Yong-chol to Land in Washington, DC, for Two-Day Visit," *Hankyoreh*, January 17, 2019, http://english.hani.co.kr/arti/english_edition/e_northkorea/878814.html.

59. David Ignatius, "Opinion: It Made Sense for Trump to Walk Away in Hanoi," *The Washington Post*, February 28, 2019, https://www.washingtonpost.com/opinions/2019/02/28/it-made-sense-trump-walk-away-hanoi/.

60. Michael R. Gordon, Jonathan Cheng, and Vivian Salama, "Even Before Trump and Kim Met, Nuclear Talks Had Run Aground," *Wall Street Journal*, March 1, 2019, https://www.wsj.com/articles/even-before-trump-and-kim-met-nuclear-talks-had-run-aground-11551487094.

61. "North Korea Says It Wants Partial Sanctions Relief," *Korea Herald*, March 1, 2019, http://www.koreaherald.com/view.php?ud=20190301000006.

62. John Bolton, *In the Room Where It Happened* (New York: Simon and Schuster, 2020), 319–52; Jeongmi Lee, "Choe Sun-hee, Kim Jung-eun Feels Like He Has Lost His Motivation to Negotiate with the US," *YTN*, March 1, 2019, https://www.ytn.co.kr/_ln/0104_20190301125916171.

63. "Pyongyang Declaration of September 2018," *Korea Times*, September 19, 2018, http://www.koreatimes.co.kr/www/nation/2018/09/103_255848.html.

64. "Chosun Sinbo: "North Korea Is Ready for Good in Case of U.S. Trust Building Measures," *NK News*, July 12, 2019, https://nk.news1.kr/news/articles/3668862.

65. "North Korea's Kim Gets New Title in Symbolic Move at Congress," *VOA News*, January 10, 2021, https://www.voanews.com/east-asia-pacific/north-koreas-kim-gets-new-title-symbolic-move-congress.

66. "On Report Made by Supreme Leader Kim Jong-un at Eighth Party Congress of WPK," compiled from Korea Central News Agency by National Committee on North Korea, accessed at https://www.ncnk.org/resources/publications/kju_8th_party_congress_speech_summary.pdf/file_view.

Chapter 4

South Korea's Strategy
for Denuclearizing North Korea

Uk Heo

Introduction

On January 20, 2021, Joe Biden became the forty-sixth president of the United States. His administration is expected to make various policy changes. One of the foreign policy issues that requires his immediate attention is the North Korean nuclear problem. Ned Price, the State Department spokesperson, indicated that the North Korean nuclear issue is an urgent priority.[1] Per the same issue, Secretary of State Antony Blinken in an interview with NBC stated that the North Korean (Democratic People's Republic of Korea; DPRK) nuclear issue is "a bad problem that's gotten worse across administrations . . . review the policy that we use the most effective tools to advance the denuclearization of the Korean peninsula."[2] In the interview, he indicated that the Biden administration is considering additional sanctions as well as diplomatic incentives.

As Blinken noted, the problem has been dealt with by multiple administrations, as it has been three decades since the North Korean nuclear crisis broke out. Numerous efforts by the United States and South Korea (Republic of Korea; ROK) to lead to North Korea's nuclear abandonment have been fruitless. Diplomatic means, including economic aids and building light water nuclear reactors for power generation in North

Korea, as well as pressure measures such as economic sanctions have been employed without success. Today, North Korea is practically a nuclear power as it has conducted six nuclear tests along with ballistic missile launches.

Why did the past efforts to denuclearize North Korea fail? What have been the goals and strategies of South Korea in their negotiations with North Korea? Have South Korea's strategies changed over different administrations? What leverage did Seoul have in negotiating with Pyongyang, and how did they use it? Have any aspects of the North Korean nuclear crisis changed over time? Has it been really feasible to persuade North Korea to abandon its nuclear programs? What can we learn from past failures?

In this study, I attempt to answer these questions by analyzing South Korea's negotiation strategies and their outcomes so that we can learn from past experiences. Since South Korea has not had a grand strategy utilized by all administrations thus far, I will analyze each administration's negotiation strategy. Lessons learned from the analysis might provide meaningful insights for future negotiations. Findings of this study will have significant policy implications given that South Korea continues to work with the United States and other allies in an attempt to lead to North Korea's nuclear disarmament.

South Korea's Strategies for Denuclearizing North Korea

DEVELOPMENT OF THE CRISIS AND THE KIM YOUNG-SAM ADMINISTRATION (1993–98)

The North Korean nuclear crisis began when the United States learned about North Korea's construction of the nuclear fuel reprocessing plant in Yongbyon. Under pressure from Russia, the DPRK joined the Nuclear Nonproliferation Treaty (NPT) in December 1985. To bring North Korea into full compliance with the NPT, Seoul and Washington began negotiations with Pyongyang through high level talks in 1990 and 1991 respectively. In July 1991, the DPRK foreign ministry proposed a joint declaration to denuclearize the Korean peninsula by mandating South Korea to remove tactical nuclear weapons deployed by the U.S. forces in Korea (USFK). Since South Korea did not take North Korea's nuclear program seriously, Seoul and Washington agreed to remove all tactical nuclear weapons deployed in South Korea in October 1991. Two months later, ROK president Roh Tae-woo publicly announced that South Korea was free of nuclear weapons. In 1992, Seoul and Pyongyang released the Joint Declaration on the Denuclearization of the Korean Peninsula, under which both Koreas agreed not to develop any types (plutonium-based or highly enriched uranium–based) of nuclear weapons.[3]

In January 1992, North Korea signed a nuclear safeguard agreement and granted permission to the International Atomic Energy Agency (IAEA) to conduct an inspection. After six inspections, the IAEA found some discrepancy between Pyongyang's pre-inspection reports and inspection results. The IAEA demanded further inspections, but North Korea refused to grant permission. As the negotiation between the DPRK and IAEA went nowhere, Pyongyang announced its withdrawal from the NPT. Pyongyang's move significantly raised Washington's suspicion of North Korea's intention to become a nuclear power despite the Joint Declaration on the Denuclearization of the Korean Peninsula in 1992.

In 1993, Kim Young-sam and Bill Clinton came to office in South Korea and the United States respectively. Kim Young-sam was concerned that the Clinton administration would continue his predecessor George Bush's pressure approach, which might have led to a crisis.[4] Since Kim Young-sam did not want to raise tensions on the Korean peninsula, he wanted to solve the problem through diplomatic means rather than putting pressure on Pyongyang.[5]

He also wanted to take the lead in nuclear negotiations, given that South Korea was the country that had unswervingly confronted North Korea and would be most directly affected if North Korea became a nuclear power. So, in his inaugural address, he proposed a summit meeting with the then North Korean leader Kim Il-sung. In the speech, he stated that, "No foreign ally is better than our compatriots. No ideology can bring greater happiness than our compatriots."[6] With that statement, President Kim Young-sam expressed his intention to prioritize compatriotic kinship rather than alliance in nuclear negotiations. This statement was strategically made to entice North Korea to negotiate with Seoul rather than Washington because until then Pyongyang had communicated about the nuclear issue with only Washington. Given Washington's suspicions about Pyongyang's nuclear ambition and pressure approach, Kim Young-sam's statement raised many eyebrows.

However, Pyongyang did not respond positively and continued its talks with Washington without Seoul's involvement. As talks were fruitless, North Korea announced its withdrawal from the NPT in March 1993. President Kim Young-sam condemned Pyongyang by stating, "I can never shake hands with someone who has nuclear weapons," indicating his frustration over North Korea's lack of response to his positive gestures. The Kim administration also issued a warning that South Korea was prepared to take proper actions to respond to any North Korean military provocations.[7] Nevertheless, the Kim administration returned Lee In-mo, a long-term, unconverted communist prisoner, to North Korea without condition.[8] The Kim administration also announced that Seoul would separate the nuclear issue from other issues and object to isolating Pyongyang from the rest of the world.[9] That indicated that Kim Young-sam still wanted to talk to North Korean leader Kim Il-sung.

Because of the lack of progress in nuclear negotiations, the Clinton administration began to consider a contingency plan, a surgical air strike. To avoid a military confrontation, former U.S. president Jimmy Carter visited Pyongyang. In the meeting, Kim Il-sung agreed to Carter's request to freeze its nuclear program and allow further inspections. In return, Washington committed to supply crude oil and build two light water nuclear reactors with the support of South Korea, Japan, and the Europe Union (EU). The two Koreas also agreed to hold a summit meeting on July 25, 1994, but the summit meeting was never held due to Kim Il-sung's sudden death on July 8, 1994.

In order to become a negotiating partner for the nuclear issue, Kim Young-sam proposed the Three Phase National Community Unification Plan in August 1994, an improved version of the Unification Plan for One National Community put forth by Roh Tae-woo in 1989. The three phases are: (1) reconciliation and cooperation; (2) creation of the Korean Commonwealth; and (3) a unified Korea comprising one nation and one state. Throughout the process of unification, South Korea would recognize North Korea's system and pursue coexistence and common prosperity (Ministry of National Unification). Yet, Pyongyang denounced the proposal.

In October 1994 in Geneva, Washington and Pyongyang finalized the so-called Agreed Framework, which ended the first North Korean nuclear crisis. However, South Korea was not able to participate in the negotiation, leaving little room for the Kim Young-sam administration to play a role in the negotiation process. With the Agreed Framework, the Korean Peninsula Energy Development Organization (KEDO) was created to support building two light water nuclear reactors in North Korea. For the remaining period of the Kim young-sam administration, the Agreed Framework dictated the North Korean nuclear crisis.

During the Kim Young-sam administration, South Korea played a limited role in negotiating with North Korea, for three reasons. First, the Kim Young-sam administration did not have a grand plan or strategy that could lead to North Korea's nuclear disarmament. In the early 1990s North Korea experienced a dire economic crisis due to the repeated famines and droughts. Many policymakers and North Korea experts predicted that the North Korean regime would not last long. Moreover, the Kim Young-sam administration did not consider North Korea's nuclear program seriously because the level of North Korean nuclear development at that time was not advanced. Thus, the Kim administration did not feel the need to develop a scheme to dismantle North Korea's nuclear program.[10]

Second, since the Kim administration was expecting the collapse of the regime in North Korea, Kim Young-sam wanted to take the lead in nuclear negotiations to create an environment in which he could voice South Korea's interests after the collapse of the Kim Il-sung regime. To this end, he tried to appeal to Kim Jong-il by providing economic aid in 1995 upon Pyongyang's request and sending a long-term, unconverted communist prisoner to North Korea. Yet Pyongyang was only interested in talking to Washington. To alter the situation, the Kim Young-sam administration employed a mixed strategy of positive signals and condemnations, but the strategy did not work.[11]

Finally, Pyongyang was interested in negotiating the nuclear issue only with the United States. To get into the negotiation, the Kim administration proposed the Three Phase National Community Unification Plan and four-party talks including the United States and China. To make the proposal more appealing, the Kim administration announced that if Pyongyang agreed to four-party talks, Seoul would not oppose bilateral talks between Washington and Pyongyang. This meant the abandonment of South Korea's position on the US-DPRK relationship, that improvement of inter-Korean relations must precede any direct contact between Washington and Pyongyang.[12] Despite the Kim Young-sam administration's efforts, Pyongyang was not interested in negotiations with Seoul. As a result, Seoul could not play a meaningful role in nuclear negotiations.

THE KIM DAE-JUNG ADMINISTRATION (1998–2003)

Although the Kim Young-sam administration repeatedly attempted to work with Pyongyang, he really did not have confidence in North Korea. By contrast, Kim Dae-jung was willing to work with Pyongyang as separate nations based on the compatriotic perspective.[13] Moreover, Kim

Young-sam had expected the collapse of the Kim Il-sung regime, but Kim Dae-jung witnessed its resilience. Because of the differences between the perceptions of Kim Young-sam and Kim Dae-jung and lessons learned from Kim Young-sam's unsuccessful dealing with North Korea, Kim Dae-jung employed a different strategy, which he labeled the Sunshine Policy.[14]

The Sunshine Policy was Kim Dae-jung's grand strategy toward North Korea, his ultimate unification policy. The Sunshine Policy was based on four provisions: (1) peaceful relationship with North Korea but no tolerance for military provocation; (2) institutionalization of a peaceful coexistence with North Korea; (3) separation of economics from politics for enhancement in economic, social, and cultural exchanges between the two Koreas; and (4) reciprocity in implementation of the Sunshine Policy.[15]

The first two provisions were intended to clarify that the Kim Dae-jung administration was not pursuing a regime change in North Korea. To remedy the lack of mutual trust, Kim Dae-jung proclaimed that South Korea was seeking a peaceful coexistence as separate nations. By doing so, the Kim Dae-jung government tried to persuade Pyongyang to accept Seoul as a negotiation partner.

The third provision, separating economics from politics, was deliberately designed to attract more investment from the private sector to North Korea. Given the limited government resources, the Kim Dae-jung administration wanted to bring in additional resources from the private sector so that Seoul could provide massive economic aid to North Korea. This approach was designed to earn Pyongyang's trust and make room to play a greater role in nuclear negotiations. The Kim administration also hoped that this provision would lead to improved relationships and increased economic exchanges among North Korea and the United States and Japan.[16]

Reciprocity in implementation of the Sunshine Policy was proposed to signal that Pyongyang also needed to make concessions.[17] Since success of the Sunshine Policy depended on North Korea's positive response, reciprocity was included as a principle of this strategy. However, North Korea did not reciprocate South Korea's positive moves, so the reciprocity principle was replaced with "provide first and expect later."[18] Modifying the reciprocity principle was the strategic choice to maintain the Sunshine Policy despite Pyongyang's provocations.

To implement the Sunshine Policy and facilitate increases in economic investment in North Korea, the Kim Dae-jung administration launched the creation of the Kaesong Industrial Complex and Kumkang Tourism Project. For the former, the Kim government simplified the permission procedure for business activities and removed private investment caps and item restrictions. For the latter, the Kim government eased travel restrictions to North Korea.

The Kim Dae-jung administration also provided economic aid to North Korea. During his tenure, the Kim Dae-jung administration (March 1998–February 2003) provided $855.7 million to North Korea, which is four times higher than the Kim Young-sam administration ($188 million) had spent. In addition, Kim Dae-jung illegally sent $500 million to Pyongyang for the June 2000 summit meeting.[19]

North Korea enjoyed all these benefits but expressed the lack of its confidence in South Korea by censuring the Sunshine Policy. Pyongyang mocked the Sunshine Policy by calling it "sunburn" policy because they reckoned the policy embodied Seoul's strategy as intended to undermine the Kim Jong-il regime.[20] The Kim regime even adopted "the military first" policy with a motto *Kangsong Taeguk* meaning a "strong and prosperous great power."[21] To this end, Kim Jong-il elevated the status of the National Defense Committee (NDC) to the highest government organization. As the chairman of the NDC, Kim Jong-il officially took charge of all political, economic, and military affairs in North Korea. In addition, North Korea test-fired a long-range missile, *Taepodong* 1, in 1998, and North Korean naval ships entered the ROK territorial sea crossing the Northern Limit Line (NLL), the maritime boundary between the two Koreas designated by the UN, resulting in the first Yonpyeong naval conflict in 1999.[22]

In October 2002, the second North Korean nuclear crisis broke out as North Korea admitted another type (highly enriched uranium–based) of its nuclear programs. As a result, implementation of the Agreed Framework was ceased. Although the Kim Dae-jung administration's strategy was engagement, South Korea joined the United States in condemning North Korea. As the relationship between Washington and Pyongyang became aggravated, the Kim Dae-jung administration employed a two-dimensional strategy: (1) work with the United States and Japan to resolve the issue through peaceful means; and (2) directly communicate with North Korea via inter-Korean negotiations. With this approach, Seoul tried to play a mediator's role between Washington and Pyongyang to prevent the escalation of the crisis. To this end, the Kim administration expressed its concerns about North Korea's nuclear development in the ministerial talks between the two Koreas on October 19–23, 2002. At the same time, when leaders of the United States, ROK, and Japan met at the APEC (Asia-Pacific Economic Cooperation) conference on October 27, 2002, Kim Dae-jung insisted on negotiating with North Korea under the Agreed Framework. In the meeting of the Trilateral Coordination and Oversight Group (TCOG) on November 8, South Korea opposed halting the supply of crude oil to the north. Nevertheless, the KEDO (Korea Energy Development Organization) executive board decided to suspend the oil supply. In response, North Korea reopened the nuclear facility and removed the seals from nuclear reactors and monitoring cameras.

Although the crisis escalated, the ROK government continued its efforts to mediate between Washington and Pyongyang. Seoul publicly announced its objection to North Korea's nuclear development and insisted on returning to the negotiation table. South Korea also communicated with the United States, Japan, China, Russia, and the European Union to change their approach, although without success.

In summary, during the Kim Dae-jung administration period, the relationship between the two Koreas significantly improved, and Kim Dae-jung and Kim Jong-il even had a summit meeting in Pyongyang on June 13–15, 2000, for the first time in history. However, when South Korea demanded inclusion of the nuclear issue in the discussion agenda for the defense ministers' meeting in September 2000, Pyongyang refused to do so. The only achievement of the meeting was mutual agreement to establish a hot line between the two countries' military commands.[23] It was clear that Kim Jong-il was not interested in serious dialogue with Kim Dae-jung about the nuclear issue. Moreover, George W. Bush was elected president of the United States in 2000, which made it difficult for Kim Dae-jung to sustain his engagement strategy because of Bush's skepticism about the effectiveness of the approach.

Overall, the Kim Dae-jung administration's strategy toward North Korea can be characterized by two principles: engagement and separation of politics and economics. The Kim administration persistently maintained the approach for two reasons: (1) the Kim Jong-il regime was unlikely to collapse and North Korea's engagement was necessary for peaceful resolution of the nuclear crisis; and (2) separation of economics and politics was inevitable because Pyongyang did not reciprocate Seoul's positive moves.[24] If South Korea linked politics and economics, Seoul would have to rescind its engagement strategy in response to North Korea's provocations. In that case, the improved relationship between the two Koreas would cool down, and no communication channel would remain. To continue Seoul's efforts to improve the relationship between the two Koreas and to make room for Seoul to play an important role in nuclear negotiations, the Kim Dae-jung administration decided to keep the principle of separation of politics and economics.[25]

THE ROH MOO-HYUN ADMINISTRATION (2003–08)

When Roh Moo-hyun came to office in 2003, upon U.S. insistence six-party talks (ROK, DPRK, United States, China, Japan, and Russia) embarked. Thus, South Korea was able to get involved in nuclear negotiations. The Roh Moo-hyun administration's grand strategy for dealing with the North Korean nuclear issue was to establish a peace regime on the Korean peninsula. The Roh administration perceived that the primary reason for North Korea's nuclear development was the regime's survival. Providing the guarantee of the regime's survival to Kim Jong-il would be the key to resolving the nuclear issue. To this end, the Roh government developed a three-phase plan: (1) promote peace by expanding inter-Korean economic cooperation and regularizing military talks, to establish a foundation to resolve the nuclear issue; (2) reach an agreement on the nuclear and missile issues, to mark a milestone for a peace regime on the Korean peninsula by deepening inter-Korean cooperation in order to build mutual trust; and (3) extend a security guarantee to Pyongyang for arms control and propose a joint economic development plan between the two Koreas, to lead to eventually signing a peace treaty with North Korea, which would establish a peace regime on the Korean peninsula.[26]

Rho Moo-hyun's take on the North Korean nuclear issue was well described in his interview with *Time* magazine. He said, "I don't think there is a particular reason to promote a different policy from the former President's policy. I will try to improve the methodology (of the policy toward North Korea) by consulting with the opposition party, winning more approval of the people and increasing transparency of process."[27] His idea of improved method was spelled out in the Peace and Prosperity policy, which had two goals and four principles for implementation. The two goals were promoting peace and prosperity in the Korean peninsula.[28] To this end, he intended a security guarantee along with economic aids to North Korea, which he believed would lead to a denuclearized North Korea.

Four principles guided the implementation measures designed to achieve these goals. They were: (1) employing peaceful means, such as diplomacy, as the problem-solving method; (2) enhancing mutual trust based on reciprocity to make bilateral talks meaningful; (3) seeking international cooperation (particularly from the United States and Japan), because inter-Korean relations were unlikely to improve without international support; and (4) encouraging citizen participation in the process of policymaking, because public support was crucial to increasing economic aid to North Korea.[29] These principles were aimed to answer North Korea's lack of response to the Kim Dae-jung administration's Sunshine Policy, resulting in a significant decline of public support for the engagement approach.[30]

The Peace and Prosperity policy called for expansion of economic exchanges between the two Koreas and an increase in economic aid, including cash inflow to North Korea. The results were an increase in total trade volume between the two Koreas from $724 million in 2003 to $1.8 billion in 2007. South Korea's economic aid to North Korea also went up from $322.6 million in 2002, the last year of the Kim Dae-jung administration to $439.7 million in 2007, the last year of the Roh administration. When the Kaesong Industrial Complex launched in 2004, the number of North Korean workers hired was fewer than two thousand, but it upsurged to 22,538 by the end of 2007.[31]

The rationale behind the Peace and Prosperity policy was that massive economic aid and cash flow to North Korea would improve mutual trust and change Pyongyang. The Roh administration utilized all public and private economic resources available for economic aid to North Korea. The move led to a summit meeting between Roh Moo-hyun and Kim Jong-il in 2007. At the meeting the two leaders signed a peace declaration, which included creating a common fishing area and construction of railroads, expressways, and a shipping complex. Yet, nuclear issues were not even discussed at the summit meeting, although the two leaders met in the midst of the nuclear crisis.[32]

Regardless of the Roh administration's approach, Pyongyang focused on Washington. Kim Jong-il apparently perceived that the survival of his regime depended on the United States, and South Korea was not a factor in this regard. Since the George W. Bush administration demanded the complete, verifiable, irreversible dismantlement (CVID) of North Korea's nuclear program as a precondition for any compensation talks, Kim Jong-il only used Roh Moo-hyun to get economic aid. Because of this fundamental difficulty embedded in the nuclear negotiation setting, the

Roh administration's approach was not effective. Realizing Pyongyang's perception, the Roh administration insisted that the United States provide a security guarantee to North Korea along with economic aid. But the Bush administration was not willing to do so.

The crisis escalated as North Korea conducted its first nuclear test on October 9, 2006. The United Nations Security Council (UNSC) passed Resolution 1718, demanding an end to nuclear tests and missile launches and a return to the six-party talks. The resolution also imposed economic sanctions on North Korea, including bans on weapons-related items and luxury goods.[33] After six rounds of six-party talks, little progress was made. North Korea shut down the Yongbyon nuclear reactor. In return, the United States supplied $400 million in fuel oil.[34] However, there was no discussion of North Korea's HEU (Highly Enriched Uranium)-based nuclear program, existing nuclear weapons stockpile, and assistance to other countries' nuclear programs.

THE LEE MYUNG-BAK ADMINISTRATION (2008–13)

Lee Myung-bak perceived that the previous two administrations' strategy for the North Korean nuclear crisis was largely a failure. According to Lee, given South Korea's economic and military superiority, South Korea's strategy to denuclearize North Korea should be based on confidence. According to Lee, providing massive economic aid regardless of North Korea's response did not accord with the stature of South Korea. South Korea's massive economic aid only helped the Kim Jong-il regime whose citizens hardly enjoyed the benefits. Unconditional economic aid to the north was a waste of South Korea's valuable tax revenues, which caused domestic conflicts between supporters and opponents of the policy. Thus, he pledged that his strategy would be balanced and stick to the principle.[35]

In a statement made right after he won the election, Lee Myung-bak indicated a change in policy by stating that his strategy toward the North Korean nuclear issue would be based on restoring the ROK-U.S. alliance. Unlike his immediate predecessors, he proclaimed that he would closely coordinate his policy with the United States.[36] At that time, U.S. President George W. Bush focused on pressuring North Korea to abandon its nuclear ambitions. Thus, it was clear which direction the Lee administration would go.

The official title of the Lee Myung-bak administration's North Korea strategy was The Policy of Mutual Benefits and Common Prosperity. The Policy of Mutual Benefits and Common Prosperity stemmed from the

National Community Unification Plan introduced by Kim Young-sam in 1994.[37] For implementation, Lee proposed The Vision 3,000 through Denuclearization and Openness. The Vision 3,000 through Denuclearization and Openness was a strategy to lead to Pyongyang's nuclear abandonment: if North Korea denuclearized and opened its society and market, South Korea would help North Korea to increase its per capita income to $3,000 within ten years. In other words, it was a conditional engagement approach, with denuclearization and opening the country as prerequisites for South Korea's economic aid.[38]

As an action plan for The Vision 3,000 through Denuclearization and Openness, Lee proposed a New Peace Initiative on the Korean Peninsula. The plan included (1) launching an international program to increase economic aid to North Korea; (2) holding high-level talks to establish an economic community between the two Koreas; and (3) developing programs that would facilitate economic development, educational enhancement, and improvement in fiscal health, economic infrastructure, and standard of living.[39]

The Lee administration's North Korea strategy was devised to deal with the main problem of the two previous administrations' engagement strategy, namely, North Korea's lack of reciprocity despite unconditional, massive economic aid. By proposing requirements for economic aid, the Lee administration made clear its intention to stick to the principle of reciprocity.

The Vision 3,000 through Denuclearization and Openness was an integrated strategy of stick (requirements) and carrot (rewards). It was also to satisfy the Bush administration and to maintain the momentum of the improved inter-Korean relationship, if possible. The rationale behind this strategy was that North Korea's dependence on South Korea's aid had significantly heightened in the previous decade. It would be difficult for Pyongyang to relinquish economic aid from the south, which would pressure the Kim Jong-il regime to try to meet the preconditions. To facilitate the implementation of the Lee administration's North Korea policy, Lee also proposed a Grand Bargain approach. The Grand Bargain approach entailed changing the approach to the North Korean nuclear crisis. Previous negotiations had failed because they focused on the nuclear issue only, although it was only one of many North Korean problems. Thus, instead of negotiating each issue separately, Lee suggested discussing all the issues together. Lee argued that this approach would help all parties reach a conclusion.[40]

North Korea proved the Lee administration's expectation wrong. They were willing to give up South Korea's economic aid. Pyongyang interpreted the Lee administration's strategy as indicative of its lack of interest in improving the inter-Korean relationship and resolving the North Korean nuclear issue.[41] As a result, The Vision 3,000 through Denuclearization and Openness did not work, but the Lee administration had no plan B. Thus, no progress was made on the nuclear issue.

To make matters worse, North Korea conducted its second nuclear test, along with missile test firings, in 2009. In response, the Obama administration decided not to directly communicate with Pyongyang. Instead, Washington sought coordinated alliance efforts through the UN, the so-called strategic patience. The rationale behind this approach was that North Korea was likely to abandon its nuclear programs as it would be difficult for them to endure the UN sanctions for a long time.

In 2010, North Korea further complicated the situation by sinking a Korean warship and shelling Yeonpyeong Island. Further UN sanctions were imposed on North Korea. However, the effects of all UN sanctions were rather limited, and North Korea withstood them. Yet, Washington did not introduce new policies, a sign of U.S. fatigue in dealing with the issue. Since the Lee administration declared that it would stick to the principles of close coordination with the United States and reciprocity, the ROK government did not amend its approach. As a result, the North Korean nuclear issue went back to square one.

Overall, the Lee administration's strategy suffered from a fatal weakness of requiring North Korea's cooperation in meeting the prerequisites of denuclearization and openness. Pyongyang had never cooperated with Seoul before and there was no reason for Seoul to expect Pyongyang to change. Considering the lack of mutual trust, the Lee administration's strategy of Vision 3,000 for Denuclearization and Openness was an empty slogan to Pyongyang. It is not clear that the strategy was designed to give a choice to Pyongyang. If they met the preconditions, the Lee administration would provide aid yet otherwise employ a pressure approach.

Lee witnessed that his predecessors lost public support when they discarded the reciprocity principle. Not to make the same mistake, Lee publicly pledged sticking to the reciprocity principle in his North Korea policy. Thus, he had to shift his strategy once North Korea committed provocations, such as the sinking of the ROK Naval battleship *Cheonan* and murder of a South Korean tourist at Kumkang Mountain. As a result, inter-Korean relations rapidly cooled down.

The Park Geun-hye Administration (2013–17)

The Park Geun-hye administration's strategy for dealing with the North Korea nuclear issue started with a critique of previous administrations' North Korea policies. Just like Lee Myung-bak, Park assessed that the assumption that the engagement strategy, with sustained economic aid, would end Pyongyang's hostility toward the south and lead to nuclear abandonment, was unfounded. The fact that ten years of massive economic aid had not led to the dismantling of North Korea's nuclear programs provided empirical evidence.[42]

Park Geun-hye also realized that the Lee Myung-bak administration's strategy was ineffective. Park Geun-hye recognized that nuclear abandonment in response to economic aid was not acceptable to Pyongyang considering the lack of mutual trust between the two Koreas. To address the problem, Park introduced her strategy, The Korean Peninsula Trust Process. The logic behind this strategy was that without confidence building between the two Koreas, no talks are meaningful, and no strategy will work.[43]

The Korean Peninsula Trust Process is well described by Park in her article "A New Kind of Korea: Building Trust Between Seoul and Pyongyang," published in *Foreign Affairs* in 2011. The Korean Peninsula Trust Process has two parts: Trustpolitik and Alignment Policy. Trustpolitik means "establishing mutually binding expectations based on global norms."[44] According to Trustpolitik, peace on the Korean peninsula is not possible without cooperation between the two Koreas. In the past, North Korea repeatedly violated international agreements and norms. To cope with the issue, Trustpolitk proposed two provisions: (1) "North Korea must keep its agreements made with South Korea and the international community to establish a minimum level of trust; and (2) there must be assured consequences for actions that breach the peace."[45] These provisions must be applied consistently to all issues between the two Koreas, including the nuclear problem. Considering that ten years of South Korea's unconditional economic aid did not earn much trust from the north, the approach stressed patience and incrementalism.

As a policy measure to lead North Korea to make policies that promote peace on the Korean peninsula based on international norms and to build mutual trust gradually, Alignment Policy was introduced. Given the importance of patience and the incremental nature of confidence building, Park highlighted public consensus and consistency as two necessary conditions of the policy. She reiterated that the policy must not be affected by internal and/or external shocks to maintain its consistency.

Park Geun-hye also stated that South Korea's security policy must be based on cooperation between the two Koreas, which must be achieved through dialogue. To achieve cooperation between the two Koreas, Alignment Policy necessitates flexible responses: in the case of military provocation by North Korea, South Korea must make North Korea pay for its actions, but if North Korea takes steps for cooperation, South Korea needs to reward them, a tit-for-tat strategy. In other words, if one party provokes the other by violating the agreement, that party must pay the price, thus mandating a commitment for cooperation by both parties. The policy also emphasized that South Korea's strategy toward North Korea must not be unconditional or unbalanced, reintroducing the reciprocity principle.[46]

For implementation of this strategy, Park Geun-hye proposed two measures: (1) strengthening the military as an important deterrent force and, as a demonstration of South Korea's military superiority to the north, to send Pyongyang a message that they will pay the price if they provoke; and (2) appealing to the international community for support to lead to North Korea's nuclear disarmament. Park Geun-hye clarified that South Korea would not accept North Korea's nuclearization under any circumstances. She assumed that the international community would support her strategy on the grounds that a nuclear North Korea would pose a security threat to them as well once it developed long-range missiles. In summary, South Korea and the international community must synchronize their efforts to dismantle North Korea's nuclear program based on credible deterrence force and vigorous persuasion through negotiations and economic rewards such as joint economic projects, including additional investment and trade and humanitarian assistance.[47]

Although Park Geun-hye spelled out her strategy to induce Pyongyang to work with Seoul for gradual confidence building, Pyongyang did not move in the direction Seoul hoped for. In February 2013, North Korea conducted its third nuclear test. Given the tit-for-tat nature of The Korean Peninsula Trust process, the Park administration responded by repealing the transfer of wartime operational control of the ROK military from the United States. Seoul also sought improvement in the war preparedness of the ROK troops. To demonstrate the cooperation between Seoul and Washington, the Park administration explicitly supported the U.S. position in the U.S.-China conflict in the South China Sea. As a result, the inter-Korean relationship quickly cooled down. In January 2016, North Korea conducted its fourth nuclear test. In response, the Park administration shut down the Kaesong Industrial Complex, an important cash cow for Pyongyang, and Seoul and Washington agreed to deploy THAAD (Terminal High Altitude Area Defense) in South Korea. The deterioration of inter-Korean relations escalated as North Korea conducted its fifth nuclear test in September 2016. To strengthen the trilateral cooperation among South Korea, the United States, and Japan, Seoul signed the General Security of Military Information Agreement with Tokyo, and THAAD was deployed in Seongju, South Korea.[48]

In many ways, implementation of the Korean Peninsula Trust Process was déjà vu of the Lee Myung-bak administration's Vision 3,000 through Denuclearization and Openness. Just like the Lee administration, which had few policy options once Pyongyang refused to honor the prerequisites, the Korean Peninsula Trust Process from the beginning did not go in the direction Seoul hoped for because of North Korea's multiple nuclear tests. Since both policies were based on the reciprocity principle, the south had to employ pressure policies toward North Korea.

The Moon Jae-in Administration (2017–2022)

When Moon Jae-in came to office in May 2017, tensions in the Korean peninsula heightened because North Korea conducted two nuclear tests combined with long range missile test firings and the U.S. government led the UN Security Council to impose the strongest sanctions ever on North Korea. Washington also pressured Beijing to be in full compliance with the UN sanctions. Recognizing the cooled relationship between the two Koreas in the past decade, Moon developed his strategy to improve inter-Korean relations while highlighting the role of South Korean leadership in denuclearizing North Korea. The strategy was named The Korean Peninsula Driver Theory. [49]

The Korean Peninsula Driver Theory is a two-track strategy: (1) cooperating with the United States by carrying out the UN sanctions on North Korea; and (2) improving inter-Korean relations through dialogue. The Moon administration adopted this strategy as it had little latitude because of the cycle of Pyongyang's military provocation and Washington's response of amplifying sanctions. U.S. president Donald Trump and North Korean leader Kim Jong-un also exchanged harsh rhetoric, escalating tensions in the region. Furthermore, the U.S.-China trade disputes and Pyongyang's persistent preference of direct negotiation with Washington made the situation more complicated for South Korea.[50]

The Moon administration realized that it is not possible to provide economic aid to North Korea unless North Korea takes some steps toward denuclearization, meaning that a step-by-step negotiation process must be employed. To facilitate the step-by-step negotiation between Washington and Pyongyang with Seoul's involvement, the Moon administration's Korean Peninsula Driver Theory was introduced. For implementation of the strategy, Seoul employed three measures: (1) expansion of the engagement approach; (2) a nuclear freeze at first, leading to ultimate denuclearization; and (3) a combination of dialogue and pressure.[51]

Since Moon Jae-in was sympathetic to Kim Dae-jung's and Roh Moo-hyun's strategies, his government's strategy to denuclearize North Korea was based on the engagement approach. Theoretically the engagement approach is a foreign policy strategy that attempts to induce national behavior/policy changes through various exchanges, including normalization of the formal relationship, high-level talks including summit meetings, confidence building, expanding trade and investments, military cooperation, providing economic and humanitarian aid, and cultural exchanges. The logic behind the approach is that amplified exchanges will influence the public to put pressure on the government to change its policies.

Because of this logic, Pyongyang reckoned the engagement strategy a hostile policy, and thus Kim Dae-jung's and Roh Moo-hyun's policies were not successful.[52] To alleviate Pyongyang's concern, the Moon administration prioritized assuring the Kim Jong-un regime survival. At the same time, Moon wanted to denuclearize North Korea and knew that it was not possible without U.S. support.

To this end, Moon proposed three step measures: (1) declaration of formally ending the Korean War for a symbolic end to the inter-Korean conflict, with U.S. support; (2) US-DPRK negotiation for a peace agreement to start a peace process in the Korean peninsula; and (3) a signed treaty to establish a peace regime on the Korean peninsula to expand economic and cultural exchanges between the two Koreas.[53]

To establish a peace regime on the Korean peninsula, North Korea's denuclearization is necessary. However, Pyongyang is unlikely to accept denuclearization, given the lack of mutual trust. Thus, the Moon administration asserted that efforts to lead to North Korea's nuclear disarmament should begin with discussions on a nuclear freeze, such as suspending nuclear and missile programs, and end with negotiations for complete dismantlement of the North Korean nuclear programs. To induce Pyongyang to the negotiation table, Seoul reiterated no preconditions for inter-Korean talks.[54]

As noted earlier, the Moon administration had little diplomatic leeway in terms of its North Korea policy due to the heightened tensions between Washington and Pyongyang. To cooperate with the U.S. maximum pressure policy, the Moon administration had to support UN sanctions. At the same time, Seoul tried to mediate the relationship between Washington and Pyongyang to facilitate talks, which culminated with summit meetings between Donald Trump and Kim Jong-un. For a while, Moon's strategy seemed working.

Yet it had a fundamental weakness, as Trump or Kim could unilaterally suspend all negotiations without prior consultation with Moon. To facilitate the continuation of talks between Washington and Pyongyang, as a trust-building measure, the Moon administration suggested "reciprocal exchanges involving nuclear concessions from North Korea and political, security, and economic concessions from the United States and its partners."[55] To induce the reciprocal exchanges, Seoul proposed a railroad project in August 2018. Yet, it was not welcomed by Washington given the UN sanctions.[56] In other words, Moon's strategy heavily relied on Washington's and Pyongyang's cooperation. This fallacy became clear when the summit meetings failed to produce meaningful outcomes. There was very little Seoul could do to modify the situation.

In summary, there was a structural limitation on South Korea's ability to play any meaningful role in the North Korean nuclear negotiation. Moreover, the Moon administration's two-track strategy carried an implicit assumption that Washington and Pyongyang would follow Seoul's lead. The strategy worked fine when Washington and Pyongyang negotiated the nuclear issue through summit meetings. Once they derailed the process, it was clear that the strategy had fundamental limits vis-à-vis Seoul's role in the negotiation of North Korea's denuclearization.

Conclusion and Discussion

There have been two types of strategies South Korea has employed to deal with the North Korean nuclear crisis: (1) engagement; and (2) pressure.

Progressive administrations (e.g., Kim Dae-jung, Roh Moo-hyn, Moon Jae-in) employed the engagement approach, seeking gradual changes in North Korea through economic aid and trade expansion while maintaining stability in the Korean peninsula. Kim Dae-jung and Roh Moo-hyun were the strong proponents of this strategy, which is based on the idea that South Korea can take the lead in denuclearizing North Korea by inducing Pyongyang to negotiate with Seoul vis-à-vis denuclearization and ultimate reunification. To this end, these administrations separated economics from politics. They started with the reciprocity principle but shifted to the principle of "provide first and expect later" to cope with the lack of positive response from Pyongyang. These two principles, separation of politics and economics and provide first and expect later, were the product of compromises made to sustain the engagement strategy despite North Korea's repeated provocations. At the same time, these two principles allowed the government to provide unconditional, massive economic aid to North Korea despite public concerns and critique (see Table 4.1).

By contrast, conservative governments (e.g., Lee Myung-bak, Park Geun-hye) preferred pressure approaches aiming for regime change or collapse. The logic behind this strategy is that economic sanctions will gradually undermine the power base of the Kim family, which will result in eventual regime collapse. The strategy has a short-term goal, denuclearization of North Korea, but also has a long-term objective, reunification via absorption by economically isolating North Korea, thus leading to bankruptcy.[57]

Implementations of the strategy by Lee Myung-bak and Park Geun-hye were different. The Lee administration employed a conditional engagement approach with Vision 3,000 through Denuclearization and Openness. The Lee administration signaled its willingness to provide economic aid if Pyongyang denuclearized first. However, the prerequisite was practically impossible for Pyongyang to accept considering the lack of mutual trust. So, Vision 3,000 through Denuclearization and Openness ended up with an empty slogan, leading to the pressure approach. It is not clear whether the Lee administration deliberately did this to join the Bush administration's pressure approach.

Park Geun-hye employed a flexible response strategy, the Korean Peninsula Trust process. It was a tit-for-tat strategy. Seoul wanted to induce Pyongyang to build trust between the two countries by starting with small-scale private sector economic exchanges, along with expressing its intention to expand the exchange with government aid to the north. This strategy also had an implicit prerequisite, Pyongyang's cooperation.

Table 4.1. South Korea's Economic Aid to North Korea
(unit: 100 million Korean won = approximately US$ 100,000)

| | Public | | Private | |
	Grant	Food Aids	Grant Aid	Total
1996	24	0	12	36
1997	240	0	182	422
1998	154	0	275	429
1999	339	0	223	562
2000	978	1,057	387	2,422
2001	975	0	782	1,757
2002	1,140	1,510	576	3,226
2003	1,097	1,510	766	3,373
2004	1,313	1,359	1,558	4,230
2005	1,360	1,787	779	3,926
2006	2,273	0	709	2,982
2007	1,983	1,505	909	4,397
2008	438	0	725	1,163
2009	294	0	377	671
2010	204	0	200	404
2011	65	0	131	196
2012	23	0	118	141
2013	133	0	51	183
2014	141	0	54	195
2015	140	0	114	254
2016	2	0	28	30
2017	0	0	11	11
2018	12	0	65	77
2019	106	0	170	277

Source: e-National Statistics (Statistical Table Aids to North Korea); Ministry of National Unification (http://www.index.go.kr/potal/main/EachDtlPageDetail.do?idx_cd = 2784).

The paths of Lee's and Park's strategies relied on Pyongyang's decision, as they both required Pyongyang's cooperative behavior. When Kim Jong-un refused, both Lee and Park administrations had no choice but to resort to pressure.

In a nutshell, all South Korea's negotiation strategies for denucle-arizing North Korea have failed, as North Korea is practically a nuclear power today. There might be three reasons for the result. The first is incorrect assessment of North Korea's intention to develop nuclear weapons. Policymakers and security experts in South Korea as well as the United States perceived that North Korea developed its nuclear programs in order to receive economic aid for the regime's survival. Thus, it would be possible to denuclearize North Korea with massive economic aid and the guarantee of regime survival. That is why unconditional economic aids were provided (see Figure 4.1). In hindsight, it was an incorrect assessment, given that Pyongyang just enjoyed the aid without making progress toward denuclearization.[58]

Second, successive administrations have underestimated the risk embedded in providing economic aid to North Korea. In February 2016, the Korean Ministry of National Unification revealed that $560 million was invested to the Kaesong Industrial Complex between 2005 and 2015. Three hundred ninety-two million dollars out of the $560 million went to the North Korean government, and is suspected to have been used for the nuclear and missile programs.[59] In addition, the Kumkang Mountain tourism project also supplied a substantial amount of cash to North Korea. Thus, it is possible that South Korea's engagement policy measures assisted North Korea's nuclear programs, which made South Korea's efforts to denuclearize North Korea difficult to succeed.

Finally, both Seoul and Washington underestimated the resilience of the Kim regime in North Korea. Kim Young-sam anticipated the regime's collapse in the near future due to the economic difficulties caused by repeated famines and droughts occurred in the early 1990s. Lee Myung-bak and Park Geun-hye as well as U.S. Republican presidents assessed that unwavering economic sanctions would undermine the power base of the Kim family, resulting in the regime collapse.[60] However, it turned out that the North Korean regime is far more durable than Seoul and Washington expected.

In conclusion, negotiations are meaningful only when both parties are willing to compromise in order to resolve the issue in contention. Pyongyang's behavior thus far suggests that North Korea was determined to become a member of the nuclear club. Thus, it was extremely difficult to lead to North Korea's nuclear abandonment regardless of South Korea's negotiation strategies. Furthermore, Pyongyang has persistently preferred to negotiate the nuclear issue with Washington, without Seoul's involvement. As a result, South Korea has had difficulties in playing a significant role in the nuclear negotiations.

Notes

1. "US Says North Korea an Urgent Priority," *VOA News*, February 12, 2021. https://www.voanews.com/usa/us-says-north-korea-urgent-priority.

2. "Secretary of State Blinken: North Korea is 'A Problem That's Gotten Worse Across Administrations,'" *NBC*, February 1, 2021. https://www.msnbc.com/andrea-mitchell-reports/watch/secy-of-state-blinken-north-korea-is-a-problem-that-s-gotten-worse-across-administrations-100352581598.

3. Min Cho and Jinha Kim, *Chronology of North Korea's Nuclear Development 1955–2014* (Seoul: Korea Institute for National Unification, 2014).

4. Leslie Gelb, "Foreign Affairs: The Next Crisis." *New York Times*, March 21, 1992. https://www.nytimes.com/1993/03/21/opinion/foreign-affairs-the-next-crisis.html?searchResultPosition=8.

5. Ok-nim Chung, *The North Korea Nuclear Crisis 588 Day* (Seoul: Seoul Press, 2015).

6. Recited from Uk Heo and Terence Roehrig, *South Korea Since 1980* (Cambridge: Cambridge University Press, 2010).

7. Jong-hyuk Kim and Youngjong Lee, "We Can't Be Spectators." *Joongang Daily*, December 27, 2002. https://www.joongang.co.kr/article/4402340#home.

8. Wankyu Choi, "The Kim Young-sam Administration's North Korea Policy: Assessment and Suggestions," in *Inter-Korean Relationship in the 21st Century*, ed. Baek Young-cheol (Seoul: Beopmoonsa, 2000).

9. Kim Young-sam, Interview with *CNN*. April 23, 1993. https://imnews.imbc.com/replay/1993/nwdesk/article/1754581_30684.html.

10. See Uk Heo and Chong-Min Hyun, "An Analysis of South Korea's Policy towards North Korea." *Pacific Focus* 16, no. 1 (2001): 89–102; Jung-bok Lee, *Solution of the North Korean Nuclear Crisis and Its Prospect* (Seoul: Joongang M&B, 2003).

11. Youngsoo Park, "Limits of the Kim Young-sam Administration's Response to the North Korean Nuclear Crisis Revisited," *Korean Political Studies* 20, no. 3 (2011): 55–78.

12. Bon-Hak Koo, "Challenges and Prospects for Inter-Korean Relations under the New Leadership," *Korean Journal of Defense Analysis* 10, no. 1 (1998): 75–93.

13. Kenneth C. Quinones, "South Korea's Approaches to North Korea: A Glacial Process," in *Korean Security Dynamics in Transition*, ed. Kyung-Ae Park and Dalchoong Kim (New York: Palgrave, 2001): 19–48.

14. Jung-hyun Shin, "Engagement Approach to North Korea," Unpublished manuscript (2002).

15. Uk Heo and Terence Roehrig, *South Korea's Rise: Economic Development, Power, and Foreign Relations* (Cambridge: Cambridge University Press, 2014).

16. Young Whan Kihl, "Seoul's Engagement Policy and US-DPRK Relations," *Korean Journal of Defense Analysis* 10, no. 1 (1998): 21–48.

17. Chung-in Moon, "Understanding the DJ Doctrine: The Sunshine Policy and the Korean Peninsula," in *Kim Dae-jung Government and Sunshine Policy: Promises and Challenges*, ed. Chung-in Moon and David I. Steinberg (Washington, DC: Georgetown University Press, 1999).

18. Uk Heo and Chong-Min Hyun, "The 'Sunshine Policy' Revisited: An Analysis of South Korea's Policy Toward North Korea," in *Conflict in Asia: Korea, China-Taiwan, and India-Pakistan*, ed. Uk Heo and Shale Horowitz (Westport, CT: Greenwood, 2003).

19. Heo and Roehrig, *South Korea Since 1980*; Heo and Roehrig, *South Korea's Rise: Economic Development, Power, and Foreign Relations*.

20. Samuel Kim, "North Korea in 2000," *Asian Survey* 41, no. 1 (2001): 12–29.

21. Choong Nam Kim, *The Korean Presidents: Leadership for Nation Building* (Norwalk, VA: East Bridge, 2007).

22. Heo and Roehrig, *South Korea since 1980*; Kim, *The Korean Presidents: Leadership for Nation Building*.

23. Howard French, "Defense Chiefs of Two Koreas Meet on Reducing Tensions," *New York Times*, September 26, 2000. A10.

24. Jung-hyun Shin, "Engagement Approach to North Korea."

25. Jung-bok Lee, *Solution of the North Korean Nuclear Crisis and Its Prospect* (Seoul: Joongang M&B, 2003).

26. Government Information Agency, "Leap into Pace and Prosperity," March 17, 2003 (Seoul: Government Information Agency, 2003).

27. "Hello, Mr. Roh: Getting to Know South Korea's New President," *Time*, March 3, 2003, 41.

28. Ministry of National Unification, *The Participatory Government's Peace and Prosperity Policy* (Seoul: Ministry of National Unification, 2003).

29. Min Cho, "Roh Moo-hyun Government's Peace and Prosperity Policy: Prospects and Tasks," *Unification Policy Studies* 12, no. 1 (2003): 1–27.

30. Hong-Suk Yoon, "The Peace and Prosperity Policy and the South-North Relationship: Evaluation and Future Tasks," in *Peace and Prosperity Policy and Peace Regime on the Korean Peninsula: The Limits of Coercive Diplomacy in Korean Peninsula*, ed. In-Duk Kang (Seoul: Institute for East Asian Studies, 2005).

31. Heo and Roehrig, *South Korea Since 1980*; Heo and Roehrig, *South Korea's Rise: Economic Development, Power, and Foreign Relations*.

32. Norimitsu Onish, "Korea Summit Results Exceed Low Expectations," *New York Times*. October 5, 2007. https://www.nytimes.com/2007/10/05/world/asia/05korea.html.

33. Anthony Faiola and Maureen Fan, "North Korea's Political, Economic Gamble," *Washington Post*, October 10, 2006. https://www.washingtonpost.com/wp-dyn/content/article/2006/10/08/AR2006100801169.html; UN Security Council Resolution, 2006. https://www.undocs.org/S/RES/1718%20.

34. Jim Yardley and David E. Sanger, "In Shift, Accord on North Korea Seems to Be Set," *New York Times*, February 13, 2007. https://www.nytimes.com/2007/02/13/world/asia/13korea.html?searchResultPosition=1.

35. Hongmei Tan, "A Study on North Korean Policy in South Korea: Compare with Kim Dae Joong, No Moo Hyon, and Lee Myong Bak Government," *Global Political Studies* 3, no. 1 (2010): 93–115.

36. Yon-se Kim, "President-Elect Vows Creative Diplomacy," *Korea Times*, December 19, 2007. https://www.koreatimes.co.kr/www/common/printpreviews.asp?categoryCode=113&newsIdx=15851.

37. Jung-rho Kim, "The Lee Myung-bak Administration's North Korea Policy: Denuclearization, Opening, and 3,000 to Grand Bargain," *Unification*, December 2009.

38. Scott Snyder, "Lee Myung-bak's Foreign Policy: A 250-Day Assessment," *Korean Journal of Defense Analysis* 21, no. 1 (2009): 85–102; Jae Jean Suh, *The Lee Myung-bak Government's North Korea Policy—A Study on its Historical and Theoretical Foundation* (Seoul: Korea Institute for National Unification, 2009); Hongmei Tan, "A Study on North Korean Policy in South Korea: Compare with Kim Dae Joong, No Moo Hyon, and Lee Myong Bak Government," *Global Political Studies* 3, no. 1 (2010): 93–115.

39. Moon-young Huh, Jung-ho Bae, In-gone Yeo, Byung-gon Chun, and Woo-taek Hong, *Implementation Strategy of The Lee Myung-bak Administration's North Korea Policy and Unification Policy* (Seoul: Korea Institute for National Unification, 2010).

40. Huh et al., *Implementation Strategy of The Lee Myung-bak Administration's North Korea Policy and Unification Policy*.

41. Tan, "A Study on North Korean Policy in South Korea: Compare with Kim Dae Joong, No Moo Hyon, and Lee Myong Bak Government."

42. Young-ho Park, "The Park Geun-hye Administration's North Korea Policy: The Korean Peninsula Trust Process and Its Policy Direction," *Unification Policy Studies* 22, no. 1 (2013): 1–25.

43. Park, "The Park Geun-hye Administration's North Korea Policy: The Korean Peninsula Trust Process and Its Policy Direction."

44. Geun-hye Park, "A New Kind of Korea: Building Trust between Seoul and Pyongyang," *Foreign Affairs* 90, no. 5 (2011): 13–18.

45. Park, "A New Kind of Korea: Building Trust between Seoul and Pyongyang."

46. Park, "A New Kind of Korea: Building Trust between Seoul and Pyongyang."

47. Park, "A New Kind of Korea: Building Trust between Seoul and Pyongyang."

48. Sung-min Hong, "Park Geun-hye's Strategy of Dismantling North Korean Nuclear Programs Covered by Impeachment," *Donga Ilbo*, February 5, 2019. http://www.donga.com/news/article/all/20190205/93987840/1.

49. Donggil Cha, "Research on Execution Strategy of Moon Jae-In Administration's 'Korean Peninsula Driver Theory,' " *Korea-Japan Military Culture Studies* 25, no. 1 (2018): 61–90; Kwang Kyu Nam, "The Moon Jae-in administration's North Korea Policy and Korea-US Relations," *Asian Education and Development Studies* 8, no. 1 (2019): 59–74.

50. Nam, "The Moon Jae-in Administration's North Korea Policy and Korea-US Relations."

51. John Hemmings, Ramon Pacheco Pardo, and Tat Yan Kong, "Negotiating the Peace: Diplomacy on the Korean Peninsula," *Henry Jackson Society and Asia Studies Center Report*, September (2018): 1–44. https://www.ies.be/files/Negotiating_the_Peace.pdf.

52. *North Korea Labor Daily*, May 25, 2017; recited from Seung-hyun Lee, "The Moon Jae-in Administration's North Korea Policy Based on Five Keyword," *Legislative Politics Review* 13, no. 1 (2018): 163–86.

53. Hemmings et al., "Negotiating the Peace: Diplomacy on the Korean Peninsula."

54. Lee, "The Moon Jae-in Administration's North Korea Policy Based on Five Keyword."

55. Uri Friedman, "The Mystery at the Heart of North Korea Talks: The Parties Have Yet to Agree on What Exactly Should Be 'Denuclearized.' But One South Korean Official Has a Plan to Close the Gap," *The Atlantic*, June 26, 2018. https://www.theatlantic.com/international/archive/2018/06/denuclearization-korean-peninsula-moon/562601/.

56. Brian Padden, "S. Korea Plans to Start Railway Project with North This Year," *Voice of America*, August 15, 2018. https://www.voanews.com/east-asia-pacific/s-korea-plans-start-railway-project-north-year.

57. Sung-ryol Cho, "Huddles and Prospects of the Moon Jae-in Administration's North Korea Policy: Analysis of the Korean Peninsula Denuclearization and the Vision of the Peace Regime," *Unification Policy Studies* 26, no. 1 (2017): 1–28.

58. Bon-Hak Koo, "Process of the North Korean Nuclear Issue and Its Solution," *Unification Policy Studies* 24, no. 2 (2015): 1–24.

59. Kyung-im Woo, Wan-joon Yoon, Min-ji Jung, "Seventy Percent of the Fund Invested to the Kaesong Industrial Complex Transferred to Kim Family . . . Used for Nuclear Programs and Luxurious Consumer Goods," *Donga Ilbo*, February 15, 2016. https://www.donga.com/news/Politics/article/all/20160215/76441953/1.

60. See Bong-Keun Chun, "An Assessment and Lessons of the North Korean Nuclear Negotiations for the Past Twenty-Years," *Korea and World Politics* 27, no. 1 (2011): 183–212.

Chapter 5

Continuity and Change in American Nonproliferation Policy toward North Korea

PAIGE PRICE CONE

Introduction

Historically, American presidents have generally shared an overarching preference for nonproliferation: preferring that no new countries pursue or, especially, acquire nuclear weapons. Interestingly though, how U.S. leaders choose to approach this goal differs across administrations, both when the incumbent's political party switches and when it remains consistent. While some U.S. presidents emphasize positive incentives, others give more weight to negative sanctions. Importantly, due to the nature of electoral turnover in the United States, leaders often enact policies that depend on the actions of future administrations. While this is true for many foreign and domestic policy concerns, from tax cuts and healthcare in the United States to human rights abuses and tariffs abroad, one enduring foreign policy concern stands out: North Korean nuclear weapons and the fear of instability they generate.

Though the United States has had some level of foreign policy interest in North Korea since the breakup of the Korean peninsula given its defense alliance with South Korea, tensions between the two states soared in 1980, when North Korea began to pursue a nuclear weapons program. Active pursuit of nuclear weapons began in 1980, with the construction of a reactor at Yongbyon that was capable of producing plutonium suited to bomb quantities, which was discovered by a U.S. spy satellite in 1980.[1] From that point forward, the United States has attempted to garner the reversal of DPRK's weapons program through diplomacy, positive economic and military incentives, economic sanctions, and the threat of military bombing. Thus far, while U.S. presidents have run the gamut of the tools employed, none have been effective in leading to denuclearization or nonproliferation.[2]

In this chapter, I explore why this may be the case. In order to do so, I first lay out the two level nature of foreign policy in the United States and touch on background factors that affect each new incoming American president—factors such as political party, past experiences, religion, and whether or not the U.S. Congress's majority shares the same political party as the president. Next, I discuss outside pressures that weigh on U.S. leaders such as alliances, changes in nuclear capabilities of adversaries, and other crises that affect American interests abroad. Finally, I walk through each administration's approach to North Korea, from Carter to Trump. In these vignettes, I highlight what the United States' primary goal was toward North Korea, how other interests might impact that goal, and what strategies the United States employed in an effort to reach it. I end with a discussion on what the lessons learned from prior administrations might mean for future interactions with the DPRK.

Domestic and International Constraints on U.S. Nuclear Policy toward North Korea

In order to determine the goals, motives, and strategies employed by the United States in negotiating with North Korea on denuclearization, it is first necessary to discuss the factors that affect American nuclear nonproliferation policy. Two bodies of literature are useful here—scholarship on material inducements in nonproliferation and scholarship on constraints to decision making. In this chapter, I focus on U.S. presidents with the assumption that leaders matter for foreign policy decision making. Though I focus on leaders as a way to examine both domestic and international constraints facing these individuals, I also pay attention to other substate level actors as well, as their interests and bargaining help define how outcomes are reached.[3] Due to this choice in level of analysis, I must lay out both domestic and international constraints facing leaders.

In the following sections, I outline these dual pressures, including individual experiences and biases, political partisanship, and public perception along with international events, alliances, and adversarial balancing that influence American interests.

CARROTS AND STICKS IN NONPROLIFERATION

Here, nuclear reversal is defined as "the phenomenon in which states embark on a path leading to nuclear weapons acquisition but subsequently reverse course, though not necessarily abandoning altogether their nuclear ambitions."[4] Importantly, Levite's definition includes an official governmental decision to slow down or stop a nuclear weapons program. Further, it allows for the option that in the future a state might decide to restart its program. Concurrently, Levite's definition is attractive because it provides a theoretical and empirical bound for nuclear programs: a state must begin active pursuit of a nuclear weapon, and subsequently abandon or discontinue its proliferation activity, to be considered to be engaging in nuclear reversal.

Scholars have debated the question of what factors influence nuclear reversal, including domestic constraints or changes in preferences, a change in a proliferator's threat environment, or the use of positive or negative inducements by a major power to influence reversal.[5] The first two explanations largely mimic the determinants of proliferation literature, placing the rationale for abandoning a program squarely within the reasons for beginning it—changes to a state's internal domestic preferences and/or capabilities or changes to a state's external security environment. The third factor provides a less deterministic explanation, allowing for a proliferator to change its preferences based on the external provision of rewards or punishment. This explanation is the focus of my argument, and I turn now to defining what inducements are and the types that make up the United States' toolkit.

Inducements, colloquially referred to as "carrots and sticks," are defined as external instruments of statecraft extended to a target state with the goal of persuading its leaders to change their behavior.[6] Positive inducements for nuclear reversal come in two forms: (1) transferring resources such as technology, money, or knowledge to influence a leader to give up their weapons program (economic incentives); or (2) offering security assurances to remove a perceived threat, such as placing a state under the nuclear umbrella of a nuclear power, building confidence by creating or strengthening alliances, or offering diplomatic recognition (security incentives). Negative inducements come in both economic and security forms as well. Strategies for negative inducements include imposing economic sanctions (either unilaterally or multilaterally) on a state, threatening to withhold promised aid, or threatening or using military intervention.[7] Further, both positive and negative inducements have a diplomatic component. In both cases, diplomacy can be used in conjunction with the offer or withholding of other inducements. Here, diplomacy acts to strengthen the inducement by adding an element of trust and by making public declarations to the receiving state. Diplomacy can also be a tool, whereby direct communication or other shows of partnership might be used either on their own or prior to offering other inducements.[8]

Scholars largely disagree about what types of inducements are most effective at leading to nuclear reversal. Some[9] have argued that positive incentives are stronger than negative sanctions, while others[10] contend that negative pressures carry more weight, and still others[11] argue that a combination is needed in order to be effective, where the timing of their use is paramount. For the purposes of this chapter, I am agnostic to the type of tools being used and examine them all in relation to U.S. objectives in addressing North Korean denuclearization.

Domestic Constraints

In order to best understand how U.S. presidents have attempted to negotiate North Korean disarmament, it is important to first lay out the constraints to foreign policy and decision making in the U.S. context. The making of foreign policy is always constrained in some fashion by external factors—be they domestic or foreign. Factors that affect foreign policy at the domestic level include both the environment in which a U.S. president operates, such as organizations vying for interest and resources or congressional partisanship as well as factors inherent to a leader such as past experiences, beliefs about nuclear weapons, and personal characteristics. Concurrently, U.S. leaders face external pressures including alliance commitments, crisis resolution, wars, and foreign trade policies. These dual pressures are best thought of as a "two level game" as defined by Robert Putnam.[12] As Putnam demonstrates, a leader, or "chief negotiator" engaged in negotiations at the international level must simultaneously negotiate at the intranational level, weighing the preferences of both audiences concurrently. The logic of two level games holds that any negotiation taking place at the international stage will ultimately need to gain domestic approval at the ratification stage, whereby the interests of constituents matters. Thus, "the political complexities for the players in this two level game are staggering."[13]

Broadly, leader level scholarship on nuclear weapons has examined a host of contexts, including why states proliferate, when leaders might be more likely to use nuclear weapons, and whether leaders are more prone to preventative war or positive engagement to prevent proliferation. This literature explores substate level factors affecting foreign policy decision making and is helpful for understanding how past U.S. administrations have negotiated with North Korea. For instance, a strain of organizational and bureaucratic politics scholarship has shown how organizational politics and parochial interests can muddy the waters for deterrence and nuclear accidents,[14] give prominence to policy experts and nuclear scientists,[15] and exaggerate the role of veto players in nuclear policy.[16]

Further, a second strain of scholarship looks directly at the role of leaders in foreign policy, focusing on the individual level of analysis. Here, the role of past experiences, beliefs about nuclear weapons, political partisanship, religion, and rhetoric are examined as ways to understand leaders' choices. For instance, looking at nuclear decisions directly, Hymans explores the psychology of seeking nuclear weapons and shows how certain national identities make some leaders more prone to nuclear pursuit than others.[17] Similarly, past experiences have been shown to matter for nuclear pursuit. Fuhrmann and Horowitz show that past participation in a rebellion exponentially increases the likelihood that a leader will seek nuclear weapons, as these leaders are more predisposed to a higher risk tolerance and an inclination toward national independence.[18] Other scholars have explored the role of morality and ethics in the attitudes of leaders toward nuclear use.[19]

The individual level of analysis is not only useful for understanding nuclear proliferation decisions, it has equal utility in explaining arms control decisions. For instance, Whitlark examines the role of leader beliefs to determine what types of leaders are more likely to consider preventative war as a counterproliferation option.[20] Leaders are predisposed to beliefs about both the general spread of nuclear weapons (proliferation) and the consequences of particular adversarial acquisition of nuclear weapons on the national security. For instance, as will become apparent in the cases below, former presidents Clinton and Bush 43 came into office with very different beliefs about nuclear weapons and the role of the United States in the international system and these beliefs shaped how each president approached the problem of North Korean nuclear weapons.

Equally important to what leaders choose to do is what they say. Recent scholarship has highlighted the role of presidential rhetoric and signaling in shaping the outcomes of nuclear decisions. For instance, McManus shows that visits by leaders to foreign governments sends a stronger signal of a credible commitment than other types of signals, while Berkemeier and Cone demonstrate that U.S. presidents' public rhetoric has a significant and direct impact on the nuclear proliferation and reversal decisions of states seeking the bomb.[21]

Finally, to sum up the domestic level of analysis, scholars have shown that partisanship and public opinion are both important to understanding nuclear policy decisions in the United States. For instance, partisanship has been shown to be increasingly important in the outcomes of arms control treaty ratification in the U.S. Senate.[22] Similarly important for treaty ratification is the partisanship of the executive, where presidents have a credibility hurdle to overcome in Congress that their counterparts do not share.[23]

Taken together, the domestic level of analysis and its subcomponents are useful for understanding how the United States has approached the problem of North Korean nuclear weapons. This body of scholarship offers fertile ground for exploring the variation in negotiating strategies among presidents Clinton, Bush 43, Obama, and Trump, including a focus on individual beliefs and experiences, the role of partisanship in both the executive and congressional branches, and how constituent and organizational interests constrain leader decision making.

INTERNATIONAL CONSTRAINTS

A leader concurrently faces constraints at the international level. These external pressures might come directly in the form of bilateral or multilateral constraints, the balancing of interests between allies, or other crises that vie for time and attention. As I will show in the following sections, each of these pressures played a role in stymieing successful negotiations with North Korea.

Foreign policy does not operate in a vacuum, and most bilateral negotiations at least tangentially involve other third parties. For instance, even when North Korea and the United States negotiated directly, the interests of South Korea, Japan, and China were discussed among U.S. policymakers in the Clinton administration.

Similarly, in weighing the interest of allies' preferences for extended deterrence versus an indigenous nuclear program, U.S. policymakers have been concerned about the ripple effect on other allies in the region. This was one reason that President Ford was especially concerned about South Korea abandoning the extended deterrent relationship and producing its own nuclear bomb, citing the concern that Japan might follow suit.[24] This concern holds for matters beyond extended deterrence, where similar balancing considerations are made for trade agreements and weapons sales.

Finally, a president often juggles many crises simultaneously, and must weigh the pros and cons of expending time and resources for any one crisis against the others on his plate. For example, toward the end of Clinton's second term, he had to decide whether to spend his last months engaging North Korea or focusing on issues in the Middle East.[25] Similarly, Bush 43 juggled the Iraq invasion, ballooning war in Afghanistan, and the successful nuclear test by North Korea. In examining the relationship between the United States and the Democratic People's Republic of North Korea (DPRK), I incorporate scholarship from both the domestic and international levels of analysis to explain the constraints present in negotiations.

Examining the Record:
Strengths and Pitfalls in Negotiating DPRK Denuclearization

North Korea's nuclear program spanned several decades before successfully testing a nuclear capable device in 2006. Correspondingly, the United States' interest in DPRK nuclear weapons, urgency over responding to the program, and methods for negotiating with the DPRK varied greatly over the past four decades based on factors both domestic and foreign. For the purposes of this analysis, the time frame analyzed is 1980 to 2020, with concluding comments on future negotiations in 2021 and beyond. Over the past four decades of negotiating with North Korea, the United States has seen seven presidential administrations, each with its own goals and strategies for dealing with the DPRK.

In the sections that follow, I loosely divide the analysis by presidential administration based on the assumption that leaders matter in the

decision making on nuclear policy[26] and thus the best way to make sense
of U.S. decision making in its dealings with the DPRK is to compare it
across presidential administrations. This comparative approach is descriptive and is not intended to be causal; rather, the goal is to understand
what factors made negotiating more or less successful. I use a combination of primary source archival material alongside excellent second source
scholarly works to analyze the goals and strategies of U.S. presidents and
their advisors in dealing with North Korea. Some administrations are
given more time and attention as their interests in and negotiations with
the DPRK ramped up. As will become apparent, U.S. interest in North
Korea's nuclear weapons program increased drastically in the early 1990s,
and though the goals and strategies have changed over time, some level
of interest has remained constant across administrations. By tracing the
past attempts at negotiating with North Korea, I have two concurrent
goals in this analysis. Firstly, to trace whether or not there was ever a
point in the negotiations where a "Yes" might have been reached, and
if so, what prevented it from happening. Secondly, I intend to utilize
the lessons garnered to provide policy recommendations for the Biden
administration moving forward.

The 1980s to Early 1990s: Carter, Reagan, and Bush 41

In 1980, a U.S. satellite discovered the construction of a reactor at Yongbyon that was capable of producing plutonium in bomb quantities.[27]
Though North Korea had been interested in nuclear weapons since at
least the early 1960s, this marked a new level of active pursuit and meant
a heightened level of interest from the United States. The early years of
DPRK's nuclear weapons program saw three U.S. presidential administrations: Carter from 1980 to 1981, Reagan from 1981 to 1989, and G. H.
W. Bush from 1989 to 1993.

President Carter's focus on North Korea was predominately for the
purpose of easing tensions between it and its neighbor to the south, while
balancing these tensions with those of the Cold War. He favored a multilateral approach that would bring together the United States, North and
South Korea, and China to help ease tensions on the peninsula. A year
before the reactor at Yongbyon was discovered, he outlined his policy
toward North Korea in a press report:

> Let me state our policy toward North Korea quite simply. We
> are prepared to participate in discussions with North Korean

officials aimed at reducing tensions on the Korean peninsula, but only if officials of the South Korean Government are full and equal participants. We have also said that to promote an atmosphere conducive to the reduction of tensions, the United States Government is prepared to improve our relations officially and unofficially with North Korea, provided that there are parallel improvements by the Soviet Union or China in relations with South Korea. We are not hostile toward North Korea. However, we are not going to take unilateral steps which are unreciprocated by North Korea's major allies, nor allow ourselves to become manipulated in a manner which ignores the rights and sovereignty of our ally, the Republic of Korea. We recognize that solution of the problems on the Korean peninsula can only be resolved through the direct involvement of the Governments of both North and South Korea.[28]

By 1980, Carter's focus was directed toward his reelection, and most accounts of his rhetoric and policies toward North Korea focus on comparing his approach to that of his Republican opponent, Ronald Reagan. While Carter favored multilateral talks and engagement with North Korea, he was quick to point out that his opponent favored military intervention, mentioning this in several debates.[29] Carter lost the campaign for reelection, and the executive branch saw a change in administrations and political party, with Ronald Reagan taking office in January 1981.

Several things happened over the 1980s to alert President Reagan to North Korea's seriousness about acquiring a nuclear capability. In 1986, its first reactor became operational and construction of two larger gas graphite reactors was begun. The following year, a radiochemical laboratory with a sizable reprocessing capacity was discovered.[30] At the same time, the United States pushed for North Korea to sign the Nonproliferation Treaty (NPT) and join the nonproliferation regime. North Korea joined the NPT in 1985, but refused to ratify the treaty unless the United States withdrew its nuclear weapons from the Korean peninsula.[31]

Though Kim Il sung steadily moved forward with developing Pyongyang's nuclear capabilities, Reagan's focus was on the Soviet Union and the Cold War raging between the two superpowers. For Reagan especially, the threat of North Korean nuclear weapons was viewed through the lens of Cold War tensions and preventing the spread of communism. As a reporter put it after Reagan's reelection, "Mr. President, during the last year, your successful campaign, you told the audience the past 4 years not 1 inch of soil has been lost to the Communist operation."[32]

Things changed in 1991 when the Soviet Union collapsed. When the USSR fell, North Korea lost its principal patron and faced a food shortage crisis. Concurrently, China, another friendly patron, rushed to establish diplomatic relations with Seoul in an effort to normalize relations on the continent after the fall of the Soviet Union. These two blows left North Korea very vulnerable and Kim Il-sung more open to negotiations. By this time, Reagan's vice president, George H. W. Bush (hereinafter Bush 41) had succeeded him in the office. The years of the Bush 41 presidency resulted in some easing of tensions between the United States and the DPRK. In September 1991, Bush 41 announced the unilateral withdrawal of all U.S. naval and land based tactical nuclear weapons deployed abroad. Though this initiative was broader in its scope than just the Korean peninsula, it resulted in the DPRK formally ratifying the NPT and the safeguards agreement with the International Atomic Energy Agency (IAEA), following through with its demand from 1985. At the same time, the easing of tensions was not linear, and both sides took steps backward as well. On North Korea's part, it conducted upward of seventy explosive tests at its Yongbyon facility in 1992, and the United States imposed sanctions on two North Korean firms for missile proliferation.[33]

In the wake of the collapse of the USSR, Bush 41's policy toward North Korea vacillated. On several occasions, he spoke highly of the progress made in North Korea to ratify the NPT and his hope that the nation would go a step farther toward peace by fully implementing the IAEA safeguards and enforcing the denuclearization of the Korean peninsula proposed by South Korean president in 1991. Though Bush 41 seemed hopeful, he took a backseat approach to dealing with North Korea—publicly stating that the onus was on Pyongyang to comply with international standards and that a multilateral dialogue with regional players was necessary.[34] Further, he made it very clear that the United States was an ally of South Korea and saw no problems if North Korea did not want to engage in a dialogue with the United States. Take, for instance, his response at a press conference held in Seoul with President Roh in his last year in office: "Our policy is not going to shift. We're not going to start having dialog with North Korea. We're dealing as we have in the past, and progress is being made. We salute the [ROK] President for that progress. And we're not about to take some end run around our staunch ally in order to accommodate Kim Il-sung. And if he doesn't want it, so much the better. That just suits the heck out of us."[35]

Ultimately, U.S. interest in North Korea in the 1980s is best seen through the prism of the Cold War. For President Reagan in particular, the main concern was North Korea gaining nuclear capabilities while still under the patronage of the Soviet Union. Though there is evidence that the United States kept a watch on North Korea through its intelligence services, North Korea's nuclear weapons program was not its main foreign policy concern during the Cold War. As Bush 41 began to manage a post–Cold War environment, the issue of North Korean nuclear weapons gained some traction in Washington. It is impossible to say if his administration would have given the issue more time and consideration had he won reelection. However, as will be shown below, the issue of loose nukes and nonproliferation became a cornerstone of the next administration's foreign policy.

THE 1990S: CLINTON, BELIEFS ABOUT THE ROLE OF THE
UNITED STATES IN NONPROLIFERATION, AND THE
AGREED FRAMEWORK

Perhaps no U.S. administration came closer to solving the problem of North Korean nuclear weapons than Bill Clinton's. From 1993 to 2000, his administration made nonproliferation in general, and dealing with North Korean nuclear ambitions specifically, a cornerstone of his foreign policy. As the dust of the Cold War began to settle, Clinton began to worry about the possibility of "loose nukes" in the former Soviet republics of Belarus, Kazakhstan, and Ukraine, where he was especially concerned that nonstate or rogue actors might get hold of these weapons without proper safety precautions in place to guard them. Further, the United States was left as the sole superpower, or the hegemon of the international system. Clinton had a vision for what a responsible hegemon should look like, with emphasis given to promoting democracy, human rights, and nonproliferation.[36]

Though the fight against proliferation was crucial to his foreign policy, Clinton did not take a clear path toward dealing with North Korea. His engagement with the DPRK went through several phases, from showing a willingness to talk bilaterally and strengthen diplomatic ties, to making talks conditional on relations between Pyongyang and Seoul, and at one point even seriously considering military intervention to bomb nuclear facilities. Which of the Clinton administration's strategies were most successful in negotiating with North Korea? What prevented the two states from achieving an agreement?

Early into Clinton's presidency, on March 12, 1993, the DPRK announced plans to withdraw from the NPT and IAEA safeguards regime—a tactic that successfully brought the United States to the negotiating table. One week before the announcement would take effect, Kim Il-sung suspended the decision after the United States granted assurances against the threat or use of force and further promised not to interfere in North Korea's internal affairs. Pyongyang then indicated that it would consider a deal with the United States involving light water reactors, though it pushed heavily for the talks between the two countries to be bilateral and leave out Seoul.[37] Clinton was very interested in negotiations with North Korea as his administration was highly concerned by the level of development of its nuclear program. Intelligence in 1993 estimated that the DPRK had separated twelve kilograms of plutonium—an amount sufficient to produce one or two nuclear weapons.[38] In 1994, things escalated when North Korea refused to allow IAEA inspectors to inspect a plutonium plant at Yongbyon.[39] It was at this point that Clinton seriously considered taking military action against North Korea. His security team began private talks considering a surgical strike that would destroy key components of the reactor site at Yongbyon. The plan was serious enough that the United States reached out to its ally and requested cooperation for such a strike from Seoul.[40]

Concurrently, Clinton pursued a diplomatic route to ease tensions with North Korea and prevent it from acquiring a nuclear capability. In early 1994, Track II diplomacy made some headway with several visitors meeting with Kim Il-sung, including Billy Graham, Selig Harrison, and former president Jimmy Carter. Carter's visit was especially fruitful, laying the groundwork for the Agreed Framework. He brought a CNN television crew with him that offered publicity to Kim Il-sung and defused the crisis brewing between the United States and DPRK.[41] However, shortly after these visits, Kim Il-sung passed away and Clinton worried that his son and successor, Kim Jongil, would not continue forward in good faith with negotiations. However, a third round of bilateral talks between the two countries lasted from July to October, with Kim Jong-il maintaining his father's desire for normalizing relations.

In October 1994, an agreement was reached, giving a symbolic victory to North Korea in that the United States recognized it as a sovereign country. The historic account of the Agreed Framework has been laid out in previous chapters of this book, so I will not go into too much detail about the agreement. For the purposes of understanding the U.S. position and negotiation tactics, and why the agreement ultimately failed, two things are crucial. Firstly, congressional midterms took place that year, and the Republicans retook control of Congress. This had dire implications for the ratification and funding of the Agreed Framework, highlighted in more detail below. Secondly, many officials in Clinton's administration believed that North Korea would collapse as a result of Kim Il-sung's death and were similarly reticent to fund the light water reactors and provide an alternate energy source that Clinton had agreed to.

Thus, the United States was slow to meet its end of the bargain and the light water reactor project stalled for three years. A domestic constraint highlighted by Kreps, Saunders, and Schultz (2018) argues that democratic presidents face greater credibility hurdles with Congress for treaty ratification than their Republican counterparts. This proved true for Clinton. The Republicans controlling Congress balked at funding the project, so Clinton sought a new solution. Working with South Korea and Japan, a trilateral organization was formed in 1995, the Korean Peninsula Energy Development Organization (KEDO). KEDO worked with other countries and international organizations to help fund the light water reactor project and meet the stipulations of the Agreed Framework. Though the Clinton administration worked with KEDO to move the project forward, lifted a trade embargo, and provided economic aid to the DPRK, Kim Jong-il was not satisfied and the DPRK felt that the United States had reneged on its agreement. Even in 1997, in the midst of a severe famine, North Korea doubled down and demanded the withdrawal of U.S. troops from the peninsula and the cancellation of U.S.ROK military exercises. Or as Clemmons puts it, it was an "intensification of the juche syndrome," whereby Pyongyang felt the need to be even more self reliant in the face of hardship.[42]

By Clinton's second term, relations with North Korea were stalled at best, and a Korea task force was formed. The task force's top recommendations to the Clinton administration were to renew ties with the ROK and to form a broader coalition of friends and allies in the region.[43] Clinton tried working with China from December 1998 through August 1999 to gain traction on the problem of North Korean nuclear weapons, but this initiative ultimately proved unfruitful. Further, the South Korean president enacted a Sunshine Policy meant to engage North Korea that coincided with a new "Perry Initiative" in the White House that proposed economic and diplomatic benefits to North Korea if it would agree to the "verifiable cessation" of its missile program.[44] This 1999 initiative led to the lifting of some U.S. sanctions on North Korea.

It seemed that the tide was turning. Clinton's final year in office ushered in negotiations that were as close to getting to a "Yes" for denuclearization as the United States has ever come. Firstly, Secretary of State Madeleine Albright spearheaded a "grand bargain" effort to successfully negotiate with Kim Jong-il, visiting with him personally in North Korea before inviting Vice Marshal Jo Myong Rok (thought to be the second most powerful figure in Pyongyang at the time) to visit the White House. While there, the vice marshal presented a letter to Clinton to invite him to Pyongyang, noting that "if the president and secretary came together we will be able to find a solution to all problems."[45] Unfortunately, as Albright noted, "North Korea's topdown decision making style did not fit with our practice of trying to 'precook' arrangements before committing the president."[46] In Clinton's final months, he wanted to visit Kim Jong-il and to bring to fruition the negotiations that had been conducted by Secretary Albright and others on his team, but he was faced with choosing between foreign policy crises. The president elect, George W. Bush, did not object to Clinton visiting in his final months. Ultimately, though, Clinton chose to spend his last remaining days and political capital on crises brewing in the Middle East and instead invited Kim Jong-il to visit Washington, D.C. Kim promptly declined, viewing the invitation as an insult. The biggest obstacle for the Clinton administration in reaching a breakthrough seems to have ultimately been a lack of time coupled with juggling too many crises at once. For North Korea, the normalization of relations with the United States was its top priority. Unfortunately for the Clinton administration, preventing the proliferation of nuclear weapons in North Korea was only one priority among many, leading to an asymmetry of attention between the two. As Clemmons notes, the Clinton team "opened the door partway to yes. In 2001, the Bush administration slammed it shut."[47]

THE EARLY 2000S: BUSH 43, A SPLIT ADMINISTRATION, AND THE SIXPARTY TALKS

When George W. Bush (hereafter Bush 43) took office, he and several of his top advisors entered the White House with an "ABC policy"—

Anything But Clinton—with the mindset to steer away from or reverse any deal nurtured by the Clinton administration. From the start, Bush's administration was divided between those who were more hawkish in their approach and motives toward North Korea and those who were more dovish. This divide could be seen even before Bush 43 officially entered office. Colin Powell, his choice for secretary of state, declared at his confirmation hearing in the Senate his willingness to maintain the policy directives of the Clinton administration, while the incoming secretary of defense, Donald Rumsfeld, publicly stated that the new administration would take a tougher stance on North Korea.

This division among administration officials initially led to some confusion in policy signaling, but it quickly became apparent that the hardliners' message would be the party line. This can be seen from a change in rhetoric from Secretary Powell, who months into the administration announced that his team would pick up where Clinton's left off. A day later, he recanted his statement, joking that he had "gotten ahead of himself," and he too began to toe the party line. From 2001 to 2005, unilateralist hardliners controlled U.S. policy toward North Korea, and their ultimate goal in dealing with the DPRK was no longer simply the dismantlement of its nuclear weapons program.[48] Rather, the Washington hawks wanted nothing short of regime change. These officials, including Vice President Dick Cheney, Secretary of Defense Rumsfeld, and Bush 43 himself, shared a general belief that North Korea was evil and should cease to exist. The rhetoric coming out of the Bush 43 White House was markedly different from its previous inhabitants, with phrases such as "We don't reward bad behavior" and "We don't negotiate with evil, we destroy it" being quite common.[49] James Kelly, the assistant secretary of state for East Asian and Pacific Affairs, perhaps highlighted the "ABC Policy" most clearly when trying to sort out the new administration's approach. " 'Peace Talks' is a Democratic term. This is a Republican administration. We need to think of something different to use."[50]

North Korea initially had a difficult time with this change, not understanding why the Bush administration would approach it differently than Clinton had. By early 2002 though, Pyongyang had fully gotten the message: it was now at the top of George W. Bush's "Axis of Evil" list, along with Iraq and Iran. Bush first used the phrase at his 2002 State of the Union address, less than five months after the September 11 terrorist attacks. It is interesting to note that the goal of the Bush administration was very similar to that of Clinton's, to prevent the proliferation of nuclear weapons. However, the impetus behind this goal was markedly different with the focus now on eradicating evil and fighting terrorism rather than behaving as a more benign superpower promoting peace and democracy.

This shift in perspective had dramatic implications for North Korea. Conducting a review of policy toward the Korean Peninsula in June 2001, Bush 43 determined that the door would be left open for talks with North Korea, but with the stipulation that other things such as human rights abuses must be discussed at any meeting as well.[51] Further, on December 31 of the same year, the administration submitted its Nuclear Posture Review (NPR) to Congress. The NPR, leaked to the public in March 2002, focused on updating U.S. forces, adopting a first strike doctrine, and advising that weapons testing might be necessary. Further, and probably more concerning for the DPRK, North Korea headed the target list of states that might be targeted with nuclear weapons. A second strategic document was released in September, the National Security Strategy (NSS). The NSS offered a comprehensive rationale for preemptive action against rogue states possessing WMDs, and it identified North Korea as a prominent example. Far from easing tensions with North Korea, the Bush team's strategic doctrines intensified Pyongyang's quest for a nuclear deterrent. Meanwhile, the State Department continued to insist that the United States would engage with North Korea "any time, any place, without preconditions."[52] North Korea agreed to talks, which were originally scheduled for April 2002 but postponed until October in the wake of a gun battle between DPRK and ROK naval vessels. By the time the talks came to fruition in October, however, the United States had learned that the DPRK had successfully created a clandestine highly enriched uranium program, and this issue dominated the U.S. position. When Assistant Secretary of State James Kelly went to Pyongyang for the meeting, he followed a script closely, with no room to maneuver, and told his North Korean counterpart that Washington had evidence of the HEU plant.[53] The DPRK admitted to the program during this meeting and it was apparent to both sides that the Agreed Framework was officially null and void. North Korea rounded out the year by withdrawing from the NPT.

At the end of Bush 43's first term, it was still difficult to discern what the ultimate goal toward North Korea was. Bush vacillated from saying that all options, including military, were on the table to emphasizing the need to engage other countries in the region for a peaceful solution. There were several themes that were consistently emphasized by his team, however: (1) the insistence that North Korea's nuclear program was a regional problem and required a multilateral not a bilateral forum for talks; (2) a refusal to reward bad behavior; and (3) a diplomatic emphasis on gaining China's support and cooperation. This vacillation can largely be seen as a lack of focus—Bush 43's attention was on the invasion of Iraq. In 2004, it withdrew twelve thousand troops (one third of the existing force) from South Korea for deployment in Iraq, and North Korea feared it was doing so to remove a tripwire and prepare for war.[54]

However, a change of personnel in top positions in Bush's second term created space for multilateral diplomacy, which ultimately became the SixParty Talks. I will not go into the details of the historical timeline of the talks nor the position of each of the actors, as a previous chapter has laid out both. For the purposes of understanding the U.S. position, however, it is important to note the continued resistance by hardliners in Bush 43's administration and their insistence on regime change for North Korea. Importantly, once a joint statement was released by those party to the talks, hawks in the U.S. administration changed their tactics to financial pressure. In 2005, heavy sanctions were imposed, including sanctions related to North Korea's nuclear program and others that more generally dealt with illicit activities, such as the September 2005 sanctions dealing with money laundering and drug trafficking.[55] These sanctions coincided with renewed rounds of the SixParty Talks and a joint statement that looked to embody strong positive progress. However, the harsh sanctions seriously weakened the doves' position favoring diplomacy—though they wanted to restart another round of talks, the diplomats could not openly challenge the sanctions. For North Korea's part, it officially maintained that as long as the United States continued to impose financial sanctions on Pyongyang, there was no hope for holding another round of talks. It responded to the sanctions by conducting two missile tests that year, one on July 4 and one on October 9 (less than a month after the September 15 sanctions and September 19 joint statement).

Bush's urgency in dealing with North Korea changed in 2006 when the DPRK successfully conducted a nuclear test. The same year, Republicans lost heavily in midterm elections as the American public's support of the Iraq and Afghanistan wars began to wane. One day after the elections, Bush 43 accepted Donald Rumsfeld's resignation and less than a month later accepted another policy hawk, John Bolton's as well. The result of these personnel changes and a Democrat controlled Congress meant that a more dovish policy toward North Korea emerged. The SixParty Talks reconvened, and the 2005 sanctions were put on the table as a carrot for removal. Concurrently, bilateral discussions at these talks between the United States and DPRK became integral. As Bush 43 entered his final years in office, his policy objectives toward North Korea gained clarity. In 2007, his administration came up with a three stage plan for dismantling Yongbyon in exchange for economic aid and security. The policy goal ultimately became known as "complete, verifiable and irreversibly denuclearization through dialogue and diplomacy," or "CVID" for short. The plan relied on an action for action rule that allowed for incremental increases in economic and political incentives in response to positive actions taken by North Korea, and this was made official in a February 2007 agreement. Two of the most positive actions to come out of this agreement were the lifting of the Trading with the Enemy Act and the removal of North Korea from the list of state sponsored terrorists.

Though some positive dialogue came at the end of Bush 43's presidency, it was ultimately too little, too late. The majority of his administration's two terms focused on unilateral, hardline policies toward dealing with regimes such as North Korea's. For those in top positions, including Bush himself, regime change remained the only palatable solution for dealing with North Korea. This myopic view put blinders on the administration and allowed North Korea to successfully acquire and test nuclear weapons rather than to engage in diplomatic discussions that might work toward normalizing relations. By the time Barack Obama entered office, the American public was sick of U.S. intervention abroad, the American economy was in tatters, and the incoming president would not be attempting to negotiate the reversal of a nuclear weapons program but rather the dismantling of a functioning nuclear weapons arsenal.

The Obama Years: Negotiating with a Nuclear Armed North Korea

Barack Obama entered office in January 2009, and his foreign policy team did not have the same stark divisions between hawks and doves as seen in the Bush years. Rather, accounts of his team's foreign policy decision making are similar to descriptions of John F. Kennedy's, with a collegial atmosphere that encouraged dissent and the desire for every voice to be heard at the table before a conclusion was reached. Once a decision was made, there was less infighting and more shared ownership of the decision.[56] Further, the top five officials in Obama's foreign policy team remained consistent after midterm elections; when Republicans won Congress it was a result of domestic economic unhappiness and not foreign wars. This collegial strategy for making foreign policy decisions meant that there was more clarity about an approach, both for the American public's consumption and signaled abroad.

Obama's interest in nonproliferation began before he even ran for president. As a junior senator, he got the opportunity to work with a legend in the nonproliferation policy community, Richard Lugar, and to travel with him to Russia and the former nuclear Soviet Republics to observe American nonproliferation efforts coming to fruition. He used these travel opportunities to learn from Senator Lugar, asking him what the biggest challenges facing nonproliferation were at the time.[57] These conversations left an indelible impression on him and shaped his views of nonproliferation entering office. Early in his tenure, he gave a disarmament speech in Prague in which he pledged to make concrete steps toward a world without nuclear weapons. His administration's NPR was starkly different than his predecessor's, focusing on reducing risks to the United States and its allies, reducing the role and numbers of nuclear weapons, and working to strengthen the nonproliferation regime internationally.[58]

Though Obama's overarching nonproliferation message was clear, his administration had a difficult time negotiating with North Korea on disarmament. Early in his administration he indicated that the Bush 43 goal of CVID would remain in place and that the main tactic for bargaining would be a multichannel pressure that incorporated friends and allies. The only difference was that the Obama administration would not sit down at the negotiating table unless the DPRK changed its behavior first—this was a stipulation that neither Bush 43 nor Clinton had issued when entering talks bilaterally or multilaterally.[59] In his first year in office, President Obama relied on both Track I and II diplomacy to try to normalize relations and ease tensions. In 2009, he sent both Stephen Bosworth, a newly appointed special representative for North Korean policy, and former president Clinton to meet with Pyongyang. In 2011 he sent former president Carter and a new special representative, Glyn Davies. The 2011 meeting with Carter was productive and the Obama administration regarded Davies's October meeting as a decisive step toward resuming the SixParty Talks. Unfortunately, the death of Kim Jong-il prevented the resumption of meetings from taking place.

While he relied on several means of diplomacy, Obama was not opposed to exercising negative pressure in dealing with the DPRK. He issued several rounds of increasingly harsh sanctions from 2009 to 2011 and again from 2015 to 2016, expanding the scope of sanctions to include blocking of property and interests, strengthening export and trade restrictions, and a comprehensive blocking of the North Korean government and Workers Party of Korea. Further, Congress passed the first statute on sanctions toward North Korea in 2016, adding teeth to the executive orders. Though the Obama Administration's NPR was markedly different from its predecessor, calling for eventual global disarmament, it did leave room for the use or threatened use of nuclear weapons against those who were nonsignatories to the NPT, sending a clear signal to North Korea.

The Obama administration utilized both positive and negative means of negotiating with North Korea, but to no avail. Ultimately, like U.S. presidents before him, Obama had several crises to juggle at once—both foreign and domestic. Domestically, Obama faced a flailing economy inherited from the Bush 43 presidency and an overhaul in healthcare that was to be his legacy. In foreign policy, and specifically in regard to nonproliferation policy, Obama's interests were divided. He had the twin threats of North Korean and Iranian nuclear weapons to deal with and ultimately decided to put his time and attention toward preventing Iran from acquiring nuclear arms. In 2015, he signed a landmark executive agreement with Iran, which included China, France, Germany, Russia, and the United Kingdom and provided sanctions relief in exchange for Iran's agreeing to stringent verification measures from the IAEA. The Joint Comprehensive Plan of Action (JCPOA) sent a clear, positive signal to Kim Jong-un highlighting the United States' willingness to negotiate and offer concessions in exchange for denuclearization. However, shortly after taking office, Obama's successor Donald Trump pulled out of the JCPOA and sent an equally clear message to North Korea—the United States cannot be trusted to abide by its agreements.

Trump Shakes Things Up, from "Fire and Fury" to a Presidential Handshake

Many drastic changes in policy and rhetoric were seen under the Trump administration. Donald Trump entered office and began undoing many of his predecessor's initiatives, much like the "ABC Policy" of the Bush 43 administration. From the Paris Climate accord to JCPOA, from Obamacare to diplomatic relations with allies—Donald Trump reversed policies and goodwill. Longtime allies of the United States, especially NATO, South Korea, and Japan, began questioning the credibility of America's commitment while the Trump administration seemed to become friendly with adversarial dictators, particularly Russian president Vladimir Putin and North Korea's Dear Leader, Kim Jong-un.

The Trump administration's approach to negotiating with the DPRK was by no means linear, and the two sides saw several ups and downs. It is too soon to fully capture the administration's negotiations and tactics, but there is enough publicly available information to at least describe the broad picture. President Trump's first year in office came out strongly hostile to North Korea, and his words and actions harshly reflected this. He built on the sanctions imposed in the Obama years, coming out with a "maximum pressure campaign" designed to get other states to not do business with North Korea. As Treasury Secretary Stephen Mnuchin noted about the policy, "Foreign financial institutions are now on notice that, going forward, they can choose to do business with the United States or with North Korea but not both."[60] Further, the Countering America's Adversaries through Sanctions Act was passed in the same year and imposed more sanctions still on North Korea. In a similar vein, Trump responded to the assassination of Kim Jong-un's half-brother by returning North Korea to the official list of state sponsored terrorism. Trump's first year also included harsh rhetoric, particularly as expressed in the 240character format of Twitter. In August 2017, he threatened to launch "fire and fury" on North Korea and noted that "military solutions are now fully in place, locked and loaded, should North Korea act unwisely."[61] In September, he taunted Kim Jong-un by referring to him as "Little Rocket Man," and in October, he publicly denounced his own secretary of state, Rex Tillerson, for trying to engage with North Korea diplomatically. His tweet on October 1 noted, "Save your energy Rex, we'll do what has to be done," and "Being nice to Rocket Man hasn't worked in 25 years, why would it work now? Clinton failed, Bush failed, and Obama failed. I wont fail."[62] A tweet in January 2018 takes a similar vein, with a new taunt for Kim Jong-un comparing the size of the U.S. nuclear button to that of North Korea.

However, Trump abruptly switched gears in 2018, agreeing to meet Kim Jong-un for a summer summit in Singapore that resulted in the suspension of high profile joint military exercises in South Korea and a signed declaration with North Korea. The declaration had no tangible steps for either denuclearization or sanctions relief, but Trump still declared the summit a success: "There is no longer a threat from North Korea, everybody can now feel much safer than the day I took office."[63]

There was a second summit in 2019 when President Trump extended a twitter invitation for a handshake across the DMZ. These overtures had mixed effects. During the Trump years there was a moratorium on North Korean nuclear tests and the escalation between the two harsh postures was stymied, though this followed Trump's own escalation. The United States and South Korea suspended military exercises and worked toward positive north south relations. However, North Korea is now a fully capable nuclear armed state and wants to be seen as such. The Trump administration's unwillingness to accept anything short of denuclearization as success hampered its ability to create meaningful change.

Lessons Learned: Comparing across Administrations

What does this mean for future relations between the US and North Korea? How should Joe Biden's and future administrations approach negotiations with Kim Jong-un? I explore these questions in the concluding section. First, it is useful to summarize the lessons learned across U.S. administrations spanning four decades of negotiating with North Korea. In this section, I compare domestic and international constraints faced by each administration as well as the goals, motives, and strategies of each. Recall that any U.S. president faces both foreign and domestic constraints to their ability to negotiate with an international actor. The case histories tracing each administration's approach to North Korea highlight these constraints. Here it is useful to categorize them and compare across administrations in order to see what strategies have been more or less successful, to determine whether there was ever a moment when the United States might have reached a "Yes" with North Korea, and to illuminate the best strategy for moving forward. Please see Table 5.1 below.

Predominant Goals and Constraints

For Carter, Reagan, and Bush 41, the overarching foreign policy goal was to prevent the spread of communism, and dealing with North Korea's fledgling nuclear program is best understood in this light. In the case of Reagan in particular, his main concern was North Korea gaining greater capabilities while the USSR was still its patron. As Bush 41 began to manage a post–Cold War environment, more attention to North Korea was given and the concern gained some traction in D.C. Constraints in the

Table 5.1. Seven U.S. Administrations Negotiate with DPRK

	Domestic Factors	International Factors	Strategy/Goals
1980–1993 Carter Reagan Bush 41	Reelection campaign; CW Balancing	Cold War Balancing; Fall of S.U.	Prevent Spread of Communism
1993–2001 Clinton	Personal Moral Values; Hawkish Congress	"Loose Nuke"; Tensions in M.E.	Prevent Proliferation
2001–2009 Bush 43	Divided Admin; "ABC Policy"	DPRK 2007 Nuke Test	Regime Change; CVID
2009–2017 Obama	Resource Constraints; Obamacare	JCPOA	CVID
2017–2021 Trump	"ABO Policy" constant turnover	JCPOA withdrawal	Denuclearization

Source: Author.

1980s were also a product of Cold War balancing, which left not enough time and resources to devote to North Korea directly.

Presidents Clinton and Obama each came into office with strong moral goals of pursuing nonproliferation. Clinton viewed the threat of North Korean nuclear weapons through the lens of the newly hegemonic United States and what role such a hegemon should play in the international system. For him, spreading democratic and peaceful values was paramount. Concurrently, he became increasingly concerned over the threat of "loose nukes" in the former Soviet republics and the potential for nonstate or rogue actors to acquire them. Specifically for North Korea, the Clinton administration's overarching goal was to prevent proliferation. In dealing with North Korea, the Clinton foreign policy team perhaps came closest of all to reaching a deal, but time was not on their side. In his final month in office, Clinton had to choose between putting his resources toward North Korea or the Middle East and decided to deal with budding Middle Eastern tensions. Domestically, Clinton was constrained by a hawkish Republican Congress that was unwilling to ratify the Agreed Framework or fund the light water projects negotiated by his team. Obama, having been mentored by a Clinton era nonproliferation icon, held similar views on the necessity of nonproliferation. His policy visions were bold, and he sought the eventual dismantling of nuclear weapons around the world. In dealing with North Korea, however, Obama weighed the efforts and strategy of a counterforce campaign against a nuclear weapons state versus nonproliferation efforts against a nuclear weapons program and he placed more import on negotiating with Iran over its nuclear program. His overarching goal was CVID, a carryover from the later years of Bush 43. Domestically, Obama faced constraints in resources as the American public was severely displeased with the U.S. economy, and his first initiative was to improve it. Similarly, he wanted to overhaul the American healthcare system and felt his legacy was in passing Obamacare. This initiative used up domestic political capital, time, and resources. Similar to Clinton, Obama had to choose which foreign policy goals to give more weight to, and he chose to deal with Iran over North Korea.

Presidents Bush 43 and Trump held similar views of America's place in the world and felt particularly that their predecessors had approached that role incorrectly. Both presidents sought to undo the foreign policy directives of their predecessors. For Bush 43, this meant undoing the positive efforts of the Clinton administration in negotiating with North Korea and refusing to have bilateral discussions until well into his second term. For Trump, it meant reversing several executive agreements. Particularly pertinent for North Korea was pulling out of JCPOA and the signal it sent announcing America's flightiness as a partner. Both Bush 43 and Trump also had harsh rhetoric for North Korea that escalated tensions. Another similarity between the two administrations was an all or nothing approach to negotiations that stemmed from their predominant goals. For Bush 43, nothing short of regime change was acceptable, viewing the dictatorship as evil. This goal changed in 2007, both as a result of North Korea's successful nuclear test the previous year and a change in top officials domestically that allowed more space for positive negotiations. This resulted in the goal of CVID and carried through to Obama's administration. Bush 43 was constrained domestically by infighting among his top officials that muddied its foreign policy approach to North Korea. Further, and perhaps most importantly, he was constrained internationally by other crises he deemed more urgent, particularly invading Iraq and the subsequent so called War on Terror. Trump's ultimate goal was denuclearization, and nothing short of it was acceptable. On a personal level, Trump was driven to show that his negotiating tactics were superior. From a national security standpoint, his administration had a renewed focus on deterring adversaries and viewed North Korea as having a distinct willingness to use its nuclear arsenal.[64] Domestically, Trump was constrained by a constant merry go round of senior level advisors. His cabinet saw more turnover in his first two years in office than his five immediate predecessors saw in their entire first terms.[65] This constant turnover made developing a clear strategy difficult. Further, several important diplomatic posts remained unfilled, including the ambassador position for South Korea. These challenges further hampered his administration's ability to get a full picture of dealing with the DPRK.

Taken together, it can be seen that both domestic and international factors constrained each of the U.S. presidents who have attempted to negotiate with North Korea over its nuclear programs. From a domestic level of analysis, Congress played an important role in either helping or stymieing the executive's ability to negotiate with North Korea. This was particularly apparent in the hawkish Congress that Clinton faced and its unwillingness to fund a deal with North Korea. From an individual leader perspective, the prior beliefs about nuclear weapons and proliferation held by each U.S. president had a profound impact on their willingness to engage with North Korea and on how they chose what tactics to pursue. Those who came in with more hawkish beliefs, such as Bush 43, were less willing to engage with North Korea directly while those who valued the role of diplomacy, as Clinton did, placed much more emphasis on Track I and II channels. Importantly, one implication to come out of this comparative analysis is that "anything but [my predecessor's]" policies are incredibly counterproductive for arms control negotiations. If U.S. presidents actually care about nonproliferation or denuclearization, they should strive for consistency in foreign policy. Further, each administration faced international constraints. Predominately, these constraints came in the form of juggling several foreign policy crises at once, which can be seen particularly in the Bush 43 and Obama administrations. However, the role of balancing alliance interests and other parties privy to negotiations with North Korea also weighed on several administrations. As noted at the outset, foreign policy decision making is a complex, multifaceted issue, and each administration had to weigh domestic and international interests when deciding how to approach North Korea. In the concluding section, I offer implications for future negotiations as well as recommendations for the Biden administration.

Implications and Recommendations
for the Biden Administration and Beyond

Four decades of negotiating with North Korea have revealed that denuclearization is a complex issue. Engagement with the country, and particularly engagement that makes Kim Jong-un feel that he is being taken seriously, will seemingly be most effective. Previous approaches that have focused on maximum pressure through economic sanctions or threats of force have proved ineffective in dealing with North Korea. These approaches have led to maximum escalation by North Korea and should be avoided by the Biden administration. Other approaches used in the past have included incremental negotiations, or the "action for action" approach of the Agreed Framework and SixParty Talks. These approaches have some value and might work to ease tensions in the immediate term. The Trump administration's approach of leader level negotiation might have some advantages for building trust between Biden and Kim Jong-un.

However, there are two approaches that have not been tried by previous administrations that may have more positive effects. The first is to change the bilateral relationship between the two countries before attempting to make a deal. The Trump administration came closest to this approach, but fell short of changing relations before negotiating. Here, the Biden team might pursue talks that focused on changing the political relations between North Korea and the United States, which would avoid front loading the issue of denuclearization, which has always been a sticky issue with North Korea.

A second approach, and potentially the most promising, might be for President Biden to move away from negotiating denuclearization and instead focus on negotiating arms control.[66] Forty years of negotiations have been unsuccessful in leading to first nonproliferation, then denuclearization. At this point, a counterforce war is a real possibility as an outcome of tensions with North Korea and would be incredibly costly. Thus, while they do not come without difficulties, arms control measures might have real merit in dealing with the DPRK.[67] Though unprecedented in dealing with North Korea, an arms control regime has been used quite effectively in negotiating with the former USSR. An arms control strategy has several attractive advantages. It shows North Korea that it is being dealt with as a nuclear power, giving it status and recognition in the international system, which might make Kim Jong-un more willing to negotiate. Further, this goodwill garnered can be used to focus on containing the most dangerous elements of North Korea's weapons program to avoid inadvertent nuclear war, spreading nuclear materials, or accidental use. While some will question this approach for legitimizing North Korea as a nuclear power, the United States needs to accept the reality of North Korean nuclear weapons and focus on increasing the stability of their nuclear deterrent through positive arms control discussions.

Notes

Thanks to Molly Berkemeier and Rachel Whitlark for their excellent comments and advice. All errors are my own.

1. I rely on Philipp Bleek, *When Did (and Didn't) States Proliferate? Chronicling the Spread of Nuclear Weapons* (Harvard: Belfer Center for Science and International Affairs, 2017) for the distinction between exploration and pursuit. Exploration is defined as whether leaders open the door to potential nuclear weapons programs and is captured when leaders authorize studies, or lowlevel activities that fall short of launching programs, and pursuit refers to active programs authorized by leaders with the aim of acquiring nuclear weapons or capacity to construct them on short notice. It is captured by authorizing work to develop capacity to produce weapons.

2. There is some confusion between the two terms *nonproliferation* and *denuclearization*. In many contexts, they are used interchangeably, but in the case of North Korea it is important to distinguish between them. *Nonproliferation* prevents the spread of nuclear weapons. Horizontal nonproliferation prevents their spread to other states and vertical nonproliferation prevents the buildup of more and more weapons in a single state. Conversely, *denuclearization* occurs when a nuclear weapons state dismantles its nuclear weapons and rids itself of the ability to produce more. Historically, South Africa is the only indigenous weapons state to have denuclearized, though the former Soviet republics went through a similar process after the fall of the Soviet Union.

3. Graham Allison and Philip Zelikow, *Essence of Decision: Explaining the Cuban Missile Crisis*, 2nd ed. (New York: Pearson Press, 1999).

4. Ariel E. Levite, "Never Say Never Again: Nuclear Reversal Revisited," *International Interactions* 28, no. 3 (2003): 237–60.

5. e.g. Rupal N. Mehta, *Delaying Doomsday: The Politics of Nuclear Reversal* (Oxford: Oxford University Press, 2020); Nicholas L. Miller, *Stopping the Bomb: The Sources and Effectiveness of US Nonproliferation Policy* (Ithaca: Cornell University

Press, 2018); Nuno P. Monteiro and Alexandre Debs, *Nuclear Politics: The Strategic Causes of Proliferation* (Ithaca: Cornell University Press, 2018); Matthew Fuhrmann and Sarah E. Kreps, "Targeting Nuclear Programs in War and Peace: A Quantitative Empirical Analysis, 1941–2000," *Journal of Conflict Resolution* 54, no. 6 (2010): 831–59; Etel Solingen, *Sanctions, Statecraft, and Nuclear Proliferation* (Cambridge: Cambridge University Press, 2012).

    6. Solingen, *Sanctions, Statecraft, and Nuclear Proliferation*, 5.

    7. David A. Baldwin, "The Power of Positive Sanctions." *World Politics* 24, no. 1 (1971): 19–38; Daniel W. Drezner, *The Sanctions Paradox: Economic Statecraft and International Relations,* (Cambridge: Cambridge University Press, 1999); Mehta, *Delaying Doomsday*; Miller, *Stopping the Bomb*; Monteiro and Debs, *Nuclear Politics.*

    8. For instance, see Ann Sartori, *Deterrence by Diplomacy* (Princeton: Princeton University Press, 2005) for a discussion of diplomacy on its own and Leon V. Sigal, *Disarming Strangers: Nuclear Diplomacy with North Korea* (1998) for a more iterative look at diplomacy in arms control.

    9. e.g., Miroslav Nincic, *The Logic of Positive Engagement* (Cornell: Cornell University Press 2011); Thomas Bernauer and Dieter Rulo, *The Politics of Positive Incentives in Arms Control* (South Carolina: University of South Carolina Press, 1999).

    10. e.g., Miller, *Stopping the Bomb*; Fuhrmann and Kreps, "Targeting Nuclear Programs in War and Peace."

    11. Mehta, *Delaying Doomsday*; Monteiro and Debs, *Nuclear Politics.*

    12. Robert Putnam, "Diplomacy and Domestic Politics: The Logic of TwoLevel Games," *International Organization* 42, no. 3 (1988): 427–60.

    13. Putnam, "Diplomacy and Domestic Politics."

    14 Scott Sagan, "Why Do States Build Nuclear Weapons? Three Models in Search of a Bomb," *International Security* 21, no. 3 (1996/97): 54–86; Lynn Eden, *Whole World on Fire: Organizations, Knowledge, Nuclear Weapons Devastation* (Ithaca: Cornell University Press, 2004).

    15. Robert Gilpin, *American Scientists and Nuclear Weapons Policy* (Princeton: Princeton University Press, 2015).

    16. Jacques E. Hymans, "Veto Players, Nuclear Energy, and Nonproliferation: Domestic Institutional Barriers to a Japanese Bomb," *International Security* 36, no. 2 (2011): 154–89.

    17. Jacques E. Hymans, *The Psychology of Nuclear Proliferation: Identity, Emotions, and Foreign Policy* (Cambridge: Cambridge University Press 2006).

    18. Matthew Fuhrmann and Michael C. Horowitz, "When Leaders Matter: Rebel Experience and Nuclear Proliferation," *The Journal of Politics* 77, no. 1 (2015): 72–87.

    19. Brian C. Rathbun and Rachel Stein, "Greater Goods: Morality and Attitudes toward the Use of Nuclear Weapons," *Journal of Conflict Resolution* 64, no. 5 (2020): 787–816.

20. Rachel E. Whitlark, "Nuclear Beliefs: A Leaderfocused Theory of CounterProliferation," *Security Studies* 26, no. 4 (2017): 545–74.

21. Roseanne W. McManus, "Making It Personal: The Role of LeaderSpecific Signals in Extended Deterrence," *The Journal of Politics* 80, no. 3 (2018): 982–95; Molly Berkemeier and Paige Price Cone, "Do As I Say, Not As I Do: The Impact of Divergent Rhetoric and Policy on Nuclear Reversal," Working draft 2022.

22. C. James DeLaet and James. M. Scott, "TreatyMaking and Partisan Politics: Arms Control and the U.S. Senate, 1960–2001," *Foreign Policy Analysis* 2, no. 2 (2006): 177–200.

23. Sarah Kreps, Elizabeth Saunders, and Kenneth Schultz, "The Ratification Premium: Hawks, Doves, and Arms Control," *World Politics* 70, no. 4 (2018): 479–514.

24. US Department of State Cable, "ROK Plans to Develop Nuclear Weapons and Missiles," March 12, 1975, History and Public Policy Program Digital Archive, Gerald Ford Presidential Library, National Security Adviser Presidential Country Files for East Asia and the Pacific, Box 11, Korea—State Department Telegrams, to SecState—NODIS (4). Obtained by Charles Kraus. http://digitalarchive.wilsoncenter.org/document/114615.

25. Ramon Pacheco Pardo, *North KoreaUS Relations under Kim Jong II: The Quest for Normalization?* (London and New York: Routledge, 2014).

26. Whitlark, "Nuclear Beliefs"; Kreps, Saunders, and Schultz, "The Ratification Premium"; Berkemeier and Cone, "Do as I Say, not as I Do."

27. Bleek, *When Did (and Didn't) States Proliferate?*

28. Jimmy Carter, Korean and East Asian Issues Questions and Answers for Publication in the Orient Press Online by Gerhard Peters and John T. Woolley, The American Presidency Project, accessed March 26, 2022, https://www.presidency.ucsb.edu/node/249080.

29. See for instance Jimmy Carter, Philadelphia, Pennsylvania Interview with Correspondents of WCAUTV. Online by Gerhard Peters and John T. Woolley, The American Presidency Project, accessed March 26, 2022, https://www.presidency.ucsb.edu/node/252064 and Jimmy Carter, Addison, Illinois Remarks and a QuestionandAnswer Session with Du Page County Residents. Online by Gerhard Peters and John T. Woolley, The American Presidency Project, accessed March 26, 2022, https://www.presidency.ucsb.edu/node/250697.

30. Bleek, *When Did (and Didn't) States Proliferate?*

31. Pacheco Pardo, *North Korea.*

32. Ronald Reagan, QuestionandAnswer Session with Reporters on Foreign and Domestic Issues Online by Gerhard Peters and John T. Woolley, The American Presidency Project, accessed March 26, 2022, https://www.presidency.ucsb.edu/node/260756.

33. US Treasury North Korea Sanctions Record, accessed March 26, 2022, https://home.treasury.gov/policy-issues/financial-sanctions/sanctions-programs-and-country-information/north-korea-sanctions.

34. Pacheco Pardo, *North Korea*; Walter Clemens, *Getting to Yes in North Korea* (Boulder: Paradigm, 2010).

35. George Bush, The President's News Conference with President Roh Tae Woo of South Korea in Seoul Online by Gerhard Peters and John T. Woolley, The American Presidency Project, accessed March 26, 2022, https://www.presidency.ucsb.edu/node/266393.

36. Richard Saccone, *Negotiating with North Korea* (Elizabeth, NJ: Hollym, 2003); Clemens, *Getting to Yes in North Korea*.

37. This was a precursor to the Agreed Framework, a germ of the agreement was born in these discussions.

38. Pacheco Pardo, *North Korea*.

39. The DPRK avoided UN sanctions by allowing the inspectors to come in the first place. The inspectors were permitted to inspect seven reported sites but were refused entry to the plutonium plant.

40. Fuhrmann and Kreps, "Targeting Nuclear Programs in War and Peace."

41. Clemens, *Getting to Yes in North Korea*; Pacheco Pardo, *North Korea*.

42. Clemens, *Getting to Yes in North Korea*.

43. Morton Abramowitz and James Laney, "Meeting the North Korean Nuclear Challenge: Report of an Independent Task Force sponsored by the Council on Foreign Relations," (Council on Foreign Relations Independent Task Force, 2003).

44. Pacheco Pardo, *North Korea*.

45. Pacheco Pardo, *North Korea*.

46. Pacheco Pardo, *North Korea*.

47. Clemens, *Getting to Yes in North Korea*.

48. Clemens, *Getting to Yes in North Korea*.

49. Saccone, *Negotiating with North Korea*.

50. James Kelly, Quoted in Charles Pritchard, *Failed Diplomacy: The Tragic Story of How North Korea Got the Bomb* (Washington, DC: Brookings Institute Press, 2007), 45.

51. Clemens, *Getting to Yes in North Korea*.

52. Pacheco Pardo, *North Korea*.

53. Pacheco Pardo, *North Korea*; Clemens, *Getting to Yes in North Korea*.

54. Pacheco Pardo, *North Korea*; Pritchard, *Failed Diplomacy*.

55. Kelsey Davenport, "Chronology of U.S.North Korean Nuclear and Missile Diplomacy," Arms Control Association, July 2020, https://www.armscontrol.org/factsheets/dprkchron.

56. Pacheco Pardo, *North Korea*.

57. Barack Obama, *A Promised Land* (New York: Crown Press, 2020).

58. Nuclear Posture Review Report, April 2010, accessed March 26, 2022, https://dod.defense.gov/Portals/1/features/defenseReviews/NPR/2010_Nuclear_Posture_Review_Report.pdf.

59. Pacheco Pardo, *North Korea*.

60. Mark Moore, "Mnuchin: Companies Working with North Korea Are 'On Notice,'" *New York Post*, September 21, 2017, https://nypost.com/2017/09/21/mnuchin-companies-working-with-north-korea-are-on-notice/.

61. Twitter Archives, the Real Donald Trump, August 8, 2017, and August 11, 2017, https://www.thetrumparchive.com.

62. Twitter Archives, the Real Donald Trump, October 1, 2017, https://www.thetrumparchive.com.

63. Twitter Archives, June 13, 2018, https://www.thetrumparchive.com.

64. Nuclear Posture Review, February 2018, accessed March 26, 2022, https://media.defense.gov/2018/Feb/02/2001872886/-1/-1/1/2018-NUCLEAR-POSTURE-REVIEW-FINAL-REPORT.PDF.

65. Kathryn Tenpas, "Tracking Turnover in the Trump Administration," Brookings, January 2021, https://www.brookings.edu/research/tracking-turnover-in-the-trump-administration/.

66. For similar discussions, see Victor Cha, "There's a Simple Option for Defusing the Coming Crisis with North Korea," *The Washington Post*, September 15, 2021, https://www.washingtonpost.com/opinions/2021/09/15/victor-cha-defusing-coming-crisis-with-north-korea/ and Bonnie Kristian, "North Korea's Nukes Aren't Going Anywhere, and the US Needs to Get Over It." *Business Insider*, February 20, 2021, https://www.businessinsider.com/us-should-drop-denuclearization-to-make-progress-with-north-korea-2021-2.

67. There are concerns that should be explored, both internally for the United States, whether this is an option that can gain enough domestic traction, and externally in regard to U.S. allies' concerns, particularly South Korea and Japan. While the policy would prove a marked change, it is still worth considering if the ultimate goal is creating stability for the region.

Chapter 6

Talking the Talk and Walking the Walk

China and the Effort to Denuclearize North Korea

Peaceful Denuclearization of North Korea: The Role of the PRC

The world witnessed a number of highly dramatic events in 2018–19 directly involving none other than all the top leaders of North Korea (the DPRK, Democratic People's Republic of Korea), South Korea (the ROK, Republic of Korea), China (the PRC, People's Republic of China), and the United States. The very reclusive North Korean leader Kim Jong-un in particular suddenly became a frequent international traveler, meeting U.S. president Donald Trump three times within a year in Singapore, Hanoi, and Panmunjom. He also traveled to China three times in one hundred days to wine and dine with Xi Jinping, the top leader of the PRC. Kim met his counterpart from South Korea, President Moon Jae-In, three times in just five months. The focus of all these dazzling summits was the perennial issue of the DPRK's nuclear program and the preservation of the NPT (Treaty on the Non-Proliferation of Nuclear Weapons) in Northeast Asia.

A window of opportunity seemed suddenly wide open for a solution to the problem of denuclearizing North Korea, after two decades of frustrating and fruitless diplomacy including six rounds of Six-Party Talks involving the two Koreas, China, the United States, plus Japan and Russia.[1]

However, not unlike before, great theatrics and grand promises quickly faded. The highly touted "breakthrough" did not materialize, as there has been basically zero real progress toward denuclearization of North Korea. Even the very concept of "denuclearization" was not really clarified.[2] The diplomatic shows staged for TV failed to help the American leader get reelected a year later in 2020. The ROK leader achieved little meaningful progress either and was succeeded in Spring 2022 by Yoon Suk-Yeol, who is likely to be more confrontational to North Korea, while the DPRK leader is poised to stay in power for life as is his renewed benefactor, the PRC leader. Moreover, Pyongyang seems to continue to be the winner, and has become more determined than ever to defiantly keep and grow its nuclear arsenal, including new delivery systems, vowing "to double down on its nuclear program" in 2021.[3] In 2022, Pyongyang continued its ballistic and cruise missile tests.[4] The Biden administration so far seems to have become "more realistic" about denuclearizing North Korea, with Vice President Kamala Harris openly suggesting an arms control first and Secretary of State Antony Blinken calling for a focus on freeze now rather than denuclearization.[5] A "calibrated, practical approach," something between Obama's "strategic patience" and Trump's "grand bargain," emerged in mid-2021 as the new American approach.[6]

If all this earnest, direct diplomacy at the highest level with its hefty financial incentives has come up with nothing to advance the all-important denuclearization of North Korea, does peaceful prevention of nuclear proliferation still have a chance in Northeast Asia at all? A key factor has been the critical, "indispensable" role played by the PRC in the effort, as Washington readily admitted.[7] With a proper understanding of Beijing's policy, particularly its underlying motivation and reasoning, as this chapter attempts to do, the answer seems to be negative, unless and until some major political changes take place in Beijing and Pyongyang, or some miracles happen, or both. Fundamentally driven by the political interest of the ruling party in the PRC, the CCP (Chinese Communist Party), rather than the Chinese national interest, Beijing has always walked the tightrope of opposing nuclear proliferation in Northeast Asia while seeking to resist, reduce, and replace American power in the region. The PRC has thus oscillated between supporting and sabotaging the course, making it long and arduous, avoiding the requisite price of possibly ruining or losing its only treaty ally, North Korea, and trying to milk as much international prestige for its own geopolitical gains as possible. As the intensified strategic rivalry between the more alarmed United States and the enriched and more assertive PRC has unfolded in recent years, Beijing has quickly returned to its North Korean comrades in the interest of its own top strategic goal of regime survival. The hasty U.S. move to stage the ill-prepared Kim-Trump Summit in fact offered Pyongyang great leverage to facilitate Beijing's swinging back, as the CCP clearly dreads a strengthened American position on the Korean Peninsula far more than the North Korean bomb. As long as this deep institutional and ideological incompatibility remains between the PRC-DPRK alliance and its strategic competitor, the USA-ROK/USA-Japan alliances (and the emerging new alliance of "like-minded democracies" in the Indo-Pacific),[8] Beijing is fully expected to continue to talk the talk and walk the walk, even abandoning the talk altogether, with little to no real effort toward denuclearizing North Korea.

Was there ever a window of opportunity for a peaceful solution to the DPRK nuclear problem that emerged in the mid-1990s? In hindsight, there was probably one window of opportunity, albeit small and transitory, from the late 1990s to the early 2010s. Though still driven by the same motivation of preserving the CCP regime but with a different power calculus in a different international environment, based on its strategy of "hiding-and-biding-for-time," Beijing behaved differently during that time. The PRC's Korea policy then was influenced by a rare overlap of the CCP's political interests with China's national interests. Beijing sought to maintain a constructive relationship with the United States and its allies that was critical to its regime survival and security, while also benefiting the Chinese nation and the Chinese people. Foreign trade and investment, external peace and recognition, and good relations with neighbors such as the ROK motivated Beijing to formulate and facilitate a policy that was largely cooperative with the United States in the effort to denuclearize the DPRK. The genuinely nationalist concerns over the presence of the North Korean bomb on the border of the Chinese heartland and the possibility of the chain reaction of a nuclear arms race in East Asia also helps to explain China's participation in actions such as the Six-Party Talks and the UN-approved sanctions. After Xi Jinping assumed power in 2012–13, China's overall foreign policy became decidedly more assertive and Beijing acted accordingly, boldly hoping to trade its comrades' bomb for closer ties with the ROK so as to weaken or even dismantle the U.S. security networks in East Asia.[9] Beijing both talked and walked in a tough way toward Pyongyang, applying sanctions even beyond what was stipulated by the UN Security Council resolutions. The PRC declared its "resolute opposition" to the North Korean nuclear program in 2013 and periodically halted the export of oil to and the import of coal from the DPRK until 2017.[10] To teach the stubborn and treacherous Pyongyang a lesson and set an example for other neighbors through a display of power and leadership was also quite befitting Xi's ambition to "lead" the world and humanity.[11]

However, as this chapter attempts to analyze, that window was always very small, inherently limited and conditional, and highly expedient; it was subject to other, larger, factors and considerations. Given our understanding of the rationale behind China's foreign policy, it is deeply dubious that that small window could ever have led to an effective, let alone successful, joint U.S.-PRC effort to denuclearize Pyongyang peacefully. To be successful, this would have required the United States to pay a hefty price, such as militarily abandoning the Korean Peninsula, strategically conceding the Western Pacific to the PRC, and politically ceasing to denounce the CCP. In that case, the window of opportunity might have opened wide enough to allow for effective Chinese action to genuinely help with denuclearizing North Korea. Absent that, it will require the United States and its allies to creatively think outside of the box with new approaches and actions to revitalize the now seemingly hopeless preservation of the NPT in Northeast Asia.

To be sure, denuclearizing the DPRK is clearly in China's national interest and, by extension, also in the political interest of the CCP-dominated PRC. Yet, Beijing has always viewed Northeast Asia, and particularly the Korean Peninsula, as a key component in its overall strategic competition with the United States and thus critical to its top goal of regime security. Nuclear nonproliferation in the region has been a legitimate diplomatic objective for the PRC, but subject to its other pursuits in and beyond the region. At times, including the first three years of Xi Jinping's "New Era," which started in Fall 2012, Beijing has moved to align with the United States and its allies to jointly sponsor UN sanctions against the DPRK, for the four-pronged purpose of winning over South Korea, removing yet another nuclear power on its border, leveraging a common interest shared with the United States, and preventing the chain reaction of a nuclear arms race that might possibly involve Japan. However, Beijing soon grew frustrated by South Korea's reluctance to switch sides, as symbolized by Seoul's defiant decision to deploy the U.S. THAAD (Terminal High Altitude Area Defense) system in 2016.[12] The smell of a possible relative gain of influence in the game by the United States, with the announcement of the Kim-Trump summit that tantalizingly implied a possible defection of the North Koreans, was enough to prompt Beijing to quickly swing back to, in Xi's words, rekindle the spirit of comradeship and the "family-like relationship" it had had with Pyongyang.[13] To be sure, Pyongyang had long flirted with the United States with the idea of doing to Beijing what Beijing did to Moscow in the 1970s–1980s.[14] It openly accused the PRC of "dancing to the tune of the U.S." as recently as in 2017.[15] Trump's imprudent move seemed concrete evidence to sufficiently frighten the CCP. Beijing quickly walked in the opposite direction to reopen its spigot, with massive aid and supplies to the DPRK, and used its power to shelter Pyongyang from international pressures. In June 2019, Xi made his long-overdue first visit to Pyongyang with great fanfare.[16] North Korea once again "are getting everything they want right now" from the PRC, without giving up their bomb at all.[17] So much for whatever chance there ever was for a joint U.S.-PRC effort to peacefully denuclearize the DPRK.

It is tempting to say that the Kim regime shrewdly exploited the eagerness of the United States to successfully reel China in, in order to secure its bombs and supplies. It is also likely that the cooling down of Sino-American relations since 2018 altered Beijing's calculus. The long-shared ideological and political commonalities between the CCP and the KWP (Korean Worker's Party), as well as the CCP's pragmatic realism, remain a powerful rationale for Beijing to shield the DPRK regime. A lingering sense of "gratitude" for KWP's help to the CCP during the Chinese Civil War (1947–49) and the not-so-hidden admiration among many in Beijing for the DPRK's approach to governance also help to explain the PRC behavior. In addition, and more fundamentally, as this chapter argues, to peacefully denuclearize the DPRK has always been a low priority for Beijing. Put another way, the CCP is more willing to risk a rather unpredictable and eccentric nuclear power bordering the Chinese heartland, than to let the United States and its allies score against it on the international stage. Once again, the shocking divorce of the CCP's political interest from China's national interest has characterized PRC foreign policy.

In the following pages, I will outline the key motivational factors behind Chinese action and policy and trace Beijing's talkings and walkings on the DPRK nuclear issue. For the CCP, a clear hierarchy of policy preferences has existed for years, as I have analyzed elsewhere:[18] First, the political interest of the ruling CCP to stay in power forever, a goal that is as obvious and distasteful as it is at odds with the West and often exists at the expense of China's national interest, which requires the forging of good relations with the West and especially the United States.[19] Second, the resultant Chinese foreign policy of resisting, reducing, and replacing U.S. power in East Asia, which leads to a rather realpolitik calculus that necessarily often views the Washington-Pyongyang disputes as an asset rather than a problem, as in "my enemy's enemy is my friend," especially when this enemy's enemy happens to be a longtime and now rare ideological and political comrade. Third, the maintenance of the Korean status quo of political division in order to preserve its treaty ally as an anti-American companion, at least until Seoul switches sides to leave the U.S. camp, which serves both the CCP's political interests and China's geostrategic interests. Finally, the commitment to seek a denuclearization of the Korean Peninsula so as to, mostly, prevent the chain reaction of a nuclear arms race that might potentially empower Japan. This hierarchy of policy preferences is at odds with that of the other involved parties. The possibility for a peaceful denuclearization of the Korean Peninsula, therefore, seems slim as long as Beijing remains an integral part of the process. Accordingly, if Washington simply returns to the half-Obama and half-Trump policy, it is probably unlikely to be much more successful in its effort to denuclearize the DPRK peacefully.[20] If, as PRC analysts worryingly speculated in 2021, the Biden administration acts with a new approach and a new determination to reduce and minimize, rather than rely on, Beijing's role and influence,[21] the management and resolution of the North Korean nuclear problem could, counterintuitively, have a fresh start.

Big Talks and Long Walks with the China Dream

Under the general banner of the "China Dream," the ambitious CCP leader Xi Jinping has personally spearheaded the assertive foreign policy of "the New Era" since 2013. "To make China strong" is now the official goal so as to set Xi at least equal to Mao Zedong, who "made China stand up," and to Deng Xiaoping, who "made China rich." The grand course of rejuvenating China's past power and glory in the whole known world would fully befit a Mao-like personal rule; it might be even more glamorous and majestic than Mao, who in fact failed miserably in his pursuit of world leadership.[22] Big talks have therefore colored PRC foreign policy in an effort to justify grandiose moves and plans for Beijing's new role of leadership in the world.[23]

Much of the CCP's big talk might be merely a clever tactic in furtherance of its political interest in monopolizing power in China forever. As the logic of authoritarian and totalitarian politics would predict, a dictatorship inherently needs a great mission or a grand vision to create a perpetual warlike atmosphere in order to continue its domination and extraction. This open-ended course might take the form of hating an internal enemy (such as "class enemies" in the Maoist PRC), or fighting a mighty external foe (such as "Western imperialists"), or constructing a communist paradise on earth. The CCP's big talk about constructing a "community for common human destiny," about being "at the center of the world stage," about "leading humanity," and about "building a better and more just world order" may be just empty talk and slogans to cover up their true intention of power grabbing and self-service.[24]

To at least back up the big talk, which is critical to the CCP's regime security, with concrete action and demonstrable gains, Beijing has become increasingly assertive around the globe with an impressive walk of new demands and more actions.[25] Financed by its huge foreign-currency reserves, earned primarily from its lopsided trade with the United States, the PRC has engaged in big leaps forward with feats such as island-construction in the South China Sea, enhanced propaganda and United Front activities in the West (particularly in the United States and international organizations), and the enormous scheme of One Belt One Road (OBOR) or the Belt and Road Initiative (BRI), which encompasses the entire Eurasian continent, Africa, and Latin America.[26] A critical component of all this is for Beijing to increase its influence and control in its own neighborhood. A rerun of China's imperialist tradition in the region or some kind of a new Monroe Doctrine in the Western Pacific is increasingly taking place.[27] The PRC is now indeed talking the talk and walking the walk as a confident hegemon in South, Southeast, Central, and Northeast Asia, and particularly in the South China Sea, the Taiwan Strait, and the Korean Peninsula.

Still, the PRC's foreign policy has characteristically been cost-ineffective in securing allies and friends, even in its own neighborhood. It seems that money alone can only procure so much good will and friendship. Its big talks and long walks have repeatedly led to direct and indirect collisions with India and Japan concurrently, for example, the two neighboring powers that Beijing traditionally has tried to play against each other rather than antagonizing both simultaneously.[28] The massive money that Beijing has showered on the rulers and elites in neighboring countries such as Cambodia, Burma, Pakistan, the Philippines, and other Central Asian nations has typically purchased unreliable support that has mostly been just lip service. The largest recipient of Beijing's money, Russia, cleverly dragged China into a strategic bind with its invasion of Ukraine in 2022.[29] More importantly, Beijing still encounters the powerfully confining East Asian security structure that was born during the Cold War many decades ago. The treaty alliances that anchor this structure deeply involve the "outsider" United States, the main ideological and political adversary of the CCP in Beijing. In fact, the United States has always been a chief threat to the CCP-PRC regime, ever since its creation. Recent developments such as the bipartisan U.S. legislation targeting Beijing with regard to trade and technology transfer and China's actions in Hong Kong and Xinjiang have only intensified the old fear and animosity.[30] Under the Biden administration, the U.S. has largely continued the Trump administration's China policy.[31] Geopolitically, the U.S.-led alliances, such as the U.S.-South Korea Alliance and the U.S.-Japan Alliance, powerfully stabilize the region and frustrate Beijing's "great power" ambitions. The American security protection of Taiwan has now become increasingly firm and transparent after decades of "strategic ambiguity."[32] That alone has always been viewed in Beijing as both a key obstacle to China's rise of power and a direct challenge to the CCP's always insecure political legitimacy at home. It still remains to be seen what consequences the 2020–22 bipartisan American condemnation of the CCP as a perpetrator of genocide and "crimes against humanity" in Xinjiang, the emergence of a new Western consensus viewing the PRC as "a systemic challenge" in 2021–22, and the White House–ordered investigation of the origin of the COVID-19 virus will bring to U.S.-China relations.[33]

It is, therefore, only natural and predictable for the CCP-dominated PRC to pursue a top foreign policy objective of resisting, reducing, and replacing the presence and influence of the United States in its neighborhood, even at the expense of China's national interests and the Chinese people's best interests. With all of its big talk and long walks, including its perhaps justifiable efforts to assume a regional and world leadership in the pursuit of worthy causes such as nonproliferation, the CCP-PRC has firmly put its Three-R (resisting, reducing, and replacing) Strategy of competing with the United States far ahead of the denuclearization of the

DPRK. The deterioration of the U.S.-PRC relationship will only solidify and enhance that hierarchy of priorities in Beijing. The only formal treaty alliance involving both Beijing and Pyongyang, the 1961 *PRC-DPRK Treaty of Friendship, Cooperation and Mutual Assistance*, therefore, was automatically and unceremoniously renewed in 2021 for another twenty years.[34]

Beijing's Korea Policy

Contrary to the conventional wisdom espoused by many pundits and advocates based on their different purposes and wishes, the PRC has had a rather consistent Korea Policy as outlined in this chapter. This author for one has been proposing that view for more than two decades, with regard to Beijing's strategic thinking about the U.S.-ROK alliance, Korean unification, and the North Korean bomb.[35] The key reason for this remarkable consistency is that both the CCP's underlying motivations and the external (mostly American) challenges have remained largely unchanged. The PRC has walked acrobatically with regard to the North Korean nuclear issue quite predictably since the late 1990s, while it has changed its talk periodically and tactically employed a variety of rhetoric. A further analysis and assessment of the varying Chinese talk may help to understand Beijing's efforts, or the lack thereof, toward denuclearizing North Korea.

Since the early days of the Korean War, the Beijing-Pyongyang relationship has been filled with conflict, discord, and disputes.[36] Since the early 1990s, as I have demonstrated elsewhere, Beijing has pursued a highly pragmatic realist policy. While it clearly prefers the continued survival of the DPRK regime for its ideological, political, and strategic ends, Beijing has developed ever-closer relations with the ROK since 1992 both for the sake of important economic interests and for cultivation of a counterweight to Japan and the United States.[37] To befriend the archrival of its only treaty ally and ideological comrade, Beijing has been literally talking the talk and walking the walk on the Korean Peninsula for three decades. Nominally supporting Korean unification, the PRC in fact has actually sought to maintain the status quo of political division.[38] As reiterated by Xi Jinping in 2016, "China will absolutely not allow chaos [associated with unification] on the Korean Peninsula."[39]

Such a self-centered but pragmatic Korea policy has brought Beijing great economic benefits and considerable strategic maneuverability in

dealing with the United States. With a South Korea that is eager to cooperate, China has built a Greater East Asian chain of production to enable
its highly lucrative exports to the United States and thereby to finance its
ambitious programs at home and abroad. At the same time, the policy
has faced a backlash. Feeling shortchanged and even betrayed by its Russian and Chinese comrades after the Cold War ended, the DPRK started
in the early 1990s to gamble on nuclear weapons to bolster its regime
security and bargaining position. This critical move of regime preservation inevitably weakened and harmed the power of the PRC, which had
been the only legitimate nuclear power in East Asia. While it is arguably
rational for the security and survival of Pyongyang's Kim dynasty, the
North Korean bomb challenges Beijing's national interests in the region
and also threatens the CCP's political interest in its regime security. As
mentioned earlier, an overlap of China's national interest and the CCP's
political interest prompted PRC's participation in the efforts toward denuclearizing North Korea. Beijing also skillfully seized the opportunity to
cultivate a rare but real common strategic interest with the United States
to strengthen its relations with Washington.[40] North Korea's desperate
and daring defiance thus somehow created an asset for the CCP's eternal
rivalry with the United States, though incurring a heavy cost to Chinese
national interests, as Beijing continued to talk the talk and walk the walk
with regard to denuclearizing North Korea.

With just some crude nuclear weapons, North Korea has succeeded
in elevating itself to become a less inferior partner in the PRC-DPRK alliance, and acquired more bargaining, even extortion, power over Beijing.
China's national interests and even national security have suffered: China
has now become the only country in the world with four nuclear powers on its borders. The DPRK-initiated nuclear proliferation in East Asia
would further undermine China's power position and freedom of action in
the region. The U.S.-led East Asian security framework, dreaded by both
the CCP and Chinese nationalists, was strengthened by the justification of
reacting to the North Korean bomb, from the U.S. "pivot to Asia" and the
Indo-Pacific Priority, and efforts such as the "U.S.-Japan-ROK Trilateral
Dialogue," to the upgrades of military technologies by the American and
Japanese militaries in the Western Pacific.[41] The rising China is therefore
further confined by its only ally's desperate but rational—and seemingly
effective—drive for regime survival through acquisition of the bomb. In
order to check the United States, Beijing is now ironically checked by its
perceived and professed strategic asset. Furthermore, for Beijing, a nuclear

Japan would be a major nightmare, not to mention a possible effort to make Taiwan nuclear. And unfortunately for China, it has to rely on the goodwill of the United States to prevent Tokyo and Taipei from moving in that direction.

The complicated Chinese efforts toward denuclearizing but preserving North Korea peaked in early 2016. After Xi made his highly celebrated visit to Seoul in 2014 without visiting Pyongyang first, as has been customary, ROK president Park Geun-Hye made her much-touted visit to attend Beijing's grand military parade in fall 2015. Yet, Pyongyang defiantly tested a "hydrogen bomb" and ballistic missiles. Other than angrier talks criticizing the "outrageous" DPRK, Beijing still refused to fully cooperate with the United States.[42] This is probably because the CCP was deeply unsure about its key strategic objective of turning and switching South Korea. More likely, as a PRC analyst put it bluntly, the North Korean bomb might indeed have been "violating China's wish and interests . . . but it is a price [that] must be paid for China to support [North] Korea to oppose and check the United States," since the security threat posed by the North Korean bomb "is much larger to the United States than to China."[43] Furthermore, the CCP seems to harbor a rather cynical view about the NPT with the zero-sum belief that someone else, read the United States and its allies, will suffer more, even though many Chinese worry that China itself might actually be the first and real victim of the DPRK bomb or a North Korean nuclear accident.[44] Even before the rewarming of Beijing-Pyongyang ties prompted by the failed Trump-Kim summits, Beijing had already tacitly accepted a nuclear North Korea by 2017 despite its open rhetoric otherwise. Since 2018, the CCP has seemed to simply have given up the strategic intention or political will to really denuclearize North Korea.

To observers, Beijing may have indeed failed a litmus test of Chinese power and leadership as it has been unable to stop and reverse an "outrageous" nuclear program on its border, despite the fact that it probably has the only chokehold on Pyongyang's lifeline and is supposedly rising up to be a mighty new superpower. Beijing's "failure" so far, however, reflects its unwillingness more than its inability. The gap between its talk and its walk epitomizes the gap between the CCP's political interest and China's national interest. The North Korean nuclear program, while seriously threatening to South Korea, Japan, and the United States, clearly spells a loss for China as a nation. Both China's national security environment and freedom of action in East Asia are negatively affected. The

North Korean bomb undercuts China's power and prestige every day, as it poisons PRC-ROK relations and undermines Chinese leadership in the region and beyond, with more and graver uncertainties and chain reactions down the road. But for the CCP, the game of foreign policy is all about safeguarding its autocratic rule, the stalemate and danger of the DPRK nuclear program are secondary to the grand strategy of fending off the United States. As long as Washington is not gaining power over the CCP, expensively feeding Pyongyang and grudgingly accepting the North Korean bomb seem tolerable prices for the CCP to pay.

It is therefore fully understandable for Beijing to merely talk about denuclearizing the DPRK. Useful and somewhat sincere on the part of Beijing, such talks and even some companion walks always stop, however, before possibly causing its only treaty ally and ideological comrade in Pyongyang to collapse or defect. The demise of the DPRK or a Pyongyang rapprochement with Washington would mean strengthening the hands of the United States and its allies—automatically viewed in Beijing as a dreadful blow to the CCP regime.[45] This highly politicized, suboptimal PRC foreign policy may serve the CCP regime well but at the heavy expense of China's national interest.[46] To be sure, the excruciating gap between Beijing's talk (reflecting more of the Chinese national interest) and walk (ultimately determined by the CCP's political interest) has not gone painlessly unnoticed in China. Fieldwork suggests that many Chinese analysts and officials are aware of this gap and have been agonizing over the disconnection. The United States, South Korea, and the world at large might have been rightfully hoping for China to act as a rising but still "normal" power, based on its calculation of national interests and taking Beijing's talk of denuclearizing North Korea seriously as a rare but genuinely shared common preference. Seoul, Tokyo, and Washington seem to have injudiciously rewarded Beijing for its perceived cooperation in the effort to denuclearize North Korea.

Of course, talks without much real walk are just talks. What has happened since the dramatic, showy acts in 2018 has once again revealed the reality: Beijing has refocused on its traditional policy of resisting and reducing U.S. influence first, while pursuing denuclearization second, if ever. In 2020–21, Beijing seemingly suddenly, but actually predictably, raised the tone of anti-American propaganda and Beijing-Pyongyang solidarity by celebrating its participation in the Korean War more than six decades ago. In fact, if the Trump-Kim summits accomplished anything, it is by acknowledging that the true nature and unique style of Chinese foreign policy, talk the talk and walk the walk, all for the Party's political interest, has been laid bare for everyone to see.

To Change the Chinese Walk: Any New Window of Opportunity?

However abnormal, the rising power of China with its inevitable nationalist and even imperialist aspirations, will necessarily still consider the North Korean nuclear program a liability and threat. Beijing's talk of denuclearizing the DPRK therefore is fully expected to continue, with varied tones and pitches at different times and to different audiences. There is still some shared interest between the United States and China on this issue for some coordinated if not cooperative effort to peacefully preserve the NPT in Northeast Asia.[47] But, based on the analysis presented in this chapter, no one should really hold out any real hope for China to assist in the peaceful denuclearization of North Korea, as long as the CCP's political interests continue to dictate China's strategic rivalry with the United States. With Beijing's lack of real action, the standard American objective of a peaceful CVID (complete, verifiable, irreversible denuclearization) of the DPRK, upheld once again by the Biden administration after its policy review in 2021, remains as distant as ever.[48] Improved diplomatic skills, thoughtful new approaches, and more coordination with allies to negotiate more effectively may be useful,[49] but likely only at the margins.

The various efforts made by the United States and its allies, with a real but transient window of opportunity or without one, so far have been largely ineffective for the reasons I have attempted to outline. It of course never hurts to keep trying but, short of some miracle happening, fundamental political changes in Beijing (to reduce the CCP's dictation of Chinese foreign policy) and Pyongyang (to reduce the regime's needs for the nuclear bomb) remain the key to any success of the U.S.-led diplomatic efforts. The DPRK bomb could only be removed together with the debilitating insecurity that has been plaguing both the CCP autocracy and the Kim dynasty. Yet, a U.S.-DPRK rapprochement, even with provisions to assure Pyongyang of international recognition, security guarantees, and economic aid, might not be as effective in persuading the DPRK to give up its bomb as many may hope. Economically lagging behind its main rival Seoul and politically viewed worldwide as a pariah state, Pyongyang perhaps rightfully has reasoned that only the asymmetric and terrifying power of nuclear weapons can give it regime security and bargaining power; Kim Jon-un has said so explicitly.[50] In fact, as Pyongyang worries about regime-destabilizing threats from both the South and the North, even with U.S. security guarantees, in light of what happened to Muammar Gaddafi of Libya and, to a different extent, Ukraine, the Kim regime probably cannot really be persuaded to give up its bomb. In addition, for Beijing not to use its immense power to derail and sabotage any major U.S.-DPRK deal, the CCP would have to feel thoroughly secure and content as well, something the United States can hardly provide without causing a cascade in its strategic positions in the Western Pacific and permanent damage to the core interests of its alliance network in the region. In fact, as I have analyzed elsewhere, the nature of the rising Chinese power determines that the CCP would never be fully content without itself leading and reordering the world in its image, something fundamentally at odds with the United States.[51] To change Beijing's actions by making more concessions to satisfy the CCP is probably too high a price to pay for denuclearizing North Korea, and would soon come back to haunt the United States and its allies.

Looking forward, are there any possibilities to synchronize Beijing's talk with its walk? Any chance to change China's foreign policy regarding the DPRK nuclear issue and create a new window of opportunity for the peaceful denuclearization of North Korea? Even without a political miracle in Beijing and Pyongyang or a grand American capitulation to the CCP, there still seem to be some new, narrow ways for the United States and its allies to denuclearize North Korea, in stages if necessary. These ideas are neither foolproof nor cost-free nor risk-free. They require vision, courage, and good execution. One idea is to treat Beijing as part of the problem based on its actions, rather than part of the solution based on its rhetoric. A concerted competition with and smart decoupling from the PRC might give the United States and its allies powerful leverage to induce Beijing to make tradeoffs over the North Korean bomb. The sanctions against Pyongyang might have a real chance of effect only if Beijing is also part of the sanctions and when the CCP feels the full consequences of the DPRK bomb. If Beijing demands a carrot that is simply too big for the United States to offer, perhaps a bigger stick would make a difference. This way, the DPRK nuclear problem itself is reframed, becoming part of a much larger, likely lengthy and complex, long game between the rising PRC and the United States. The window of opportunity for peacefully denuclearizing North Korea may reopen when *both* Beijing and Pyongyang realize that the DPRK bomb has decreased, not increased, their bargaining power, international statue, economic fortune, and particularly regime security. How the allies, especially South Korea, act and react in this scenario will be critical.[52]

Another idea is to leverage Beijing-Pyongyang discord and to exclude rather than rely on China to address the North Korean bomb. Could the United States and its allies go farther to explore and maximize the possibility of a North Korean defection? The NPT might have a better chance in Northeast Asia if the allies moved away from their fixation on denuclearizing North Korea with China's supposedly "indispensable" help. With a "swift shift" in the Biden administration's "principled diplomacy" of multilateralism, Washington and Seoul seem to have moved in the direction of "upgrading" the US-ROK alliance and developing, along with Tokyo, a trilateral partnership to face China and North Korea in a holistic way.[53] More thorough and tougher efforts like the 2018 Vancouver Foreign Ministers' Meeting on Security and Stability on Korean Peninsula, attended by twenty nations while excluding China, Russia, and the DPRK,[54] might create a new path forward. The Vancouver decision on using force, including naval blockade and financial cutoff of North Korea, halted by the futile Kim-Trump summit, uncertain consequences notwithstanding, could likely bear new fruit, as PRC analysts have dreaded.[55]

Finally, there is the idea of carefully magnifying and exploring nationalist concerns in China over the possible chain reaction of a nuclear arms race in East Asia. This will likely alter the CCP's political calculus and nudge Beijing into behaving as a "normal" nation with regard to the DPRK nuclear program. If the Chinese could put up with its ally, however erratic and estranged, having nuclear weapons right on their border, why wouldn't the Americans feel the same way about their much more stable allies thinking about going nuclear? If, starting with the Bush administration, Washington could accept nuclear arsenals in South Asia, perhaps it should also consider the same in East Asia? Indeed, many have long argued in private and public for countries like Japan and South Korea to arm themselves with nuclear weapons for their own national security and their power position versus the DPRK and the PRC.[56] Such a bold move would be a retreat and revision, albeit measured and reversible, of the NPT regime, and create new issues to be managed in the U.S.-ROK and U.S.-Japan alliances, for sure. It might be more symbolic than actual, well controlled and paced, and firmly conditional on Pyongyang's nuclear program to minimize its impact on the NPT. In fact, well executed, this innovative move would enhance the U.S.-led alliance network by creating a better balance of power in the region to deter North Korea and facilitating a more robust collective security regime to counter the rising PRC power. Moreover, it would actually increase the likelihood of denuclearizing North Korea so as to ultimately preserve the NPT in Northeast Asia. Once Japan and South Korea (and perhaps eventually even Taiwan) start to contemplate and even plan for going nuclear as their legitimate response to match and deter the DPRK, with the United States watching attentively with sympathy and tacit nonobstruction, Beijing would have to really seriously reevaluate its priority list to reconsider its policy toward the North Korean bomb. After all, an NPT that exempts and ignores, de facto, the PRC ally of the DPRK but restricts and disadvantages the U.S. allies by disallowing exploration of options seems neither stable nor desirable in the long run.

Conclusion

The long-lasting Cold War–era security framework in East Asia, anchored by the U.S.-ROK and U.S.-Japan alliances, has structurally confined the rising power of the PRC. While that framework is inconvenient but not necessarily threatening, much less detrimental, to China's national security and economic prosperity, the U.S. presence and leadership in the region always represents a sharp contrast, stark challenge, and implied mortal threat to the CCP-PRC party-state's political system. Both the U.S. presence and the U.S.-anchored East Asian security framework have thus naturally become the leading targets for Beijing. Clearly not always obedient or reliable or trouble-free, the DPRK has managed to survive on the Chinese supply and sheltering, as a rare ideological companion and a geostrategic asset to the CCP's foreign policy in the region.

With that backdrop, the Chinese policy toward the DPRK's nuclear program (and also the issue of Korean unification) has been driven by two sets of interests that sometimes overlap but are often in serious conflict: the national interest of China as a sovereign nation like many others in the constant pursuit of security and power, and the political interest of the CCP autocracy, which is an ideological loner facing a persistent threat from the presence of the United States. Chinese foreign policy in general and Beijing's actions concerning the Korean Peninsula in particular are peculiarly politicized to promote the CCP's regime security first and foremost. It is the CCP's political interest, not China's national interest, that has been fanning animosity between Beijing and Washington/Tokyo, and the same holds for China's long and expensive but largely unreciprocated support of the Kim regime. Indeed, in its seven decades of history, Beijing has repeatedly ceded Chinese land and water, not to mention many other tangible and intangible Chinese national interests, for the CCP's regime survival and security without many qualms.[57] Historians have documented that Chinese foreign policy has always been "shaped by the CCP's domestic political agenda."[58] The gap, even divorce, between China's national interests and the CCP's political interests is striking and persistent. It has determined that Beijing talks the talk but walks the walk about denuclearizing North Korea. The PRC clearly would like a denuclearization of the Korean Peninsula and Northeast Asia, but the CCP wants much more to resist, reduce, and replace American power in the region even at the price of grudgingly tolerating the North Korean bomb so close to the heartland of China.

There was at times only a small and transient window of opportunity as Beijing tried to balance the two sets of interests, as exhibited by its hosting of the Six-Party Talks and participation in the UN-organized sanctions against Pyongyang. In the early 2010s, having exhaustively milked the doomed multilateral Six-Party Talks, the CCP under Xi Jinping had the ambitious plan to possibly trade the nuclear arsenal of its DPRK comrades for a breakthrough in Beijing's political and strategic relationship with South Korea, at the expense of the U.S.-ROK Alliance. As one PRC analyst succinctly stated, it is simply in Beijing's strategic interest "to weaken the U.S.-led military alliances [in East Asia] and pull South Korea off the American track."[59] A new, strengthened Chinese cooperation with the UN sanctions thus developed, and Beijing showed an unusually cold shoulder to Pyongyang, until Xi's personal overtures were frustrated and even "humiliated" by Seoul's decision to deploy THADD in 2016–17. Once Pyongyang seized upon the U.S. offer of a Trump-Kim summit in 2018 and craftily maneuvered with it, that small window of opportunity was quickly closed. The CCP realigned its talk with its walk to oppose the United States and its allies. The smaller player in the game, the DPRK, seems to have won again against its mighty opponents with its bombs and missiles intact and the Chinese supply surged.

Beijing's big talk has never been matched by its long walk with regard to denuclearizing the DPRK. Decisively oscillating toward sabotaging the course of denuclearization, the CCP is now preparing for more strategic rivalry with the United States. As long as the deep institutional and ideological incompatibility remains between Beijing and Washington, without a sea change of sociopolitical institutions and values on either or both sides, perhaps only some new, innovative though somewhat risky moves could now reopen the window of opportunity for a peaceful or partially peaceful denuclearization of North Korea and the preservation of the NPT in East Asia.

Since the CCP has often been a spoiler sabotaging the efforts of peaceful denuclearization of North Korea, as acknowledged openly by a senior PRC specialist in Korea studies, it may indeed be better to try new, holistic ways that combine more confrontation with and further "exclusion" of Beijing.[60] By the same logic, the United States and its allies could think and act creatively to specifically maximize the negatives of the North Korean bomb on the CCP. If the allies moved away from their fixation on denuclearizing North Korea with China's supposedly "indispensable" help, the North Korean nuclear issue and the preservation of the NPT in East Asia might be, perhaps paradoxically, managed and even resolved more effectively in the overall context of the Sino-American strategic competition. Only when Beijing deems that the damage caused by the North Korean bomb to China's national interests and national security starts to impair the CCP regime and reduce, or even cancel, the payoffs from upsetting and costing the United States in the region, the PRC might then be realistically expected to deal more seriously with North Korean denuclearization. The CCP's political interests and pursuits, after all, determine PRC foreign policy.[61]

Notes

The author wants to thank Terence Roehrig, Su-Mi Lee, and the anonymous reviewers for comments and suggestions, and Pooja P. Patel and Paul Goldsman for research and editorial assistance.

1. Kelsey Davenport, "Chronology of U.S.-North Korean Nuclear and Missile Diplomacy," Arms Control Association, July 2020, https://www.armscontrol.org/factsheets/dprkchron.

2. Evans Revere, "Kim's 'New Path' and the Failure of Trump's North Korea Policy," *East Asia Forum*, January 20, 2020.

3. Rafael Mariano Grossi, "DPRK Nuclear Activities Still 'Cause For Serious Concern,'" *UN News*, September 21, 2020; Celine Castronuovo, "North Korean Plant May be Building Nuclear Components, Report Finds," *The Hill*,

December 18, 2020; Josh Smith, "Mysterious N. Korea Site May Be Building Nuclear Components," *Reuters*, December 18, 2020; "North Korea Unveils New Submarine-launched Missile," BBC, January 15, 2021; Sang-Hun Choe, "Kim Jong-un Uses Party Congress to Double Down on Nuclear Program," *New York Times*, January 14, 2021, A10.

4. Sang-Hun Choe, "Why Is North Korea Suddenly Launching So Many Missiles?" *New York Times*, January 25, 2022.

5. Ramon Pacheco Pardo and Jihwan Hwang, "Seoul Sees Hope in Biden's North Korea Approach," *The Hill*, March 8, 2021.

6. Scott A. Snyder, "Biden's Policy Review Leaves North Korea Challenge in Limbo," Council on Foreign Relations Blog, May 19, 2021, https://www.cfr.org/blog/bidens-policy-review-leaves-north-korea-challenge-limbo.

7. "Secretary of State Michael Pompeo's Remarks to the Silicon Valley Leadership Group," San Francisco, January 13, 2020, https://id.usembassy.gov/wp-content/uploads/sites/72/Remarks-by-Secretary-Pompeo-on-Technology-and-the-China-Security-Challenge.pdf.

8. Jason Scott and Isabel Reynolds, "Australia Seeks to Build Defense Ties to Counter China Squeeze," *Bloomberg*, November 16, 2020.

9. Author's interviews with People's Republic of China officials and analysts, 2013–16.

10. People's Republic of China Foreign Ministry, "Statements," Beijing, February 12, 2013 and January 6, 2016; Sang-Hun Choe, "China Suspends All Coal Imports from North Korea," *New York Times*, February 19, 2017, A6; Ryan Woo and Muyu Xu, "China Halts Oil Product Exports to North Korea in November," *Reuters*, December 26, 2017.

11. The Chinese Communist Party Central History and Archives Bureau, ed, *Digest of Xi Jinping's Treaties on Great Power Diplomacy with Chinese Characteristics* (中共中央党史和文献研究院: 习近平关于中国特色大国外交论述摘编) (Beijing: Zhongyang wenxian, 2020). CCP Department of Propaganda, "Fully Promoting Great Power Diplomacy with Chinese Characteristics in the New Era [中共中央宣传部: 新时代中国特色大国外交全面推进]," *Renmin Ribao* (人民日报), September 30, 2022.

12. "THAAD on the Korean Peninsula," *Backgrounder* (Stockholm), Institute for Security and Development Policy, October 2017.

13. "Xi Jinping and Kim Jung-un Held a Meeting (习近平同金正恩举行会谈)," *Xinhua*, March 3, 2018.

14. Author's conversations with the Democratic People's Republic of Korea diplomats and representatives, 1999–2006.

15. Jonathan Cheng and Chun Han Wong, "North Korea Mocks China for 'Dancing to U.S. Tune,'" *Wall Street Journal*, February 23, 2017.

16. Tao Jiang, "Xi Jinping's 'Time in Pyongyang' (蒋涛: 习近平的"平壤时间")," *China News* (Beijing), June 21, 2019.

17. Dan De Luce and Ken Dilanian, "China Eases Economic Pressure on North Korea, Undercutting the Trump Administration," *NBC News*, September 5, 2018.

18. Fei-Ling Wang, "China and the Prospects of Denuclearization of North Korea," *Asian Journal of Peacebuilding* (Seoul, Korea) 6, no. 2 (2018): 267–88.

19. Yi Wang, "Analyzing the Building and Institutional Construction of a New Type of Global Governance System (王毅: 试析新型全球治理体系的构建及制度建设)," *Guowai lilun dongtai* (State of Foreign Theories) 8 (2013): 5–11.

20. Frank Aum and Joseph Yun, "Nuclear Diplomacy with North Korea: What's Ahead for the Biden Administration?" U.S. Institute of Peace, December 21, 2020.

21. Wu, Xinbo ed., *Crisis and New Situation* (吴心伯: 危局与新局: 复旦国际战略报告), Shanghai, January 13, 2021; Zhang, Liangui, "Biden's New Policy towards Korean Nuclear Issue Will Lead to New Crisis on The Peninsula" (张琏瑰: 拜登朝核新政策将引发半岛新危机)," *Dunjian wang* (钝角网) (Beijing), June 9, 2021.

22. Fei-Ling Wang, *The China Record: An Assessment of the People's Republic* (Albany: State University of New York Press, 2023), ch. 1.

23. The Chinese Communist Party (CCP) Central Document Studies Bureau, *Selections of Xi Jinping's Words on Realizing the China Dream for the Great Rejuvenation of the Chinese Nation* (习近平关于实现中华民族伟大复兴的中国梦论述摘编) (Beijing: Zhongyang wenxian, 2013); Fei-Ling Wang, *The China Order: Centralia, World Empire, and the Nature of Chinese Power* (Albany: State University of New York Press, 2017), 195–218.

24. For those grand worldviews and plans, see CCP Central History and Archives Bureau ed, *Digest*. For an interpretation of the slogans in Chinese foreign policy, see Jinghan Zeng, *Slogan Politics: Understanding Chinese Foreign Policy Concepts* (London: Palgrave Macmillan, 2020).

25. Ely Ratner et al., *More Willing and Able: Charting China's International Security Activism* (Washington, DC: Center for a New American Security, 2015).

26. The latest to join BRI was Argentina in 2022. "Argentina Officially Joins BRI in Major Boost for China–Latin America Cooperation," *Global Times* (Beijing), February 6, 2022.

27. Yuan-kang Wang, *Harmony and War: Confucian Culture and Chinese Power Politics* (New York: Columbia University Press, 2010); Steven Walt, "Dealing with a Chinese Monroe Doctrine," *New York Times*, May 3, 2012.

28. John W. Garver and Fei-Ling Wang, "China's Anti-Encirclement Struggle: The U.S., India, and Japan," *Asian Security* 6, no. 3 (October 2010): 238–61.

29. Chris Buckley, " 'Abrupt Changes,' China Caught in a Bind Over Russia's Invasion of Ukraine," *New York Times*, February 25, 2022.

30. U.S. Congress, Hong Kong Human Rights and Democracy Act of 2019, November 20, 2019; Uyghur Human Rights Policy Act of (2019) 2020, June 17, 2020; and Hong Kong Autonomy Act of 2020, July 14, 2020.

31. Kurt M. Campbell and Laura Rosenberger, "Speeches on U.S.-China Relations," Oksenberg Conference, Stanford University, May 27, 2021; Yinhong Shi, "Biden Administration's China Policy Expressed (时殷弘: 拜登政府对华当今方针宣示)," *Renda meiguo yanjiu jianbao* (人大美国研究简报), March 7, 2021, No. 1.

32. U.S. Congress, *Taiwan Allies International Protection and Enhancement Initiative (TAIPEI) Act of 2019*, March 28, 2020; Yun-yu Chen and Emerson Lim, "Declassified Cables Reveal U.S. Assurances on Taiwan's Defense," *Focus Taiwan*, August 31, 2020; Richard Haass and David Sacks, "American Support for Taiwan Must Be Unambiguous," *Foreign Affairs*, September 2, 2020; Elbridge Colby, "America Can Defend Taiwan," *Wall Street Journal*, January 26, 2021.

33. Michael Pompeo, "Determination of the Secretary of State on Atrocities in Xinjiang," U.S. Department of State News Release, January 19, 2021, https://2017-2021.state.gov/determination-of-the-secretary-of-state-on-atrocities-in-xinjiang/index.html; Edward Wong and Chris Buckley, "U.S. Says China's Repression of Uighurs Is 'Genocide,'" *New York Times*, April 22, 2021; White House, "Statement by President Joe Biden on the Investigation into the Origins of COVID-19," May 26, 2021, https://www.whitehouse.gov/briefing-room/statements-releases/2021/05/26/statement-by-president-joe-biden-on-the-investigation-into-the-origins-of-covid-19/. Jo He-rim, "South Korea's Intelligence Agency Joins NATO's Cyber Defense Center as First in Asia," *The Korea Herald*, Seoul, May 5, 2022; *G7 Leaders' Communiqué*, Elmau, Germany, June 28, 2022. *NATO 2022 Strategic Concept*, Madrid, Spain, June 29, 2022: 10 and 5.

34. Sino-Korean Friendship, Cooperation and Mutual Assistance Treaty, 1961 (renewed 2021), Article 7.

35. Fei-Ling Wang, "Changing Views: Chinese Perception of the United States–South Korea Alliance," *Problems of Post-Communism* (July-August 1996): 25–34; "Joining the Major Powers for the Status Quo: China's Views and Policy on Korean Reunification," *Pacific Affairs* 72, no. 2 (1999): 167–85; "Looking East: China's Policy toward the Korean Peninsula," in *Engagement with North Korea: A Viable Alternative*, ed. Sung Chull Kim and David C. Kang (Albany: State University of New York Press, 2005), 47–72; "Resisting, Reducing, and Replacing: China's Strategy and Policy towards the United States," in *China's Domestic Politics and Foreign Policies, and Major Countries' Strategies on China*, ed. Jung-Ho Bae (Seoul: KINU, 2012), 155–86; "Between the Bomb and the United States: China Faces the Nuclear North Korea," in *The North Korean Nuclear Challenge: How the Bomb Would Influence North Korea and the Region,* ed. Sung Chull Kim and Michael Cohen (Washington, DC: Georgetown University Press, 2017), 157–78.

36. Zhihua Shen, "The Shocking Inside Story of Sino-Korean Relations" (沈志华: 中朝关系惊天内幕), *Sina lishi* (新浪历史) (Beijing), September 3, 2013.

37. Wang, "Joining," 167–85; "Looking East," 47–72.

38. Jung-Ho Bae et al., *The Perceptions of Northeast Asia's Four States on Korean Unification* (Seoul: KINU, 2014), 28–37.

39. Jinping Xi, "Speech at the Opening Ceremony of the Fifth CICA For-eign Ministers Meeting" (习近平: 在亚信五次外长会议开幕式上的讲话), *Xinhua*, April 28, 2016.

40. Scott A. Snyder, "China's Persistent Support for the Six-Party Talks," *Atlantic*, September 19, 2013; Tony Munroe and Ben Blanchard, "North Korea's Neighbors Push to Resume Six-Party Talks," *Reuters*, March 26, 2015.

41. *The DOD Focus on the Indo-Pacific*, U.S. Department of Defense, 2018; Philippe Mesmer, "Japan and South Korea Want NATO to Look toward Asia," *Le Monde*, Paris, June 29, 2022.

42. Michelle Nichols et al., "Exclusive: U.N. Lifts North Korea Sanctions on Four Ships at China's Request," *Reuters*, March 22, 2016.

43. Huilai Zhou, "It's Too Early for China to Abandon North Korea" (周慧来: 中国放弃朝鲜还为时尚早), *Lianhe* zaobao (United Daily), June 15, 2010.

44. Author's interviews with PRC officials and analysts, 2016–18.

45. "'Abandoning [North] Korea' Is an Idea Too Immature and Extreme," ("放弃朝鲜"的主张过于幼稚和极端) *Huanqiu shibao* (环球时报), April 12, 2013; Dunqiu Li, "Cannot 'Abandon' the 65-Year Old Partner [North] Korea" (李敦球: 不能"放弃"朝鲜这65年的伙伴), *Huanqiu shibao* (环球时报), November, 27, 2014; Kezhen Zhou, "China Cannot Abandon [North] Korea" (周可真: 中国不能放弃朝鲜), *ScienceNet.cn* Blog, March 10, 2017.

46. Carla Freeman, ed., *China and North Korea: Strategic and Policy Per-spectives from a Changing China* (New York: Palgrave Macmillan, 2015).

47. Tong Zhao, "What Does North Korea's Provocation Mean to China?" (赵通: 朝鲜的挑衅对中国意味着什么) Carnegie-Tsinghua (Beijing), July 15, 2020.

48. Robert Einhorn, "The Rollout of the Biden Administration's North Korea Policy Review Leaves Unanswered Questions," Brookings, May 4, 2021.

49. Rafiq Dossani, *Engagement with North Korea: A Portfolio-Based Approach to Diplomacy* (Santa Monica: RAND, 2020); Stephen J. Blank, "North Korea: Nuclear Threat or Security Problem?" *Journal of Indo-Pacific Affairs*, Air University, December 2, 2020. https://www.airuniversity.af.edu/JIPA/Display/Article/2432401/north-korea-nuclear-threat-or-security-problem/.

50. "Nukes Mean No More War, Kim Says," *Asia Times*, July 28, 2020.

51. Wang, *The China Order*.

52. Anthony H. Cordesman et al., *North Korean Nuclear Forces and the Threat of Weapons of Mass Destruction in Northeast Asia* (Washington, DC: CSIS, July 25, 2016); Toby Dalton and Ain Han, *Elections, Nukes, and the Future of the South Korea–U.S. Alliance* (Washington, DC: Carnegie Endowment for Interna-tional Peace, October 26, 2020).

53. Sangmi Cha, "South Korea's Moon Pledges to Upgrade Alliance with U.S. in Call with Biden," *Reuters*, February 3, 2021; Gabriella Bernal, "Biden seeks Tokyo-Seoul Thaw to Help End North Korea Deadlock," *Nikki Asia*, February 10, 2021; Robert Burns, "Biden's Deal with Seoul Points to a Swift Shift on Alli-

ances," *AP News*, March 11, 2021; Julian Ryall, "Will Japan–South Korea Talks Yield Improved Ties as North's Provocations Drive Them Vloser?" *South China Morning Post*, October 27, 2022.

54. "Co-chairs' Summary of the Vancouver Foreign Ministers' Meeting on Security and Stability on the Korean Peninsula," Global Affairs Canada, Government of Canada, January 16, 2018. https://www.canada.ca/en/global-affairs/news/2018/01/co-chair_s_summaryofthevancouverforeignministersmeetingonsecurit.html.

55. PRC analysts seem to have seen this point. Zhang, "Biden's New Policy."

56. Doug Bandow, "America's Asian Allies Need Their Own Nukes," *Foreign Policy*, December 30, 2020.

57. M. Taylor Fravel, "Regime Insecurity and International Cooperation: Explaining China's Compromises in Territorial Disputes," *International Security* 30 (Fall 2005): 46–83; Zhihua Shen, "China's Policy of Dealing with Land Border Disputes during the Cold War" (沈志華: 冷戰年代中國處理陸地邊界糾紛的方針), *21st Century* (Hong Kong), June 2014.

58. John W. Garver, *China's Quest: Foreign Relations of the People's Republic of China* (New York: Oxford University Press, 2016).

59. Zhao, "What Does North Korea's Provocation Mean to China?" For PRC's expedient "conciliatory" policy about its territorial disputes with South Korea in the Yellow Sea, see Shuxian Luo, "China–South Korea Disputes in the Yellow Sea: Why a More Conciliatory Chinese Posture," *Journal of Contemporary China* 31, no. 138 (2022): 913–30.

60. Jiyong Zheng, "Three Key Points of Biden Administration's Policy towards the Korean Peninsula" (郑继永: 拜登政府对朝鲜半岛政策三要点), *The Paper* (澎湃) (Shanghai), January 18, 2021.

61. Jiechi Yang, "Actively Construct Favorable External Environment" (杨洁篪: 积极营造良好外部环境), *Renmin Ribao* (人民日报), November 30, 2020, 6.

Chapter 7

Japan's Policy Dilemma vis-à-vis North Korea

Yuki Tatsumi

On May 12, 2022, North Korea conducted yet another ballistic missile test.[1] The third in the month of May alone, it was the sixteenth missile test by Pyongyang since the beginning of 2022, including the first intercontinental ballistic missile test conducted in five years, on March 24, 2022. As Prime Minister Fumio Kishida, Defense Minister Nobuo Kishi, and Foreign Minister Yoshimasa Hayashi firmly condemned Pyongyang's actions, these provocations illustrate the reality of the security threats that Japan faces from North Korea.

However, Japan has been stuck in a policy conundrum since the early 2000s, with Japan's policy goals vis-à-vis North Korea having shifted over the years. Since North Korea remains one of just a few countries with whom Japan has yet to normalize bilateral relations, diplomatic normalization with Pyongyang was Tokyo's most important policy goal vis-à-vis North Korea during the Cold War through the end of 1990s. In fact, despite the emergence of concerns over North Korea's nuclear weapon and ballistic missile programs in the 1990s, Japan continued its attempts at engagement with North Korea so that the two countries could continue to discuss a path toward diplomatic normalization. For instance, as late as 1999, a multiparty delegation led by former prime minister Tomiichi Murayama, a Social Democrat, visited Pyongyang to hold talks with North

Korean officials in hopes of paving the way toward resuming normaliza-tion talks[2] and discussions on the abduction of Japanese nationals.

It was not until North Korea first declared its intention to withdraw from the Nuclear Non-Proliferation Treaty (NPT) in 1992 that the nuclear disarmament of North Korea came to the fore of the minds of Japa-nese policymakers. Still, despite Japan's heightened concern about North Korea's nuclear and missile program following the first North Korean nuclear crisis and Pyongyang's first ballistic missile test in 1995, Japan continued to pursue diplomatic normalization with North Korea as its primary goal for North Korea throughout the 1990s. In fact, while Pyong-yang's nuclear and missile threat had become the top concern for the Japanese government by the mid-1990s, it was not until the early 2000s that the main goal of Japan's North Korea policy made a clear shift away from normalizing ties with Pyongyang.[3]

Normalization or Denuclearization?

Diplomatic normalization began to take a back seat in Japan's North Korea policy goals in the 1990s when Pyongyang's nuclear and missile programs began to raise serious concerns. In particular, a gradual shift away from normalization began when the national security establishment in Japan became acutely aware of the tangible threat from North Korea's nuclear and missile programs following North Korea's first declaration of with-drawal from the NPT in 1995, which was followed shortly thereafter by Pyongyang's first ballistic missile test over Japan.

Still, Japan was largely left on the margins as the United States and North Korea engaged in direct negotiations for the Framework Agreement in 1994,[4] followed by a U.S.-South Korea joint proposal to hold Four-Party Talks together with North Korea and China to discuss the future of the Korean Peninsula,[5] leaving Japan to search for its own window of oppor-tunity to improve bilateral relations with North Korea. Starting with the Pyongyang visit by former vice prime minister Shin Kanamaru and Social Democratic Party Chairman Makoto Tanabe in September 1990, there persisted a strong desire among Japanese political leaders to pursue dip-lomatic normalization with Pyongyang. These leaders, many of whom experienced World War II and Japan's unconditional surrender during their formative years, had been driven by their personal desire to end Japan's World War II legacies.

Normalization of Japan–North Korea relations was one such legacy close to their hearts.[6] The aforementioned North Korea visit by the Murayama delegation was another example of such persistence at the political level to create opportunities for engagement. These efforts created tension between political leaders and the Japanese government as the government moved to prioritize denuclearization of the peninsula and deterrence measures. Japan supported the implementation of the 1994 Agreed Framework through the Korean Peninsula Energy Development Organization (KEDO), while also seeking to deter further North Korean provocation by enhancing the U.S.-Japan alliance and Japan's own defense capabilities through measures such as the introduction of ballistic missile defenses and intelligence-gathering satellites.

The dynamics surrounding the Japanese government's effort to stay focused on North Korea's denuclearization dramatically changed again when Prime Minister Junichiro Koizumi visited Pyongyang in 2002. Koizumi met with North Korean leader Kim Jong-il in hopes of paving the way for the negotiation of diplomatic normalization, culminating in the two leaders signing the Japan-DPRK Pyongyang Declaration at the end of his visit. The Declaration, attempting to comprehensively address the bilateral issues of concern between Japan and North Korea, in addition to North Korea's agreement to maintain its moratorium on missiles tests, included the following:

1. Agreement to resume the normalization negotiation;

2. Japan's recognition of its behavior during Japan's colonial rule and expression of "deep remorse and heartfelt apology";

3. DPRK's agreement to "take appropriate measures" to prevent abduction of Japanese citizens from happening again; and

4. Agreement to cooperate for the peace and security of Northeast Asia, including taking confidence-building measures and confirmation of the "necessity of resolving security problems including nuclear and missile issues by promoting dialogues among countries concerned."[7]

The Pyongyang Declaration sought to achieve the Japanese government's goal toward North Korea's denuclearization by trying to address all of Japan's concerns vis-à-vis North Korea in one document, thus laying the groundwork for Japan to actively participate in the multinational framework to negotiate denuclearization with North Korea. In particular, it sought to embed the North Korean abduction issue (*rachi mondai*)[8] firmly as a part of the negotiation agenda in the multilateral framework.

The Pyongyang Declaration partially achieved the Japanese government's goal as it did provide Japan a framework upon which Japan could pursue close policy coordination with other countries. Japan joined the United States, China, South Korea, and Russia to bring North Korea to the negotiation table under the framework of the Six-Party Talks, as seen in the Joint Declaration issued in September 2005.[9] On the other hand, Koizumi's Pyongyang visits, in September 2002 and May 2004, resulted in the imposition of an unanticipated constraint on Japan's North Korea policy which continues to hamstring Japan today—the abduction issue.

The Abduction Issue Hamstrings Japan

From the 1970s until the mid-1980s, there were numerous cases of Japanese citizens going missing, primarily from Japanese coastal cities on the Sea of Japan. The families of these citizens insisted that the Japanese government should push North Korea to return their missing family members, but Tokyo, prioritizing diplomatic normalization with Pyongyang throughout the Cold War, took no meaningful action.

However, the publication of a book about Megumi Yokota—who was thirteen years old when she disappeared—by her mother in 1999 brought the issue to light among the Japanese public.[10] The heartbreaking story told by Mrs. Sakie Yokota—a gentle-mannered, soft-spoken elderly Japanese woman—about her daughter's unexplained disappearance in 1977 and her and her husband's struggle to get the Japanese government to act captured national attention, coining the issue as "the abduction issue."

As security concerns with North Korea began to grow in Japan throughout the 1990s with the growth of Pyongyang's nuclear and missile program, a group formed by the families of these abducted Japanese citizens, facilitated by conservative Japanese journalists and academics, approached conservative politicians in the ruling Liberal Democratic Party (LDP) to pressure the government. These politicians included former prime minister Shinzo Abe, Katsuei Hirasawa, and Kenji Furuya, among many others.

These family members also traveled to Washington, D.C., and met with members of the U.S. Congress and officials in the U.S. government, urging them to pressure North Korea on their behalf as well. However, North Korea continued to deny these allegations, insisting that they were nothing more than conspiracy theories.

The Koizumi-Kim summit in September 2002 drastically changed the dynamics surrounding the issue. During the meeting, Kim Jong-il admitted that North Korean security agents had indeed kidnapped Japanese citizens in the past. Kim told Koizumi that these agents acted without leadership's authorization, apologized for these actions, and expressed his intention to prevent such incidents from ever happening again.[11] Furthermore, despite Pyongyang's past denial, he told Koizumi that his government confirmed thirteen cases of abduction—eight, including Megumi Yokota, who were deceased and five survivors.[12] These five survivors returned home to Japan in October 2002 under conditions of temporary return. The survivors decided to stay in Japan, and were eventually reunited with their families who had remained in North Korea in 2004, following Koizumi's second summit meeting with Kim in May of that year.

Koizumi's two summit meetings with Kim were a diplomatic breakthrough for Japan. Indeed, the 2002 Pyongyang Declaration allowed Japan to create the framework through which Japan negotiates all its policy goals vis-à-vis North Korea—from the nuclear program to the abduction issue to diplomatic normalization—as a comprehensive package. This approach should have allowed Japan the flexibility it needed to negotiate with North Korea as it pursued multiple policy goals.

At the same time, the revelations of the abduction issue since the first Koizumi-Kim Summit also laid the foundation for Japan's current hard stance on North Korea. The public's interest in North Korea jumped after Koizumi's first summit with Kim. Public opinion polls conducted by the Cabinet Affairs Office in October 2001 showed only about 55 percent of the respondents were interested in North Korea,[13] but the same opinion poll conducted a year later showed that more than 65 percent of respondents supported normalizing diplomatic relations with North Korea, with close to 84 percent of respondents identifying the abduction issue as the issue of greatest interest with regard to North Korea.[14] By 2004, the abduction issue dominated the Japanese public's interest in North Korea, with approximately 90 percent of survey respondents identifying it as the issue they were most interested in about North Korea.[15] Such intensifying attention on the abduction issue displayed by the public, augmented by the stance taken by influential political leaders, including former prime minister Shinzo Abe, that Japan should not normalize diplomatic relations with North Korea without the complete resolution of the abduction issue, put limitations on the Japanese government's ability to negotiate with North Korea. The resolution of the abduction issue essentially became a necessary precondition for Japan to have any flexibility in its approach vis-à-vis North Korea.

Since then, Japan's North Korea policy has been hamstrung by the abduction issue. All prime ministers after Koizumi have identified the "resolution" of the abduction issue as the requirement for Japan to resume any meaningful diplomatic engagement with North Korea, including resumption of normalization talks. Most recently, Prime Minister Fumio Kishida, who took office in September 2021, remarked that the abduction issue remains "the most important issue for the government."[16] Although he expressed his government's intention to seek Japan–North Korea normalization through a comprehensive resolution of all issues of concern for Tokyo, he also mentioned that he would do all he could to realize "the homecoming of all the abductees as soon as possible."[17]

Because of the lack of flexibility in its North Korea policy, Japan has often found itself marginalized in multilateral diplomatic efforts to advance the goal of North Korea's denuclearization. Even though Japan initially was successful in including the abduction issue as an issue to be addressed in the Six-Party Talks, it has since been less and less successful in maintaining the commitment to the resolution of the abduction issue among the other Six-Party participants. When the leaders of the countries of the Six-Party Talks began to meet North Korean leader Kim Jong-un after U.S. president Donald Trump shocked the world by meeting Kim for a summit meeting in June 2018, then–Japanese prime minister Shinzo Abe was the only leader that could not meet with Kim, despite his repeated expression of his willingness to meet Kim "without any precondition." Even though Abe's successors, Suga and Kishida, reiterated Abe's stance,[18] there is no prospect for a Japanese leader to directly meet Kim.

Impacts of External and Internal Factors

As mentioned earlier in this paper, Japan's ultimate policy goal vis-à-vis North Korea is establishing diplomatic normalization and thereby ending one of the last remaining World War II legacies. The biggest external factor that has influenced this goal is the development of nuclear and missile capabilities by Pyongyang. The realization that these capabilities pose tangible threats to Japanese security prompted leaders to add denu-clearization and addressing North Korea's conventional military capabili-ties to the list of Japan's policy goals, forcing the government and political leaders to tread carefully between ensuring Japan's own security and con-tinuing to explore ways to make progress on diplomatic normalization with North Korea.

Pyongyang's nuclear and missile program impacted Japan beyond its North Korea policy, primarily in its security policy. For instance, the structural inadequacy in the U.S.-Japan alliance, which came to the attention of U.S. and Japanese policymakers during the first North Korea nuclear crisis, triggered the first revision of the U.S.-Japan Guidelines for Defense Cooperation. The revision, concluded in 1997, introduced a new frame of reference called "the situation in the area surrounding Japan" (SIAS-J), which clarified the role of Japan in support of the U.S. in a regional contingency.[19] North Korea's missile test also triggered a debate in Japan over the additional measures required to ensure that Japan has sufficient national defense capability to protect itself from the threat posed by North Korea. This debate resulted in accelerating Japan's decision to acquire its own reconnaissance satellite, as well as the decision to intro-duce ballistic missile defense, both of which took place in early 2000s.[20]

In addition, Tokyo's lack of direct communication channels with North Korea has made Japan dependent on the United States to shape its negotiating position against North Korea in a way that addresses Japan's concerns. This dynamic, which first emerged at the time of the negotiation of the Framework Agreement in the 1990s, essentially continues to the present day. It is the interplay between Japan's own security concerns and its need to closely align its negotiating position with that of the United States that eventually brought Japan to its current position of supporting complete, verifiable, and irreversible denuclearization (CVID) of North Korea's nuclear program.

Moreover, Japan's reliance on the United States in denuclearization negotiation with North Korea makes Japan very sensitive to the dynam-ics between the United States and China. In particular, as China's role as the convener of the Six-Party Talks grew, Japan became increasingly concerned that the United States and China might reach a "grand bar-gain" on North Korea's denuclearization that might not necessarily reflect Japan's own priorities, such as Pyongyang's ballistic missile capability and the abduction issue. The importance of ensuring that Washington fully take Tokyo's concerns into account has only grown since the breakdown of the Six-Party Talks and as Japan's bilateral relations with other Six-Party Talks participants—China, South Korea, and Russia—have either been aggravated (China and South Korea) or reached a stalemate (Russia).

The political repercussions of the abduction issue in Japan are the biggest domestic factor that have impacted Japan's policy toward North Korea. When the five abductees returned to Japan several months after Prime Minister Koizumi's first North Korea visit in 2002, it triggered a very emotional reaction among the Japanese public. Even though these abductees initially returned to Japan with a promise from the Japanese government to North Korea that they would be sent back to North Korea after a short family reunion, public outcry against North Korea was so intense that Japan ultimately decided to honor the five abductees' wishes to stay in Japan, breaking its initial commitment to Pyongyang. Although Koizumi managed to get North Korea to return the family members of these abductees to Japan,[21] Japan's bilateral negotiation with North Korea came to a complete deadlock. It also hardened Japanese public opinion against any engagement with North Korea, let alone providing incentives of any kind to Pyongyang, making it politically impossible for Japanese politicians to support direct negotiation with North Korea. This continues to hamstring the government's approach toward North Korea today.

Muddled Motives, Constrained Strategies

One of the challenges Japan faces in pursuing its policy goals toward North Korea is that its goals addressing national security concerns are often muddled by consideration at the political level in Japan.

On one hand, Japan's top policy goals for North Korea from a national security perspective should address the security threat posed by North Korea. This not only includes North Korea's denuclearization but also missiles, proliferation of weapons of mass destruction, cyber, and other nonnuclear security concerns. On the other hand, in a broader context of Japan's settling its legacy of World War II, diplomatic normalization with North Korea, as mentioned earlier in this paper, is one of the last remaining "must do" policies for Japan. However, given the national security threat North Korea poses to Japan with its nuclear and missile programs, as former top North Korea negotiator Hitoshi Tanaka frames it, only when these security issues have been addressed can Japan proceed to resume normalization talks with North Korea.[22]

Achieving these goals requires Japan to use various tools. For instance, Japan can negotiate with North Korea on national security threats, denuclearization, and other security concerns while complementing and reinforcing these efforts through a combination of various actions, including further strengthening Japan's defense relationship with the United States, strengthening policy coordination with the United States and South Korea, actively engaging in multinational nonproliferation initiatives such as the Proliferation Security Initiative (PSI), as well as enhancing Japan's own military capabilities to respond to these threats. Furthermore, diplomatic normalization with North Korea requires direct, bilateral negotiation with North Korea, and Japan needs to address its own World War II legacy issues, including economic reparations, during the process. As pointed out by former Japanese ambassador to the United States and former lead negotiator in the Six-Party Talks Kenichiro Sasae, Japan can only achieve both of its goals by pursuing a comprehensive agreement with North Korea that covers all issues from denuclearization to the abduction issue.[23]

In any case, it is imperative for Japan to face North Korea from a position where it can effectively negotiate with Pyongyang. Such a position requires Japan to have a degree of flexibility in the diplomatic tools it can utilize vis-à-vis North Korea, including both carrots (i.e., bilateral economic assistance and investment, resumption of normalization talks, and support for an economic assistance package in international financial institutions) as well as sticks (economic sanctions, travel restrictions, and trade embargoes).

The limitation Japan suffers in its negotiation position vis-à-vis North Korea becomes very clear when examined through the lens of negotiation theory. There are generally two approaches in negotiation—distributive (zero-sum) and integrative (positive-sum). There are also a few key components to consider—the number of actors, issues, motives and intentions, relationships, and leverages among the negotiating parties. Furthermore, in the negotiation processes, factors such as whether the negotiating parties have flexibility in their bargaining positions and how willing they are to make compromises to reach agreements are critical to determining the outcome of the negotiations. If a country has multiple policy goals vis-à-vis the other negotiating party (or parties, in cases of multinational negotiations), the chances of successfully reaching agreements will likely improve if the above key factors in negotiations are better aligned.

Table 7.1. Japan's North Korea Policy Goals in the Context of Negotiation Theory

Policy goals/issues	Resolve abduction issue	NK denuclearization	Normalization
Approach	Distributive	Distributive	Integrative
Number of actors	2	6	2
Motives/ Intentions	Return of all the confirmed abductees	Japan's national security	Resolve one of the WWII legacies
Leverage	Little	Little	Little
Flexibility	None	Little	Some
Willing to compromise?	No	No	Maybe

Source: Author created table.

In the case of Japan, however, it is not well positioned for successful negotiation in any of its three major policy goals vis-à-vis North Korea.

As Table 7.1 illustrates, Japan faces several challenges in achieving its three North Korea policy goals that are consistent. First, Japan has very little flexibility in its negotiating position in each of the three goals. In fact, its steadfast "resolution of abduction issue first" position, coupled with Tokyo's unwillingness to demonstrate flexibility, has hampered Japan's negotiating position in denuclearization as well as normalization.

As a result, Japan has little leverage of its own in all three policy goals, as it gives North Korea little incentive to engage in serious negotiation with Japan, let alone make concessions along the way. This also means Japan is very dependent on other actors, chiefly the United States, to take Japan's concerns into consideration in their negotiations with North Korea. As such, Japan's interest has been deeply affected by the lack of progress on denuclearization talks since the collapse of the Six-Party Talks in 2009, when North Korea announced its withdrawal from the discussions.[24]

What is particularly crippling for Japan's North Korea policy is the lack of flexibility in negotiation position that the abduction issue imposes on Japan, since it has only allowed Japan to resort to sticks since 2004. Some, including Hitoshi Tanaka, who worked to materialize Koizumi's first North Korea visit in 2002, criticize many political leaders, including former prime minister Abe, for having abused the abduction issue by politicizing it to gain stronger support for their hardline stance on North Korea and to shore up their domestic political support.[25] Former defense minister Shigeru Ishiba, who once chaired the parliamentary caucus on the abduction issue himself, also pointed out that many politicians in Japan, regardless of their party affiliation, have taken advantage of the prevailing perception among the Japanese public of North Korea as a "scary country" to enhance their political position, simply labeling North Korea as a dangerous country without exploring ways to resolve the existing problems between the two countries.[26] Indeed, politicization of the abduction issue by many Japanese political leaders has left Japan unable to break the current deadlock in its negotiations with North Korea, with little prospect of a breakthrough.

Final Thoughts

Japan's policy goals toward North Korea have considerably evolved over the last few decades. Beginning with the sole goal of diplomatic normalization, Japan increasingly has come to face competing policy goals as Pyongyang's provocative behavior, nuclear and missile developments, and the abduction issue grabbed public attention and created an environment that is not conducive to pursuing the policy goal of normalization, or to engaging in denuclearization talks with a full set of tools at Japan's disposal.

What has been fortunate for Japan is that it has not had to reckon with the impact of its adherence to the "resolution of abduction issue first" position since the breakdown of the Six-Party Talks. A series of provocative behaviors by North Korea—including repeated nuclear and intercontinental ballistic missile tests, as well as armed attacks against South Korea[27]—has made it easy for Japan to maintain its current negotiating position. The United States, by choosing minimal engagement and insisting on CVID with the North during the Obama and Trump administrations, also helped Japan keep its position closely aligned with that of the United States.

However, should the denuclearization negotiation be resumed under the Biden administration, Japan would quickly have to again face the fallout from its uncompromising negotiating position. Unless Japan can find its way out of the current "resolution of abduction issues first" approach, its policy dilemma vis-à-vis North Korea is likely to continue for the foreseeable future.

Notes

1. "North Korea Fires Suspected Ballistic Missiles toward Sea," *Associated Press*, May 12, 2022, https://www.nbcnews.com/news/world/north-korea-fires-suspected-ballistic-missile-sea-rcna28468

2. Ministry of Foreign Affairs of Japan, "Houdoukan Kaiken Kiroku" (Heisei 11-nen 12-gatsu), Press Briefings by Press Secretary, Ministry of Foreign Affairs of Japan, December 1999, https://www.mofa.go.jp/mofaj/press/kaiken/hodokan/hodo9912.html#index.

3. Ministry of Foreign Affairs of Japan, "Houdoukan Kaiken Kiroku."

4. "Agreed Framework between the United States of America and the Democratic People's Republic of Korea," U.S. Department of State Archive, October 21, 1994, https://2001-2009.state.gov/t/ac/rls/or/2004/31009.htm. Even though Japan was not a direct party to this negotiation, it ended up being asked to make a considerable financial contribution as the three countries established the Korean Peninsula Energy Development Organization (KEDO) to implement the Agreed Framework. For the history of KEDO, see KEDO, "History" http://www.kedo.org/au_history.asp.

5. See, for example, John Broder, "Clinton Proposes 4-Party Talks on Peace in Korea," *LA Times*, April 16, 1996, https://www.latimes.com/archives/la-xpm-1996-04-16-mn-59125-story.html.

6. " *'Issho ni Dorobune wo Katsugou' Kanemaru Houchou kara 30-nen Tai-Kitachousen Gaikou no Katsuro wa dokoni* ['Let Us Carry a Ship Made of mud' 30 Years since North Korea Visit by Kanemaru, Where Is the Opening for Diplomacy vis-à-vis North Korea?)," *Interview Series Kanamaru houchou 30-nen Ni-chou Gaikou Koremade Korekara* (Interview Series: 30 years after Kanemaru's North Korea visit—Japan–North Korea Diplomacy's Past and Future), *Asahi Shimbun Globe*, September 27, 2020, https://globe.asahi.com/article/13739946.

7. "Japan-DPRK Pyongyang Declaration," Ministry of Foreign Affairs of Japan, September 17, 2002, https://www.mofa.go.jp/region/asia-paci/n_korea/pmv0209/pyongyang.html.

8. The so-called abduction issue between Japan and North Korea is centered on North Korea's refusal to provide credible accounts of the Japanese citizens who were kidnapped by North Korea's national security agents and sent to North Korea so that they could train their agents to pass as Japanese citizens. There have been

twelve cases that were confirmed by Japanese law enforcement authority, but there are several hundred additional cases suspected to involve abduction.

9. "Joint Statement of the Fourth Round of the Six Party Talks Beijing, September 19, 2005," U.S. Department of State Archive, September 19, 2005, https://2001-2009.state.gov/r/pa/prs/ps/2005/53490.htm.

10. Sakie Yokota, *Megumi, Okaasan ga Kitto Tasukete Ageru* (Megumi, Mom Will Rescue You No Matter What) (Tokyo: Soshisha, 1999). The book was later translated into English and published as Sakie Yokota, *North Korea Kidnapped My Daughter* (New York: Vertical, 2009).

11. "Hiroku Kim Jong-Il 65" (Kim Jong-il Revealed, Part 65), *Sankei Shimbun*, March 1, 2016, https://www.sankei.com/article/20160301-JVXFGANHHVIQTO M2WTNMYGU5SA/4/.

12. However, there is still a discrepancy, as the Japanese government confirmed seventeen cases of abduction. "Kita Chousen ni yoru Nihon-jin Rachi Mondai: Rachi Mondai wo meguru Niccho-kan no yaritori [Abduction of Japanese Citizens by North Korea: Japan-North Korea Negotiation over the Abduction Issue]," Ministry of Foreign Affairs of Japan, accessed June 10, 2022, https://www.mofa.go.jp/mofaj/a_o/na/kp/page1w_000082.html.

13. "Heisei 13 nendo Gaikou ni Kansuru Yoron Chousa" (2001 Public Opinion Poll on Diplomacy), conducted in October 2001, Cabinet Affairs Office, accessed June 10, 2022, https://survey.gov-online.go.jp/h13/h13-gaikou/2-1.html.

14. "Heisei 14 nendo Gaikou ni Kansuru Yoron Chousa" (2002 Public Opinion Poll on Diplomacy), conducted in October 2002, Cabinet Affairs Office, accessed June 10, 2022, https://survey.gov-online.go.jp/h14/h14-gaikou/2-1.html.

15. "Heisei 15 nendo Gaikou ni Kansuru Yoron Chousa" (2003 Public Opinion Poll on Diplomacy), conducted in October 2003, Cabinet Affairs Office, accessed June 10, 2022, https://survey.gov-online.go.jp/h15/h15-gaikou/2-1.html.

16. "Dai Nihyaku Hachi-kai Kokkai ni Okeru Kishida Naikaku Souri Daijin Shisei Houshin Enzetsu" (Policy Address by Prime Minister Fumiko Kishida to the 208th Session of Diet), Prime Minister's Office of Japan, January 17, 2022, https://www.kantei.go.jp/jp/101_kishida/statement/2022/0117shiseihoshin.html.

17. "Dai 2-hyaku 3-kai Kokkai ni Okesu Suga Naikaku Souri Daijin Shoshin Hyoumei Enzetsu" (Speech by Prime Minister Suga at the 203th Diet Session), Prime Minister and His/Her Cabinet (*Kantei*), October 26, 2020, https://www.kantei.go.jp/jp/99_suga/statement/2020/1026shoshinhyomei.html.

18. Prime Minister and His/Her Cabinet (*Kantei*), "Dai 2-hyaku 3-kai Kokkai."

19. "The Guidelines for Japan-U.S. Defense Cooperation," Ministry of Defense of Japan, September 23, 1997, https://www.mod.go.jp/e/d_act/us/anpo/19970923e.html.

20. It is a common observation that Japan decided to introduce its own reconnaissance satellite following North Korea's ballistic missile launch in 1998. For alternative analyses, see, for example, William W. Radcliffe, "Origins and

Current State of Japan's Reconnaissance Satellite Program," *Studies in Intelligence* 54, no. 3 (Extracts, September 2010). https://www.cia.gov/static/aca9997a3231f-8682380c970a5ab831a/Origins-and-Current-State.pdf.

21. The husband of Hitomi Soga, one of the abductees, did not come to Japan right away, as he had deserted his post and defected to North Korea during the Korean War, and thus needed to be court-martialed before he was free to enter Japan. Instead, he met Hitomi Soga in Indonesia, and following the conclusion of the court-martial, entered Japan to be reunited with Soga.

22. Hitoshi Tanaka, " 'Sakebu dakedeha kaiketsu Shinai' Nihon ni Tarinai Tai-Kita Chousen Gaikou ni Hitsuyou na mono ['Nothing Can Be Resolved by Screaming' What Is Missing but Necessary in Japan's Diplomacy toward North Korea?]," Interview Series: 30 years after Kanemaru's North Korea visit—Japan–North Korea Diplomacy's Past and Future, *Asahi Shimbun Globe*, September 28, 2020, https://globe.asahi.com/article/13759615.

23. "Kita Chousen tono Tafu na Koushou, Utagai bukai Aite to no Sesshikata Moto Toppu Gaikoukan no me [Tough Negotiation with North Korea, How to Deal with the Counterpart Who Are Deeply Suspicious—Perspective from a Former Top Diplomat]," Interview Series: 30 years after Kanemaru's North Korea visit—Japan–North Korea Diplomacy's Past and Future), *Asahi Shimbun Globe*, September 30, 2020, https://globe.asahi.com/article/13765879.

24. Kelsey Davenport, "The Six-Party Talks at a Glance," Arms Control Association, accessed June 2018, https://www.armscontrol.org/factsheets/6partytalks.

25. Davenport, "The Six-Party Talks."

26. Shigeru Ishiba, "Kita Chousen wa Osoroshii deha Koushou wa Ugokanai Seiji wa Yoron no Yuuwaku ni Makeruna ['North Is a Scary Country' Does Not Move Negotiation; Politics Should Not Cave to the Temptation of Public Opinion]," Interview Series: 30 years after Kanemaru's North Korea visit—Japan–North Korea Diplomacy's Past and Future, *Asahi Shimbun Globe*, September 29, 2020, https://globe.asahi.com/article/13764972.

27. These provocations include the naval confrontation near Yeongpyeong Island in 2002 and the bombardment of the island in 2010.

Chapter 8

Russia and North Korean Denuclearization

RICHARD WEITZ

This chapter reviews Russia's main objectives regarding the North Korean nuclear program, assesses the motives for these goals, and presents the main strategies Moscow has pursued to realize them. The Russian government does not want North Korea to have nuclear weapons due to the elevated war risks, Western countermeasures, economic obstacles, and other problems presented by the DPRK nuclear efforts. Yet, Moscow has long joined China in opposing the vigorous sanctions and further coercive pressure designed to induce the DPRK to change its position. Russian officials argue that such measures are counterproductive by increasing North Koreans' sense of insecurity. They also do not want to see regime change in North Korea that could remove a strategic buffer for the Russian Far East. Resolving the DPRK nuclear dispute might remove international sanctions impeding realization of Russian commercial objectives in Northeast Asia, but economic goals have always been of secondary importance in shaping the policies of the Russian government toward the DPRK nuclear weapons program. Other Russian objectives have included remaining a significant player on DPRK nuclear issues, exploiting the crisis to gain diplomatic leverage with other countries, and aspiring to broker any settlement through Moscow-led mediation.

Goals and Motives

The leaders of the Russian Federation have long viewed the nuclear program of the Democratic People's Republic of Korea (DPRK) as having a negative impact on Russia's regional security, diplomatic, and economic objectives. Although Russia is not directly threatened by the DPRK nuclear weapons stockpile, as it would more likely be employed against other countries, a major military conflict in Northeast Asia due to an escalation related to the North's nuclear program, whether caused deliberately or by accident, would have extremely negative repercussions for Moscow.[1] Though Russian officials disapprove of North Korea's nuclear weapons program, they often express understanding for the DPRK's search for security and would not want to see foreign-imposed regime change in Pyongyang, even if it ended the North's nuclear program, due to the value of having a geographic buffer against the U.S. military and North Korea's potential as a junior partner in Moscow's anti-American coalition. Russian policymakers fear that the result of Seoul-led Korean unification would be disadvantageous to their country by decreasing Moscow's influence in the Koreas, removing a buffer zone separating Russia from U.S. ground forces based in South Korea, and intensifying security competition in Northeast Asia. Russian leaders also want their country to remain a major actor on DPRK nuclear issues, exploiting the crisis to gain diplomatic leverage and clout with other players, and aspiring to broker any settlement through Moscow-led mediation. Russian diplomacy has strived to induce countries with greater influence in Korean affairs to respect Russian interests and Moscow's priorities.[2]

A foundational motive behind Moscow's policies toward the DPRK nuclear issue has been that the histories of the Russian and Korean nations have been intertwined for centuries. The Russian Federation and the DPRK share a seventeen-kilometer border. The Soviet Union proved instrumental in the creation of the DPRK, which was established as a separate communist state when the Soviet armed forces occupied the northern half of Korea following Japan's surrender in August 1945. Along with the PRC, Russia was Pyongyang's leading partner during the Cold War, and helped the DPRK launch its nuclear research program, which Pyongyang subsequently exploited to pursue nuclear weapons.[3] But Moscow was largely excluded from the negotiations regarding the Korean nuclear issue in the 1990s. For instance, Russia was not a member of the Four-Party Talks that led to the DRPK LWR project consortium. Only through great exertions was Moscow able to secure membership in the Six-Party Talks launched a few years later. Following the Ukraine crisis and Moscow's annexation of Crimea resulted in a Washington-led effort to isolate Russia in March 2014, Moscow has searched for means to circumvent Western sanctions on Russian entities by seeking new partners in Asia (and the Middle East). Some Russian analysts have viewed the North Korean nuclear crisis as an opportunity to demonstrate "relevance as a central player in Asia's security environment" and avoid isolation.[4]

Russian policymakers calculate that they made a mistake during the 1990s when they let relations with the DPRK, shunned as an archaic Marxist-Leninist backwater, wither under the presidency of Boris Yeltsin. After the collapse of the USSR, the new Russian Federation ended its subsidies for DPRK purchases of energy and other Russian goods, attempted to secure payment of North Korea's Soviet-era debt to Russia, and established economic and diplomatic relations with the increasingly prosperous ROK, which Russian analysts hoped might provide needed investment and technology. Ironically, this alienation from the North reduced Russia's appeal to the ROK because South Koreans no longer saw Moscow as an optimal interlocutor with Pyongyang. Rather, ROK officials directed their diplomacy toward China to persuade or pressure Pyongyang into eliminating its nuclear weapons program. Moscow's decreased influence was apparent during the first Korean nuclear crisis in 1993–94, when it was mostly an observer. This status continued in 1997, when the Four-Party Talks began among China, the United States, and the two Korean states.

Yeltsin's successor Vladimir Putin sought to pursue more balanced relations with both Koreas. An early priority was restoring Russia's influence in East Asia, including North Korea, as part of Putin's broader ambitions to reestablish Russia as a great power. Whereas Yeltsin's government shunned Pyongyang in an effort to court Seoul, the Putin administration pursued more balanced relations, engaging with both Koreas to enhance Moscow's leverage with all the parties active in Korean affairs. In July 2000, Putin became the first Russian president to visit North Korea, where he signed a new Treaty on Friendship, Good-Neighborly Relations and Cooperation. Though not a mutual defense alliance or even a security pact like the 1961 Soviet-DPRK friendship and mutual assistance treaty (or the equivalent PRC-DPRK pact), the new accord provided for official consultations regarding common threats. Putin also attempted to end the dispute over North Korea's rocket development program by offering the DPRK opportunities to participate in Russia's space program. After announcing at the G-8 summit that Kim Jong-il had told him that the DPRK would renounce its ballistic missile programs in exchange for foreign assistance in creating a civilian space program, Putin was embarrassingly undercut when the North Korean government disavowed the pledge. In recent years, Russian officials have sought to participate in the drafting and signing of any inter-Korean peace treaty that might supersede the 1953 Korean Armistice. Many PRC and ROK leaders have seemed to prefer that only the original combatants (both Koreas, China, and the United States) negotiate and sign any peace treaty, excluding Russia and Japan. Along with Tokyo, Moscow would vehemently oppose such nonparticipation.

Russian analysts believe that North Korea wants nuclear weapons primarily for defensive purposes. In Putin's words, "They know full-well how the situation developed, for example, in Iraq . . . and they see possession of nuclear weapons and missiles as the only way to defend themselves."[5] Russian policymakers view U.S. policies as deepening DPRK insecurities and increasing the North's desire to stockpile nuclear weapons. They maintain that a long-term solution to the nuclear issue will require an enduring transformation of the Northeast Asian security environment. They also do not expect that North Korea would deliberately (and irrationally) start a nuclear war. Yet, Russian policymakers oppose the North's nuclear weapons program due to the problems it generates for Russia's defense interests in East Asia. First, Russian policymakers worry about the possibilities of an inadvertent escalatory path to nuclear use. Possessing nuclear weapons might embolden Pyongyang to take greater risks in its provocations, which would elevate the risk of war. Additionally, there is the danger that North Korea might sell fissile materials to another state or nonstate actor such as criminals and terrorists in exchange for hard currency. Above all, Russian policymakers worry that North Korean nuclear weapons might prompt, or provide a pretext for, U.S. military countermeasures. Russian leaders have also sought to constrain North Korea's testing of long-range ballistic missiles because of the proximity of their flight paths to Russian territory. Russia's most important Pacific Coast city and the main port of the Russian Pacific Fleet, Vladivostok, is located only 140 kilometers from North Korean territory. In 2006, the DPRK launched several missiles that fell within Russia's two hundred nautical miles (370 km) exclusive economic zone in the Sea of Japan. One missile reportedly veered off course and landed near the Russian port of Nakhoda. Russian armed forces subsequently stationed advanced surface-to-air interceptors near the North Korean border. In

2009, then-president Dmitriy Medvedev cited DPRK missile launches as well as its nuclear weapons tests as a "concern for us," given that, "We are located in close proximity to this country."[6]

As part of its campaign to bolster Russia's presence in East Asia, Moscow also leverages its ties with the DPRK to gain influence with South Korea, Japan, and other states. For example, Russian Foreign Minister Sergey Lavrov made the nuclear issue the centerpiece of the agenda during his visit to Seoul in March 2021.[7] Directly following this meeting, the Russian and ROK vice defense ministers adopted a bilateral defense partnership in which both nations pledged to work for Korean denuclearization. Following the Russian invasion of Ukraine starting in February 2022, Russia and the DPRK have engaged in extensive direct contacts. North Korea was also one of the few countries to oppose the U.S.-backed resolution in the UN General Assembly censoring the Russian attack. The renewed bilateral talks between Moscow and Pyongyang in the wake of the Ukrainian invasion demonstrate how both governments are using each other to counter their international isolation.

A Russian priority has been to achieve economic gains from cooperation with North Korea, both directly and by integrating Russia more pervasively into Asian economies. Russia has been striving to deepen its economic ties with the prosperous Asian region by shipping more energy eastward, joining Asian institutions, and encouraging greater Asian economic investment into Russia.[8] Russian corporations want to build rail links, energy pipelines, and other projects connecting Russia to and through North Korean territory. Russian firms also seek access to the DPRK's natural resources, such as its rare earth minerals, as well as its territory for transit projects. The Russian government supports these projects since they might serve as commercial arteries for Russian–Northeast Asian economic exchanges. Russian officials had hoped that stronger ties with other Asian countries would facilitate investment and technology transfers to Russia that would help modernize the Russian economy. Yet, Russia has not achieved its economic desires regarding the DPRK due to persistent intra-Korean tensions and external sanctions imposed on the North. Russia's invasion of Ukraine and the resulting expansion and deepening of the Western sanctions package will likely make these economic gains even more unrealizable. Therefore, it will become a less immediate Russian objective for the next few years. Russia's direct influence in Pyongyang might accordingly decline due to the decreased Russian potential to offer the North economic benefits.[9] Still, there will likely be growing Russian interest in working with the North to circumvent the sanctions on both states and in exploiting DPRK tensions with the United States and its Asian allies for political/military advantage.

Strategies and Tactics

Moscow has employed a variety of tools to attain its goals regarding North Korea's nuclear program. Russia has pursued bilateral diplomatic engagement with Pyongyang and with some other key players, especially China and the United States, regarding the DPRK nuclear issue, multilateral interactions through the United Nations and similar international institutions and groupings, limited economic sanctions to pressure Pyongyang, and offers of economic inducements to sway the DPRK leadership into taking desirable action. Unlike in the case of its policies toward some other regions, Russia has not used its military power or threats of military action extensively regarding North Korea.

Russian officials have maintained lines of communication with North Korea through both multilateral and bilateral mechanisms. In its diplomacy regarding the DPRK nuclear issue, Moscow has employed multilateral tools such as joint declarations with other governments, senior Russian officials' trips to the Korean Peninsula, and support for the Six-Party Talks as the main institutions for Korean diplomacy. Moscow has often utilized the UN Security Council, where Russia has the power to veto measures it opposes, to exclude or dilute proposed sanctions on the DPRK for its various malign actions, ranging from its nuclear and missile tests to human rights issues. Russia has blocked the use of language that might have authorized the use of force to compel DPRK compliance with UNSC resolutions. The Russian government has also strived to limit sanctions against the DPRK. Russian diplomats typically oppose using sanctions to punish foreign governments. In the case of North Korea, Russian officials state that sanctions generally provide, at best, modest leverage with Pyongyang, and certainly cannot solve the DPRK nuclear problem in isolation from negotiations and measures assuring the security of a nonnuclear DPRK. Russia often views sanctions as counterproductive, believing they contribute to North Korea's isolation and its hardline approach toward other countries. Putin has observed that it was important not to back North Korea into a corner and leave it with no option but to raise tensions.[10] Russian foreign minister Lavrov has also denigrated most coercive measures against the DPRK as bootless punishment for punishment's sake.[11] In addition to denunciatory statements and the blocking of sanctions in the UN Security Council, observers believe that Russia has helped North Korea circumvent some sanctions, such as by assisting DPRK individuals and companies to open illicit bank accounts.[12] Russian entities also have allowed DPRK laborers to continue working in Russia even after the December 2019 UNSC prohibition on such work took effect, which helps Russia to ease its labor shortage, North Korea to earn foreign revenue, and both countries to sustain mutual economic ties even as the United States has blocked their efforts to remove some sanctions.[13]

Russian experts argue that, in the long run, having a benign regional security environment can best help attain North Korea's denuclearization. Among other negative effects, sanctions can limit the resources available to Russian-backed regional economic projects. Moscow has wielded its UNSC veto power to block proposed UN resolutions that could impose severe international sanctions on the DPRK. Russian officials also oppose the unilateral sanctions adopted by the United States, South Korea, and other countries on North Korea through national measures taken without UNSC backing. In 2014, Russian officials tried to dissuade the U.S. government from retaliating for the cyberattack on the Sony Corporation after that company made a film, *The Interview,* which depicted the assassination of the North Korean leader. While casting doubt on DPRK responsibility for the attack, Russian policymakers defended North Koreans' anger at the film.[14] When some of these U.S. sanctions, which blocked DPRK access to some $25 million deposited in Macao's Banco Delta Asia, became an obstacle to denuclearization, the Russian government and Russian banks assisted North Korea in recuperating these funds.[15] Russian policymakers argue that incentive-based strategies, such as offering the DPRK guarantees of security and sovereignty based on international law, generally offer a superior means for inducing Pyongyang to denuclearize.[16] For instance, in June 2021, Putin said, "The North Korean nuclear problem is not going to be resolved by pressuring the North and toughening the sanctions against it, [but] only by ensuring the security of its people, and with patience and a careful approach."[17]

Nonetheless, Russian officials will sometimes agree to impose limited sanctions on the DPRK as a "lesser evil" than doing nothing or too much. The modest sanctions also censor DPRK actions Moscow opposes and can avert tougher Western responses, such as national sanctions or military countermeasures, outside of Russian control. For example, in

2007, Moscow banned the transfer of Russian equipment, materials, or knowledge that the DPRK could use to further develop weapons of mass destruction, and prohibited Russian entities from engaging in financial transactions with UN-designated entities assisting the North's nuclear weapons program.[18] Furthermore, after the DPRK's fourth nuclear test, Moscow backed UNSC Resolution 2270 to induce Pyongyang to return to the negotiating table regarding its missile and nuclear weapons programs. Additionally, Moscow has supported some UN punitive measures to ensure that the UNSC remains a vital instrument in the international community's response to the Korea issue. Russian diplomats fear a repeat of the Kosovo (1998) and Iraq (2003) examples, when Western governments decided to bypass the UN and employ force on their own initiative, through "coalitions of the willing," after they could not work through the UNSC due to Moscow's veto. Russian diplomats balance blocking harsh UN sanctions while sustaining Western interests in working through the UN. The experience of Iraq, Kosovo, and Syria demonstrates that, if Moscow blocked all Western-backed measures against the DPRK in the UN, the Western powers might simply pursue collective measures outside the United Nations despite Russian opposition. In those few cases when Moscow has supported the use of sanctions, Russian diplomats, wary of their endless struggle to remove the many Western sanctions imposed on Russia, have insisted that the sanctions be removed as soon as North Korea complies with them.

Another way that Russia has employed multilateral tools has been by affirming its role in Korean security affairs and bolstering its international status by referencing the DPRK nuclear issue in joint multilateral and bilateral statements with other governments. By making such joint declarations, Russia's dialogue partners affirm Moscow's role as a legitimate player on the Korea issue. For example, the Russian government attacked the North Korean nuclear test in January 2016 as a "flagrant violation of international law" that generated more tensions on the Korean Peninsula.[19] Putin therefore agreed that the international community should give a "strong and united" response to the test.[20] Russian diplomats worked with their foreign counterparts to craft an international response, centered on UNSC Resolution 2270.[21] Russian officials have also regularly called on the DPRK government to adhere to multilateral mechanisms and standards, such as the Treaty on the Non-Proliferation of Nuclear Weapons.

When advantageous, Moscow has aligned its policies with other states, particularly China, to amplify their impact. For example, Russian policymakers have recognized that North Korea is a significant security interest for the PRC and that China is the most important foreign partner of both Russia and the DPRK.[22] Therefore, Russian diplomats have traditionally allowed their Chinese counterparts to take the lead in negotiating the content of UN resolutions regarding North Korea.[23] The PRC has become a preferred Russian partner given the overlapping perspective in Moscow and Beijing on many Korean security issues.

Russia has promoted multilateral security guarantees, arms control, and confidence-building measures for the DPRK in exchange for North Korea's ending its nuclear weapons program voluntarily. Russian scholars and diplomats have also been enthusiastic about offering visions of transitioning Northeast Asia from its current state of armed confrontation to that of a comprehensive system of multilateral collective security with a cooperative concert of equal great powers who respect one another's vital interests.[24] During the 1990s, Russia unsuccessfully proposed creating an eight-party and then a ten-party conference to arrange a comprehensive solution to the DPRK nuclear crisis.[25] Moscow was more successful in pushing for a multilateral structure with equal Russian participation in the 2000s with the launching of the Six-Party Talks. A senior Russian diplomat chaired the Six-Party Working Group dealing with the issue of how these Six-Party Talks might serve as a basis for a future multilateral security system in northeast Asia. At the April 25, 2019, Putin-Kim summit in Vladivostok, the Russian delegation again backed the DPRK (and PRC) position that confidence-building measures would help promote DPRK denuclearization.[26]

Russian diplomacy has generally favored an action-for-action, step-by-step approach in which North Korea is rewarded by the other parties for any positive step taken toward denuclearization. Through a process of incremental reciprocal measures, this phased approach intends to generate trust and positive momentum toward a final resolution of the crisis through the creation of a mutually beneficial "package solution."[27] For instance, the DPRK would first freeze its nuclear program in return for a suspension of U.S. military activities in the ROK, then the DPRK could eliminate its nuclear program in return for the removal of U.S. forces from the Korean Peninsula. These measures would allow the parties to build a network of energy and logistical cooperation that could create the opportunity for long-term success. From this perspective, Russian representatives have castigated other parties that Moscow holds are not fulfilling their commitments, warning that their failure might unravel hard-won past agreements. In criticizing the United States for losing interest in the Six-Party agreements, Putin observed, "The North Korean leadership showed a constructive attitude, but the countries like the U.S. seems to have abandoned the promise (they made) to the North."[28]

Russian officials also criticized President Donald Trump's 2017 threats against North Korea as excessive, counterproductive, and potentially dangerous since they might lead to war through miscalculation.[29] That year, the Russian military reinforced its troops deployed near the North Korean border.[30] The following year, the Russian government invited Chinese and Mongolian troops to participate in its annual strategic exercises, Vostok-2018, which took place in eastern Russia, near North Korea, in September. The location was expected, since Russia rotates its strategic exercise among its four strategic commands, and the most recent Vostok (which means "East" in Russian) drill had occurred in 2014. Yet, the unprecedented invitation to the Chinese and Mongolian armed forces in early 2018 might have reflected the perceived growing risk of Korean War scenarios. Russian diplomacy offered modest support for the Trump administration's subsequent direct diplomatic engagements with President Kim, welcoming the dialogue but insisting that it should provide a foundation for wider multilateral talks among all six governments that had participated in the Six-Party Talks, including Russia.[31]

In this regard, Russian leaders have emphasized that their diplomats enjoy good access and communication opportunities with both Koreas, potentially allowing Moscow to broker intra-Korean cooperation. They have generally argued for engaging in talks with North Korea without preconditions. In 2013, Putin stated, "If we constantly set preconditions for the start of talks, they may never begin."[32] Russia has also been more open than some other parties to the idea that North Korea could continue peaceful nuclear activities with proper international safeguards and IAEA supervision, despite concerns that North Korea might again pursue weapons-related work under the guise of pursuing nonmilitary nuclear activities. Adhering to their general stance of respecting state sovereignty and refraining from interfering in other states' internal affairs, Russian officials have consistently declined to criticize North Korea's human rights situation.

Putin has been especially active regarding Korean issues and has repeatedly tried to shape developments there. He visited Pyongyang soon after becoming president and sought to broker a solution to the dispute over the DPRK's rocket launches, which the North justified as space launch vehicles. Despite this setback, Russian diplomacy strived to take advantage of the poor relations between Beijing and Pyongyang in the first years after Kim Jong-un became DPRK leader. Between 2014 and 2017, the PRC surprised the Russian foreign policy community by imposing more severe sanctions against the DPRK regime than Russia.[33] Distancing themselves from Beijing's harsh rhetoric regarding Pyongyang, Russian leaders tried to strengthen ties with Kim, who apparently saw Moscow as a potential balancer to Beijing's unwelcome influence as well as to U.S. hostility.[34] As a result, Russian-DPRK bilateral engagements—encompassing official diplomatic but also economic and social contacts—starkly increased around mid-2010.[35] The high point of Russian engagement with the DPRK occurred in the mid-2010s, when Putin's government made a sustained effort to induce Kim Jong-un to come to Moscow. This visit would have been his first trip outside North Korea since becoming the DPRK's supreme leader in December 2011. The specific occasion was an invitation to participate in the May 2015 Victory Day celebrations marking the seventieth anniversary of Nazi Germany's defeat in World War II. Deputy Foreign Minister Igor Morgulov said such a visit would "contribute to "peace on the Korean peninsula, as well as northeast Asia."[36] Since ROK president Park and PRC president Xi Jinping were preparing to attend, Putin could have tried to broker some high-level talks among the leaders of these four countries. In the end, however, the DPRK sent *a* leader (Kim Yong Nam, the symbolic head of state and president of the Presidium of the Supreme People's Assembly), instead of *the* leader, to the event. One reason might have been Russia's declining the DPRK's request to purchase Russia's most advanced fighter plane, the Su-35.[37]

The PRC foreign ministry supported the Russian invitation.[38] Despite deviating from Beijing's harsh stance in the mid-2010s, Russian policy has generally sought to align Moscow's position with that of Beijing. Russian officials have constantly consulted with their PRC counterparts. Since 2015, they have held a regular ministerial dialogue on Northeast Asian security between a Russian deputy foreign minister and a PRC vice minister. The Russian and Chinese delegations have often taken common stances in the UN, the Six-Party Talks, and other frameworks dealing with Korea. The two governments have issued numerous joint declarations regarding the DPRK nuclear program and other related issues. They have also coordinated their approach toward resisting, imposing, and more recently removing sanctions on the DPRK.[39] There are presumably recurring Sino-Russian consultations regarding various DPRK scenarios. At the extreme, it is difficult to imagine Russia intervening militarily in a Korean conflict or DPRK meltdown scenario without Beijing's approval. More likely, Moscow would expect and rely on PLA intervention to stabilize the DPRK, establish a buffer zone along the Sino-Korean border, or secure the North's WMD and leadership assets following state collapse. Perhaps the most extensive Sino-Russian collaboration regarding the DPRK nuclear program has been the peace plan they developed in 2017 and jointly pushed thereafter. This "three-stage roadmap" involved a dual freeze of the DPRK nuclear and missile tests combined with a suspension of large ROK-U.S. military exercises; then multiple series of bilateral talks including direct discussions between the DPRK and U.S. leaders; and then a return to the multilateral Six-Party Talks, which would provide a framework to address both nuclear and nonnuclear issues (military threats, sanctions, economic cooperation, confidence-building measures, foreign military presence, etc.) in order to establish an enduring and comprehensive multipolar Northeast Asian security system.[40]

Additionally, Russia has sought to use potential economic gains as leverage to secure cooperation from both Korean governments and raise its profile in intra-Korean issues.[41] Russian policymakers have wanted their exports to freely transit the Korean Peninsula in order to reach various Asian Pacific markets. For instance, Russian firms have aspired to lay power lines and energy pipelines between Russia and South Korea across North Korean territory. They have also discussed building a trans-Korean railroad and connecting it with Russia's trans-Siberian rail system. Furthermore, they wanted access to the DPRK's ice-free ports, which, in contrast to Vladivostok, Russia's main Pacific port, are accessible year-round. A Russian-DPRK joint venture to upgrade the North's Rason port, by modernizing its piers and constructing a thirty-four-mile Khasan-Rajin transit railway to the Russian border, into a special economic zone and transshipment center for northeast Asia has attracted substantial ROK interest (though not investment). Russia and North Korea even launched a ferry service between Rajin and Vladivostok that has been used by DPRK laborers working in the Russian Far East as well as Chinese and Russian tourists.

Though looking mostly at economic opportunities in other countries, Russian policymakers also hoped to boost commerce with North Korea. In 2013, the two governments set the target of increasing direct bilateral trade to $1 billion by 2020 through expanded commerce, investment, and collaborative projects.[42] The official figure reflecting direct trade fell far below that, amounting to less than $50 million.[43] Some indirect trade occurs through the much longer and more porous PRC-DPRK border and via concealed entities, but the value generated is not high. As a point of comparison, at one point during the Cold War, almost one-half of North Korea's trade occurred with the Soviet Union.[44] To boost these totals, Russian companies have explored complex barter arrangements, so far unrealized, in which Russia would contribute investment and technologies to revitalize North Korea's dilapidated power grid or railway lines in exchange for gaining the right to exploit its most valuable minerals.[45]

Rejecting the Soviet practice of subsiding commerce with North Korea, Russian policymakers have generally stood firm on charging market rather than "friendship" prices for their economic transactions with the DPRK. Nonetheless, they did write off almost all of North Korea's Soviet-era loans. For years, DPRK negotiators indicated that they wanted Moscow to write off the entire debt. The Russian government proposed various alternative debt settlement options to Pyongyang, including conditioning Russia's forgiving loans to the North in exchange for DPRK property or investment opportunities, but the North Koreans rejected these arrangements. Russian negotiators eventually agreed to waive most of the debt, since the repayment issue had impeded the launching of new projects. North Koreans were extremely unlikely to repay the debt in any case, so it seemed logical for Moscow to come to terms with a settlement. To overcome the Western sanctions on their economies, the DPRK and Russian governments subsequently agreed to employ rubles for some monetary transactions.[46] Thousands of North Korean guestworkers also continue to engage in forestry and construction in remote camps in northeastern Russia. Though their working conditions are often better than those suffered by laborers in North Korea, they must transfer most of their salaries to the DPRK government, a practice that began during the Soviet period. A bilateral agreement also obliges the Russian authorities to hand over to the DPRK authorities any North Koreans who flee the camps or who illegally enter the Russian Federation.[47]

The most direct link between Russian economic policy and North Korea's nuclear weapons program occurred in 2018, when Moscow reportedly proposed, in return for the North's curtailing its nuclear weapons program, building and operating a nuclear power plant in the DPRK. As in its other foreign nuclear energy projects, Russia would have provided fresh uranium fuel to the plant and returned the spent fuel rods to Russia to limit proliferation concerns. Besides promoting DPRK denuclearization and elevating Moscow's role in the Koreas, the move would have enhanced Russia's energy influence in Northeast Asia and nuclear energy credentials globally.[48] The Russian and DPRK governments also created a bilateral business council and signed additional bilateral economic agreements. Moscow has also been open to cooperating with Beijing's Belt and Road Initiative and former South Korean president Park Geun-hye's Eurasian Initiative to envelop North Korean economic collaboration in larger regional economic frameworks.[49] Nonetheless, though these measures have removed some Russian-DPRK economic barriers, the volatile security situation on the peninsula, and more recently the COVID-19 epidemic (which led to a drastic reduction in Russian-DPRK contacts and the departure of many Russian nationals from North Korea), have proved to be insurmountable barriers to launching sustained large-scale economic projects encompassing North Korea. As a result, Moscow lacks the economic leverage that Beijing enjoys over North Korea. Though the DPRK foreign ministry marked the third anniversary of the Kim-Putin summit in Vladivostok by committing "to expand and develop in all fields the friendly and cooperative relations with Russia, our friend and friendly neighbor," Russian analysts do not expect economic ties to improve substantially anytime soon.[50]

Still, Russia's invasion of Ukraine has shaken up many long-standing presumptions about Russian foreign policy. Until now, there has been strong support among Russia's DPRK experts that Moscow should generally cooperate with foreign partners to curtail the North's nuclear program and promote intra-Korean peace and prosperity.[51] But the deterioration in Russian-U.S. relations in recent years has increased the influence of those in the Russian foreign policy elite who see the DPRK as a potential partner in Moscow's elevated confrontation with the West.[52] The recent Japanese and South Korean decisions to support the Western sanctions against Russia over Ukraine has likely augmented this group. Until now, Russia has not played a spoiler role in international efforts to end the DPRK nuclear program, but the Kremlin under its current malign leadership might well do so in the future.

Notes

1. Dmitri Trenin, "Putin's Strategic Framework for Northeast Asia," *Joint U.S.-Korea Academic Studies*, 2020, 59, https://keia.org/wp-content/uploads/2020/12/kei_jointus-korea_2020_1_3.pdf.

2. Bobo Lo, "Russia and the Security Landscape of Northeast Asia," French Institute of International Relations, report no 29, March 2020, 13–14, https://www.ifri.org/sites/default/files/atoms/files/lo_security_asia_20201.pdf

3. Ilya Dyachkov, Leonid Kozlov, Andrei Lankov, Artyom Lukin, Georgy Toloraya, and Igor Tolstokulakov, "From Joseph Stalin and Kim Il-sung to Vladimir Putin and Kim Jong-un," in *Nuclear Weapons and Russian–North Korean Relations*, ed. Artyom Lukin et al. (Foreign Policy Research Institute, 2017), https://www.fpri.org/wp-content/uploads/2017/11/NuclearWeaponsRussiaDPRKDec2017.pdf.

4. Elizabeth Wishnick, "The Impact of the Sino-Russian Partnership on the North Korean Nuclear Crisis: U.S. Policy Implications," The National Bureau of Asian Research, March 2019, https://www.nbr.org/publication/the-sino-russian-partnership-and-the-north-korean-nuclear-crisis/.

5. Anastasia Barannikova, "What Russia Thinks about North Korea's Nuclear Weapons," *Bulletin of the Atomic Scientists*, April 24, 2019, https://thebulletin.org/2019/04/what-russia-thinks-about-north-koreas-nuclear-weapons/.

6. Dmitry Medvedev, "Interview to RAI and *Corriere della Sera*," *The Kremlin*, July 5, 2009, http://en.kremlin.ru/events/president/transcripts/4719/print.

7. Anthony V. Rinna, "South Korea's Diplomatic Balancing Act with Russia," *East Asia Forum*, May 5, 2021, https://www.eastasiaforum.org/2021/05/05/south-koreas-diplomatic-balancing-act-with-russia/.

8. Fiona Hill and Bobo Lo, "Putin's Pivot: Why Russia Is Looking East," *Foreign Affairs*, July 31, 2013, https://www.foreignaffairs.com/articles/russian-federation/2013-07-31/putins-pivot.

9. Andrei Lankov, "Russia's Waning Influence on North Korea," Carnegie Moscow Center, December 21, 2020, https://carnegie.ru/commentary/83506.

10. Olivia Beavers, "Putin Warns against Backing North Korea into a Corner," *The Hill*, October 19, 2017, https://thehill.com/policy/defense/356224-putin-warns-against-backing-north-korean-leader-into-corner.

11. "UN Needs 'Tough' N Korea Resolution: Russia," Agence-France Presse, May 27, 2009, http://www.spacewar.com/2006/090527095511.ye29xj6w.html.

12. Mathew Ha, "Treasury Designates Russian Company that Helped North Korea Cheat Sanctions," Foundation for the Defense of Democracies, June 20, 2019, https://www.fdd.org/analysis/2019/06/20/treasury-designates-russian-company-that-helped-north-korea-cheat-sanctions/.

13. Christy Lee, "Experts: Russia Skirts Sanctions on N. Korean Workers to Defy US-led Pressure," VOA News, February 1, 2020, https://www.voanews.com/east-asia-pacific/experts-russia-skirts-sanctions-n-korean-workers-defy-us-led-pressure.

14. "Russia Offers Support to North Korea amid Sony Hack Controversy Associated Press," *Fox News*, December 25, 2014, http://www.foxnews.com/world/2014/12/25/russia-offers-support-to-north-korea-amid-sony-hack-controversy/.

15. Steven R. Weisman, "The Ripples of Punishing One Bank," *The New York Times*, July 3, 2007, https://www.nytimes.com/2007/07/03/business/world-business/03bank.html?

16. "Statement by Permanent Representative Vassily Nebenzia at a UN Security Council Briefing on the Situation on the Korean Peninsula," Permanent Mission of the Russian Federation to the United Nations, December 11, 2019, https://russiaun.ru/en/news/dprk111219.

17. Kim Seung-yeon, "Putin Calls for Guaranteeing N. Korea's Security to Resolve Nuclear Quandary," *Yonhap*, June 5, 2021, https://en.yna.co.kr/view/AEN20210605000500325.

18. "Путин подписал указ о санкциях против КНДР [Putin podpisal ukaz o sanktsiyax protiv KNDR; Putin Signs Decree on Sanctions against the DPRK]," Gazeta.ru, May 30, 2007, http://www.gazeta.ru/news/business/2007/05/30/n_1075339.shtml.

19. Bill Chappell, "Russia, China, and U.S. Condemn North Korea's Nuclear Test Claims," National Public Radio, January 6, 2016, http://www.npr.org/sections/thetwo-way/2016/01/06/462121579/russia-china-and-u-s-condemn-north-koreas-nuclear-test-claims.

20. "Obama, Putin Agree on 'Strong and United' Response to North Korean Nuclear Test," *Korea Times*, January 14, 2016, http://www.koreatimes.co.kr/www/news/nation/2016/01/485_195406.html.

21. "Japan, Russia Agree to Cooperate on North Korea Issue," *Sputnik*, January 13, 2016, http://sputniknews.com/politics/20160113/1033036335/russia-japan-cooperate-north-korea.html.

22. Artyom Lukin, "Russia's Policy Toward North Korea: Following China's Lead," *38 North*, December 23, 2019, https://www.38north.org/2019/12/alukin122319/.

23. Georgy Toloraya and Vassily Gabets, "Solving the Korean Conundrum: Russia's Interaction with Major Actors in the Trump-Moon Era," *International Journal of Korean Unification Studies*, vol. 26, no. 1 (2017), 128, https://www.kinu.or.kr/pyxis-api/1/digital-files/16bd4162-9f47-47fe-8be5-d4624d0044db.

24. See for example, "Security and Cooperation in Northeast Asia: The Russian-South Korean Experts Joint Paper," Russian International Affairs Council (2015), https://www.slideshare.net/RussianCouncil/security-and-cooperation-in-northeast-asia-the-russiansouth-korean-experts-joint-paper.

25. Victor Cha, *The Impossible State North Korea Past, and Future* (New York: HarperCollins, 2018), 365.

26. Scott A. Snyder, "Where Does the Russia–North Korea Relationship Stand," Council on Foreign Relations, April 29, 2019, https://www.cfr.org/in-brief/where-does-russia-north-korea-relationship-stand.

27. Georgy Toloraya, "The Six Party Talks: A Russian Perspective," *Asian Perspective* 32, no. 4 (2008): 45–69, https://www.jstor.org/stable/i40101450?refreqid=excelsior%3Acd316998933600575e64f269192e05ee.

28. Kim Seung-yeon, "Putin Calls for Guaranteeing N. Korea's Security to Resolve Nuclear Quandary," *Yonhap*, June 5, 2021, https://en.yna.co.kr/view/AEN20210605000500325.

29. Toloraya and Gabets, "Solving the Korean Conundrum," 109–49.

30. Gaye Christofferson, "Chinese, Russian, Japanese, and Korean Strategies for Northeast Asian Cross-Border Energy," *Joint U.S.-Korea Academic Studies* 30 (2019), 97, https://keia.org/wp-content/uploads/2020/05/kei_jointus-korea_2019_1.5.pdf.

31. Sangtu Ko, "Geopolitical Motivations behind Russia's Active Engagement with North Korea," *The Korean Journal of Security Affairs* 24, no. 2 (December 2019): 151–52.

32. Vladimir Putin, Interview with Korean Broadcasting System, The Kremlin, November 12, 2013, http://www.en.kremlin.ru/events/president/transcripts/interviews/19603/print.

33. Toloraya and Gabets, "Solving the Korean Conundrum," 128.

34. "Has Russia Replaced China as North Korea's Best Friend?," *Sputnik*, March 29, 2015, https://sputniknews.com/analysis/201503291020175816/.

35. Toloraya and Gabets, "Solving the Korean Conundrum," 117–18.

36. "Kim Jong Un Moscow Visit Continuation of Russia, North Korea Dialogue," *Sputnik*, January 28, 2015, https://sputniknews.com/politics/201501281017474293/.

37. Zachary Keck, "North Korea Wants To Buy Russia's Super Advanced Su-35 Fighter Jet," *The National Interest*, January 9, 2015, http://nationalinterest.org/blog/the-buzz/north-korea-wants-buy-russias-super-advanced-su-35-fighter-12005.

38. "China Says Kim's Possible Visit to Russia 'Conducive to Peace,'" *Korea Times*, January 22, 2015, http://www.koreatimesus.com/china-says-kims-possible-visit-to-russia-conducive-to-peace/.

39. Michelle Nichols, "Russia, China to Hold More U.N. Talks on Lifting North Korean Sanctions: Diplomats," Reuters, December 29, 2019, https://www.reuters.com/article/us-northkorea-usa-un/russia-china-to-hold-more-u-n-talks-on-lifting-north-korea-sanctions-diplomats-idUSKBN1YX0LD.

40. Renslaer W. Lee III, and William Severe, "Russia and Crisis Management on the Korean Peninsula," Foreign Policy Research Institute, November 2017, https://www.fpri.org/wp-content/uploads/2017/11/RussiaCrisisMgmtDec2017.pdf; and Artyom Lukin, "Russia's Game on the North Korean Peninsula: Accepting China's Rise to Global Hegemony?," in *The China-Russia Entente and the Korean Peninsula*, ed. Jaewoo Choo, Youngjun Kim, Artyom Lukin, and Elizabeth Wishnick, The National Bureau of Asian Research, NBR Special Report No. 78, March 2019, https://www.nbr.org/wp-content/uploads/pdfs/publications/sr78_china_russia_entente_march2019.pdf.

41. Stephen Blank, "How Can Russia Contribute to Peace in Korea?," *The Korean Journal of Defense Analysis* 32, no. 1 (March 2020): 41–63, https://www.kci.go.kr/kciportal/ci/sereArticleSearch/ciSereArtiView.kci?sereArticleSearchBean.artiId=ART002561503.

42. Kang Tae-jun, "Russia Signs Economic Development Protocol with North Korea," NK News, April 3, 2014, http://www.nknews.org/2014/04/russia-signs-economic-development-protocol-with-north-korea/.

43. "Trade Turnover between Russia and North Korea Reached $42.74 Mln in 2020," February 19, 2021, https://tass.com/economy/1258635.

44. Sangtu Ko, "Geopolitical Motivations," 144.

45. "Russia Eyes Railway-for-Resources Project with North Korea," Agence-France Press, October 30, 2014, https://news.yahoo.com/russia-eyes-railway-resources-project-north-korea-110352721.html; and "Russia to Help N. Korea with Power Grid," *The Chosun Ilbo*, January 23, 2015, english.chosun.com/site/data/html_dir/2015/01/23/2015012301579.html.

46. Tae-jun Kang, "North Korea Russia Trade Takes Another Step," *The Diplomat*, January 21, 2015, http://thediplomat.com/2015/01/north-korea-russia-trade-takes-another-step/.

47. Alexander Podrabinek, "Russia Will Deport Refugees Back to North Korea," Institute of Modern Russia, November 5, 2014, http://www.imrussia.org/en/opinions/2077-russia-will-deport-refugees-back-to-north-korea.

48. John Hudson and Ellen Nakashima, "Russia Secretly Offered North Korea a Nuclear Power Plant in Exchange for Dismantling Weapons, Officials Say," *The Washington Post*, January 29, 2019, https://www.washingtonpost.com/world/national-security/russia-secretly-offered-north-korea-a-nuclear-power-plant-officials-say/.

49. Alexander Vorontsov, "Eurasia Right to Left," *Russia in Global Affairs* (January/March 2015), http://eng.globalaffairs.ru/number/Eurasia-Right-to-Left-17370.

50. "N. Korea Vows to Expand Relations with Russia on Eve of Summit Anniversary," *Yonhap*, April 24, 2022, https://en.yna.co.kr/view/AEN20220424001700315.

51. Artyom Lukin. "Why Did the Hanoi Summit Fail and What Comes Next?: The View from Russia," *Joint U.S.-Korea Academic Studies* 4, no. 3 (2019): 341–52. http://keia.org/sites/default/files/publications/kei_jointus-korea_2019_4.3.pdf.

52. Alexander Lukin and Oksana Pugacheva, "Russia's Priorities and Approaches to Issues Regarding the Korean Peninsula," *The Korean Journal of Defense Analysis* 34, no. 1 (2022): 86, https://www.kci.go.kr/kciportal/landing/article.kci?arti_id=ART002818704.

Chapter 9

The Right Coalition, the Right Time, and the Right Framework

Lessons Learned from Forty-Plus Years of Negotiation

SU-MI LEE AND PAMELA AALL

For the past four decades, the international community including South Korea, China, Japan, Russia, and the United States has attempted to persuade North Korea to give up its nuclear weapons program to no avail. This final chapter will summarize the dynamic negotiations that accompanied this period, a back-and-forth that at times broadcast hope that an agreement would be reached, at times showed the hopelessness of that aspiration, and at times simply reflected stalemate. The chapter then returns to the discussion of party cohesion and ripeness, first introduced in chapter 1, as they related to the North Korean negotiations over time. The chapter finds that there has been little ripeness and even less party cohesion over the course of the negotiations. The chapter ends with a suggestion for reframing the issues in order to allow talks to go forward.

In the mid-1980s, as evidence of visible progress on North Korea's nuclear program was found, the United States, worrying about North Korea's nuclear ambitions, urged the USSR to pressure North Korea to join the Nuclear Non-Proliferation Treaty (NPT). Requirements that came with the membership to the NPT such as the declaration of all its nuclear materials and inspection obligations prompted North Korea to reconsider its membership to the NPT. On March 12, 1993, Pyongyang threatened to leave the NPT but ended up suspending the decision to withdraw. As the crisis continued, former president Jimmy Carter traveled to Pyongyang and convinced Kim Il-sung to consent to the outline of a deal to give up his nuclear weapons. Eventually, the Agreed Framework was signed by North Korea and the United States on October 21, 1994, and included North Korea's commitment to freezing and dismantling its nuclear weapon program and the U.S. promise to help construct two light water reactors in North Korea. The deal also included energy assistance and measures to improve diplomatic ties between the United States and North Korea. Nonetheless, with growing tension between Pyongyang and Washington, the agreement collapsed in 2002 and North Korea effectively withdrew from the NPT in January 2003.

The next major negotiation talks on North Korea's nuclear program, known as the Six-Party Talks, began in Beijing in August 2003, and ended in 2009. The Six-Party Talks involved North Korea, South Korea, the United States, China, Japan, and Russia. After the first two years of negotiations, the six parties achieved a breakthrough in July 2005, leading to the conclusion of the Joint Statement in September 2005. The Joint Statement detailed a step-by-step plan to denuclearize North Korea and specified rewards to compensate for its cooperative behavior. Although follow-on talks discussing the implementation of the September agreement were futile due to the contentious exchanges between North Korea and the United States, along with North Korea's first nuclear weapon detonation and expanded missile tests in 2006, the six parties resumed their talks in February 2007 and drafted feasible implementation plans of the September agreement of 2005. Subsequent talks achieved little progress. The October joint statement of 2007 showed a slow development in the effort to denuclearize North Korea, but eventually, the Six-Party Talks came to a halt in spring 2009 when North Korea conducted its second nuclear weapon test.

In July 2011, North Korea and the United States held a series of bilateral meetings at the urging of South Korea. The two parties eventually reached the Leap Day Deal in February 2012 stipulating that North Korea would dismantle its nuclear weapons, stop ballistic missile testing, and allow inspectors in the country in exchange for U.S. food aid. However, the deal did not survive due to North Korea's insistence that a space launch was not covered by the ballistic missile testing moratorium. In early 2018, a series of bilateral dialogues between Seoul and Pyongyang led to not only Pyongyang's verbal commitment to refrain from further missile and nuclear weapons testing but also Kim Jong-un's verbal invitation to President Trump for a bilateral meeting in the near future. Two summits between Kim and Trump, the Singapore summit and the Hanoi summit, were held in June 2018 and February 2019; however, such efforts did not stop North Korea from growing its nuclear program.

As this history shows, there has been a constant stream of negotiations between and among the parties over the long period from 1980 to the present. As we suggested in chapter 1, these negotiations were both multiparty and two-sided. Although a number of direct negotiations took place only between the United States and North Korea, the other parties had very strong interests in the outcome, and were still part of the negotiation framework. Unconventional, perhaps, but we would argue that these negotiations were multilateral, with one country taking the lead on the negotiations at different times. Some of these negotiations led to agreements. There were bilateral agreements between North and South Korea—for instance, the Korean Peninsula denuclearization agreement of 1992. There were bilateral agreements between the United States and North Korea—the Agreed Framework of 1994, the Leap Day Deal, and the Singapore summit. There were multilateral agreements, such as the establishment of KEDO (1995) and the Six-Party Talks' disarmament principles (2005–09). Despite the constant flow of talk and ideas, none of the agreements have lasted for more than a few years, and some only a few days. Why was this? Why hasn't the four-decades-long efforts to denuclearize North Korea brought about any meaningful outcome? From the evidence of the preceding chapters, we identify the lack of two factors, party cohesion and ripeness, as detriments to successful North Korea nuclear negotiations.

Party Cohesion

As discussed in the introductory chapter on negotiation, a strong cohesion of positions within a coalition constitutes a form of leverage. Without it, the coalitions are not able to articulate and project their common positions or use carefully coordinated, consistent strategies to induce the other side's concessions. In this section, we will show how the lack of strong cohesion among the five interested outside parties contributed to the failure of North Korea nuclear negotiations.

As noted above, the Six-Party talks on North Korea's nuclear weapon program are essentially bilateral multiparty negotiations. Although there are six distinct parties involved in the negotiations, one side of the negotiations—consisting of the five countries—demanded North Korea be denuclearized while the other side, North Korea, demanded some forms of rewards such as economic aid as a concession. However, each of the five external countries entered the negotiations with its own motives and goals, some of which did not directly concern dismantling North Korea's nuclear weapon system. The intangibility of the issue, which is often associated with indivisibility, being negotiated did not make things easier.

GOALS, MOTIVES, AND STRATEGIES

When parties enter a negotiation, they bring to the table the goals they hope to achieve at the end. They anticipate that the outcome is positioned on their aspiration point of the bargaining range in the best scenario, while their worst scenario would land them on the reservation point. Understanding the goals helps predict what type of behavior the parties might exhibit or what type of strategies they employ throughout the course of negotiations. Parties' motives reveal the extent to which they are willing to make concessions. In bilateral multiparty negotiations, having and maintaining consistent/cohesive goals and coordinated strategies throughout the negotiation would be the key to successful negotiations.

In the case of North Korea nuclear negotiations, the goals, motives, and strategies of the five parties that participated in the negotiations with North Korea were palpably inconsistent and divergent throughout the years, and, consequently, unsuccessful negotiations were to be expected. There was no moment throughout a series of negotiations when all five parties shared a single or comparable goal they sought to achieve in the negotiations with North Korea. Their motives were divergent throughout the years; as a result, they adopted different strategies to deal with the issues concerning North Korea.

This said, however, it should be noted that South Korea's ultimate goal has been consistent throughout the years: denuclearization of North Korea. As the potential direct target of North Korea's aggressive and unpredictable behavior, South Korea did not waver about its goal when engaging in the negotiations, although its means to achieve this goal changed at times. The foundational goals of the Soviet Union/Russia and China have also remained relatively constant—to promote their countries' status and to preserve their regimes in power. Although this ultimate goal was at the foundation of their policies, their short-term goals and tactics changed fairly frequently. Japan's attention swung between establishing relations with North Korea and halting the development of nuclear weapons. And while the United States also prioritized denuclearization, its focus on this goal has not been as steadfast as South Korea's.

The 1980s

In the 1980s, when evidence of visible progress of North Korea's nuclear weapon program was discovered, the United States sought to prevent the proliferation of nuclear weapons. During the Cold War, Washington did not want a communist state such as North Korea to become another nuclear power. Yet, it did not seek direct communication with North Korea. Instead, Washington tried to pursue a multilateral approach and promote dialogues between the two Koreas. Washington also pressured Moscow to encourage Pyongyang to join the Treaty on the Non-Proliferation of Nuclear Weapons (NPT). Moscow agreed to do so to prevent any war in the Korean peninsula that might disturb the security status quo in the region. At the time, China considered the USSR as its ideological rival and sought to oppose the USSR on every front, and its policy toward Korea reflected that goal. Beijing shared and supported Washington's concern about the development of North Korea's nuclear weapon program. Yet, China's ultimate motive, which has remained constant throughout the years, was to ensure the CCP regime's security. Although both the USSR and China preferred no other nuclear powers in the region than themselves, denuclearization of North Korea was not their primary concern at the time. In the meantime, Japan was aware that North Korea was developing a nuclear weapon program in the 1980s. Yet, Japan's policy goal at the time was to normalize its relations with North Korea, which was one of the last countries that Japan hadn't normalized diplomatic relations with in the post–World War II period.

The 1990s

Significant events in the late 1980s and the early 1990s changed some of these parties' goals, motives, and strategies toward the issues concerning North Korea. The Tiananmen protests in 1989 brought sanctions on China. To get them lifted, Beijing continued to support Washington's effort to deal with North Korea. To ensure the CCP's survival, Beijing also walked a tightrope between maintaining good relations with South Korea for its economic growth and with North Korea for its ideological brotherhood, while keeping the West on its side. The United States' policy goal regarding North Korea's nuclear program remained the same, although its motive changed after the collapse of its Cold War counterpart. While Washington sought to end North Korea's nuclear program, with the end of the Cold War the United States hoped to normalize its relations with North Korea. In addition, as a responsible hegemon in the unipolar system, it hoped to lead an effort to denuclearize Pyongyang. The United States withdrew its nuclear weapons from South Korea, expecting North Korea to dismantle its weapon system in return. Such a move was not effective. Displeased by the NPT's requirements, North Korea threatened to leave the NPT in 1993. Responding to this drastic option, Washington pursued bilateral talks with Pyongyang, which eventually resulted in the 1994 Agreed Framework.

North Korea's threat to withdraw from the NPT changed Japan's priority on its foreign policy agenda toward North Korea. Once Japan realized it was a potential target of North Korea's nuclear weapons, it shared South Korea's policy goal of denuclearizing North Korea; protecting itself from North Korea's nuclear threat became Japan's primary policy objective. Allying with the United States, Tokyo explored the possibility of building trilateral cooperation among the United States, Japan, and South Korea to seek denuclearization.

South Korea's goal and motive toward North Korea did not change; it sought to denuclearize North Korea. Yet it figured that the North Korean regime was in such a dire situation following the famine years of the mid-1990s that it would collapse on its own. Likewise, Russia's goal and chief motive on the issues concerning North Korea did not change; it hoped to maintain the security status quo in the region with no conflict, particularly after the collapse of the USSR.

The 2000s

The U.S. position on North Korea took a significant turn after the 9/11 attacks. Although it continued to negotiate with North Korea, taking part in the Six-Party Talks, and eventually offered a security guarantee, it opted to use more pressure and sought to change North Korea's regime as it determined that regime change was the only way to deal with an embodiment of the Axis of Evil such as North Korea. In the late 2000s, under the Obama administration, the United States focused more on normalizing diplomatic relations and reassuring its allies in the region and, thus, stabilizing regional security. It continued with the conditional engagement approach that stated that Washington would engage in any talks with North Korea only when it agreed to proceed on denuclearization.

Since North Korea admitted kidnapping Japanese citizens, in 2002, resolution of the abduction issue became a precondition for Tokyo to engage in any talks with North Korea. Japan participated in bilateral negotiations with North Korea for the return of the abductees, and when it joined multilateral negotiations to denuclearize North Korea, Japan insisted that the resolution of the abduction issue was an integral part of those negotiations.

South Korea's goal and motive in dealing with North Korea remained the same, but Seoul realized that North Korea's regime was sturdier than previously regarded and adopted a different approach. From the late 1990s through the late 2000s, as part of the Sunshine Policy, South Korea provided unconditional economic aid to North Korea, which emerged from a prolonged severe famine, hoping that the improvement of its diplomatic relations with Pyongyang would eventually lead to the denuclearization of North Korea.

Like South Korea, Moscow did not waver about its goal and motives in approaching the issues concerning North Korea's nuclear weapon program. Although it hoped to denuclearize North Korea, its primary goal was to ensure the issues concerning North Korea would not become a trigger for any grave tension or conflict on the Korean peninsula, as it hoped to preserve the security status quo in the region. For these reasons, Russia opted to join the multilateral effort and took part in the Six-Party Talks.

Beijing's motive behind taking part in the negotiation talks with North Korea and other parties remained the same: preservation of the CCP's regime. However, Beijing's goal took a drastic turn as its global standing was raised as one of the emerging powers. Moving away from being a supportive partner to the United States, China sought to resist, reduce, and replace U.S. influence in East Asia while persuading South Korea to choose China over the United States as its ally and reinforcing its alliance with North Korea. Nonetheless, China supported the multilateral efforts to denuclearize North Korea such as the Six-Party Talks and the UN sanctions throughout the 2010s.

The 2010s

Although Seoul's goal and motive remained the same, it realized the unconditional engagement approach of the Sunshine Policy, taken from the late 1990s through the late 2000s, only did more harm than good. As a consequence, Seoul decided to adopt a conditional engagement strategy: North Korea would be rewarded only when it made a concession. In the late 2010s, South Korea offered to arrange a meeting between Washington and Pyongyang, which led to the 2018 Singapore Summit.

There was no change in the U.S. policy goal toward North Korea, although its motive and strategy changed under the Trump administration. From 2017 through 2020, Washington's motive concerning North Korea's nuclear missile system seemed to reflect Trump's personal ambition rather than the interest of the country. Instead of multilateral negotiations, bilateral talks were revived, which led to much-publicized 2018 and 2019 summits between Washington and Pyongyang.

Japan's policy goals and its motive pursuit of such goals did not change. Nor did its strategies. Resolution of the abduction issue to facilitate a full accounting of Japanese abductees remained as Japan's primary goal in regard to any issues concerning North Korea. It was willing to participate in bilateral or multilateral negotiations as long as such talks would address the abduction issues. Likewise, there was no change in Russia's policy goals, motives, and strategies toward nuclear negotiations with North Korea: no war, preservation of the security status quo, and multilateral negotiations.

China's policy objective toward North Korea continued to be motivated by the CCP's regime security. Thus, China continued to seek to resist, reduce, and replace the United States' power in the East Asian region, and in the late 2010s it began to focus more on balancing power with the United States in the region.

PARTY COHESION IN THE CASE OF NORTH KOREA

All parties involved in the Six-Party Talks brought their own agendas to the negotiation table. The five parties that were mobilized to denuclearize North Korea were in fact motivated to engage in the negotiations partly by their international and domestic situations. The primary goals they hoped to achieve in the negotiations, as well as strategies employed to accomplish such goals, varied greatly. Opposing goals actively pursued by the five coalition parties eliminated any realistic chance of successful negotiation. The divergent goals and demands that the coalition of the five parties pursued in the negotiations sent a mixed message to North Korea, failing to show a strong resolve on its position and derailing the negotiations. For instance, during the second round of the Six-Party Talks in February 2004, South Korea, China, and Russia offered to aid North Korea with its energy infrastructure if it agreed to dismantle its nuclear weapon system; Washington insisted that Pyongyang be disarmed before the United States signed on to such an agreement.[1] In another instance that occurred during the second round of the talks, China and Russia were content with a suboptimal settlement North Korea proposed that would dismantle its nuclear weapons program but allow the country to continue with its nuclear activities. The United States, Japan, and South Korea, however, were adamant that such a proposal was unacceptable.[2] Although all five parties sought denuclearization, an acceptable degree of denuclearization varied among the parties.

After the third round of the Six-Party Talks that again ended with no joint statement, in October 2004, the South Korean foreign minister stressed that the five parties "must come up with a more creative and realistic proposal," while China's counterpart made a more pointed remark that "we wish the U.S. side would go further to adopt a flexible and practical attitude on the issue."[3] In June 2005 after the Six-Party Talks had been halted for a year, as concerns about disagreements between Seoul and Washington over dealing with North Korea issues grew, then-South Korean president Roh defended the strong unity between the two countries while then-U.S. president Bush emphasized that the coalition of the five parties would have "one voice."[4] Such statements indicate the parties were all aware of the importance of cohesion within the coalition for their negotiations with North Korea to be successful; however, when multiple parties, motivated by various factors, engage in negotiations as a team, it is challenging to form and maintain cohesion. Any chance of successful bilateral negotiations with North Korea is contingent on the effective coordination of the action plans among the five parties involved in the talks as a team[5] whose goals and motives are divergent and influenced by their international and domestic situations.

It is difficult to form and maintain cohesion within a coalition in bilateral multiparty negotiations. Parties not only accommodate and deal with their own domestic actors but also coordinate their respective actions before they present their position to the opposite side. Washington did not endorse the agreement by which South Korea, China, and Russia offered to assist North Korea with its energy needs, partly because of the pressure from the hard-liners within the administration expressing their disappointment in the first round of the talks that failed to secure North Korea's commitment to dismantling its nuclear weapons system.[6] While coordinating its positions with its partners in the negotiations, Washington had to appease its domestic audience.

In essence, in bilateral multiparty negotiations, having too many players makes it difficult to coordinate and represent their diverse needs and positions. In the case of North Korea, there were the divergent goals and interests of the five parties that needed to be satisfied; their actions and strategies that aimed to fulfill their goals needed to be orchestrated. One solution might be simply to reduce the number of negotiating parties. The fewer negotiating parties, the fewer players they will have to coordinate with and appease. Having fewer negotiating parties also entails fewer issues on the negotiation table and thus more time to focus on the main issue. Yet, such a solution is not short of downsides. For one, the smaller coalition has less to offer in exchange for North Korea's concession; however, such resources could be mobilized outside the workings of negotiation. In addition, leadership within a coalition might help achieve party cohesion. The leader does not have to be the strongest party in the coalition but should be willing to bear the costs of keeping the other coalition members from pursuing their own agenda and keeping them focused on the common goal, herding them through the negotiation process. Parties might not be receptive to being told to prioritize the common goal and give up their own agenda; however, the coalition could still benefit from having a member acting as a leader that will at least ensure their position to be consistent. Nonetheless, it should be noted that it would be extremely challenging to reduce the number of negotiating parties and establish leadership among powerful, strong-willed countries such as the United States, China, and Russia in order to form and maintain party cohesion.

Conflict Ripeness: A Mutable Condition

In the opening chapter, we discussed how we have borrowed from the mediation literature the concept of ripeness as a moment in time in the course of a conflict when productive negotiations might start or might start up again. Ripeness indicates a willingness to enter into discussions, define an agenda, put forward positions, and look for solutions. That there is a ripe moment is not a guarantee of a successful outcome—the conflict parties might not be able to bridge their divides or agree on a set of negotiable issues. As we mentioned earlier, there are two conditions that encourage ripeness. The first is a mutually hurting stalemate (MHS) in which both parties experience a significant hardship but neither party can gain the upper hand. The second is the identification of a "way out" (a mutually enticing opportunity, or MEO) and the prospect of a better future if they can put the conflict behind them.[7]

It is important to recognize that ripeness is not a fixed state but can fluctuate throughout the conflict cycle due to changes in both internal and external circumstances. Ripeness can be enhanced or diminished by changes on the battlefield. For instance, a series of grinding battles that leave the military situation relatively unchanged might make the conflict parties realize that their chances of pushing back their opponent are slim to none. On the other hand, a sudden battlefield victory (or acquisition of new resources) by one party could raise hopes of complete victory and destabilize a military situation that was formerly in stalemate. Ripeness can also be affected by changes in leadership of one or more of the affected parties by providing an opening in a frozen relationship or closing the window to talks. A third factor that can induce ripeness is change in the international environment, such as shifting relations among major powers, global economic downturns, or natural disasters. Looking at these factors that affect ripeness in turn may give us a sense of how ripeness has waxed and waned over time.

CHANGES ON THE BATTLEFIELD

On the military front, there was a kind of stalemate until 2006 when North Korea tested, underground, its first nuclear weapon. Until that time, the parties had squared off not in terms of military strength (the combined power of the five other negotiating countries far outweighed the capacity of a relatively weak North Korea) but in terms of their willingness to deploy whatever weapons they had. While North Korea threatened escalation and often walked away from agreements, it also repeatedly reengaged in negotiations at a later date. While the other countries shared the goal of preventing North Korean nuclear weapons development, they were not willing to deploy the military strength necessary to deter North

Korea by force. Testing of the 2006 weapon altered that equation. It not only proved that North Korea had acquired nuclear capability but also raised the likelihood that the regime would use it as a bargaining chip. The situation on the battlefield had changed, but instead of ripening the situation, it moved the parties farther away and transformed the discussion from talks on preventing nuclearization to talks on preventing its use. Changes on the battlefield in this case did not lead to a ripe moment for successful negotiation.

LEADERSHIP CHANGES

The six countries have also experienced a number of leadership changes over the conflict period. If this dynamic were to have an impact, one would expect to see it during leadership changes in the United State, South Korea, and North Korea, the three countries at the center of the conflict. Since 1990, the United States has swung back and forth between three Republican presidents–George H. W. Bush, George W. Bush, and Donald Trump—and three Democrats: Bill Clinton, Barack Obama, and Joe Biden. Each president has differed markedly from his predecessor on dealing with North Korea, and there have been strong differences within each political party and changing policy approaches within the presidential administrations as well. South Korea too has seen shifts from one president to the next in terms of approach to North Korea. Kim Dae-jung's Sunshine Policy, an attempt to engage with the North Korean regime in the early 2000s was continued by his successor, Roh Moo-hyun. However, the policy did not result in warmer relations in the long term and the next two administrations (under Lee Myung-bak and Park Geun-hye respectively) took harder, more hostile stands. In both the United States and South Korea, leadership changes did lead to temporary thawing of relations with North Korea, providing perhaps windows of opportunity, but these efforts were not consistent over time. In both cases, alternating between engagement and a more hostile approach might have lessened the impact of either policy, as "waiting it out" became a viable option on the North Korean side. It is hard to maintain pressure on the process if one party sees an end to their pain as a possibility if they only hang on till the next transition.

North Korean leadership changes in 2011 might have changed the relationship among the negotiating parties significantly had Kim Jong-un reversed the nuclear policies of his father, or if his attempt to consolidate power had faltered in the transition period. Neither of these happened. Kim Jong-un moved quickly and with a degree of ruthlessness to assert to domestic and international audiences his authority over the country. Further, as Scott Snyder's chapter points out, four months after Kim Jong-il's death, the new regime inserted language in the North Korean constitution noting the country's standing as a nuclear state. From that moment, the regime's legitimacy and authority was explicitly linked to its possession of nuclear weapons. Far from reversing his father's policies, he expanded and strengthened them.

INTERNATIONAL IMPACTS

One event in particular at the international level also served as a potential game-changer. The end of the Cold War produced a much-weakened Russia from the remains of the Soviet Union and also provided China with an opportunity to play a larger role on the world stage. As both countries moved to recognize South Korea for the first time, North Korea reacted defensively, warning that it would pursue an independent nuclear policy. At the same time, however, North Korea also reached out to South Korea and the United States in a series of conciliatory moves, and a few years later the United States under the Clinton administration and North Korea signed the Geneva Agreed Framework. This agreement was plagued with implementation problems on the American side and, as it seems, noncompliance on the North Korean side but it did provide a different framing for the relationship that might have been possible to develop further. However, Bush administration skepticism about North Korea's intentions and North Korea's secret uranium enrichment program acted together to scrap the Agreed Framework in 2002. Any window that had been opened by the termination of the Cold War was now firmly closed, at least for a few years.

While there have been changes in each of these dimensions—battle-field changes, leadership transitions, international impacts—these potentially significant events have not created the kind of prolonged agreement that allowed parties to move beyond the conflict. What accounts for this? One factor might have arisen out of the nature of the mutually hurting stalemate, the first condition for productive negotiations. There is no doubt that the conflict has been stalemated many times over the years when both negotiations and policies have failed to produce forward momentum. But the stalemate may not hurt the parties as much as it gives them a reliable framework for their relationships, a soft, stable, self-serving stalemate, in William Zartman's words.[8]

Dean Pruitt argues that a mutually hurting stalemate is hard to reach because parties arrive at different times at the moment in which they become interested in a negotiated solution.[9] This mutual aspect of the stalemate is even more problematic in the North Korea case due to the number of participants. The five countries negotiating with North Korea are different in terms of their size, capabilities, proximity to the conflict, and national and foreign policy interests. Pruitt would suggest that it is unlikely that all five would perceive a hurting stalemate at the same time and in the same way.

THE COSTS OF DIFFERING GOALS, AGAIN

As the chapters and our discussion of party cohesion illustrate well, each country entered negotiation with its own goals. From the start, North Korea's goal was to increase its security, a goal that seems only to grow stronger as negotiations as well as threats and coercion continue, and to increase its legitimacy in the eyes of the rest of the world. It had access to alternative means to achieve these ends—for instance, entering into alliances with other countries—but preferred the independence that came with nuclear weapons acquisition. As mentioned earlier, China, Japan, Russia, South Korea, and the United States support denuclearization of North Korea, but beyond that their goals are diverse. China has been focused on the dual goals of increasing regional security and the security of its own regime. Russia, intent on increasing its profile in global affairs, wants to establish and maintain its relevance to the North Korea conflict. The Japanese have been somewhat inconsistent and thrown off track by the introduction of human rights issues into the relationship with North Korea. In South Korea, it is apparent that there has been a division of opinion in the country on how to bring the North Koreans to the table. Finally, the American approach, like the South Korean one, has alternated between wanting to punish North Korea for its human rights abuses and wishing to find ways to define a common interest over which the two countries can negotiate. As earlier noted, this diversity of interests makes it difficult to create a situation in which a hurting stalemate hits the participants equally or at the same time.

Concluding Thoughts: Providing a New Framework

The case of North Korea nuclear negotiations reaffirms that multiparty negotiations—and particularly bilateral multiparty negotiations—are difficult to conduct. For bilateral multiparty negotiations to be successful, parties on one side must prioritize common goals and use similar strategies to achieve those goals. That is far from what we have witnessed in the case of North Korea nuclear negotiations. Ripeness that occurs when parties experience a mutually hurting stalemate (MHS) and do not foresee a realistic chance of winning unilaterally is a necessary condition for successful negotiations. The parties involved in the Six-Party Talks did not experience a mutually hurting stalemate at the same time, if any of them did at all.

Do these findings suggest there would be no point to negotiations if there were no party cohesion and ripeness? In answer to this question, it is important to note one success: that there has been no sustained conflict on the Korean Peninsula during this long period of negotiations. Moreover, there are other positive aspects to these continued talks. Negotiations are a form of communication through which the parties learn about each others' interests and needs. Without such communication, parties would not be able to realize it if they experience a mutually hurting stalemate and, thus, when ripeness occurs. They might not be able to form party cohesion among the members within one coalition if they stopped communicating with each other. Although bilateral multiparty negotiations, in the absence of party cohesion and ripeness, might not bring about the outcome the parties intend, it is still important that the parties continue to engage in negotiations to learn about others' bargaining positions as well as their goals and intentions. North Korea has not given up its nuclear program and it does not seem likely that it will at any time soon. However, it is important that the international community continues to engage in negotiations with North Korea. Doing so might not lead to denuclearization of North Korea, but over time it might lead to socialization of North Korea as a member of the international community.

There is a factor that might affect the willingness of the parties to strike and keep a deal. This factor involves providing a new framework for the negotiations that leads to changes in the parties' goals, and changes in how they think about reaching those goals can also alter their perceptions of ripeness. Examples of measures that one could take to encourage ripeness would be to put pressure on the parties to recalculate benefits and risks of reaching or not reaching an agreement. Pressure might be applied through using carrots or sticks, both tangible and intangible. A tangible incentive would be to offer economic development and promises of investment and enhanced trade. A less tangible but particularly powerful piece of leverage would be to find a way to grant the recognition and respect that the North Korean regime is seeking.

Another means of providing a new framework would be to broaden the negotiations. Transforming the negotiations so that they were focused not on denuclearization but rather on arms control would allow discussion of strategic weapons to be embedded in a larger context of rules, expectations, and agreements to reduce the likelihood of conflict and build confidence among the parties.[10] This approach has been criticized because it involves recognizing North Korea as a nuclear state, but it might provide new perspectives that would help the principal parties escape from the current stalemate.

A third means of providing a new framework would be the introduction of a mediator into the negotiations. An impartial mediator could help on many fronts. In these negotiations in which there is not a common understanding of what the problems are, a mediator might help the parties define the issues. Equally, a mediator could help parties recognize how their interests might be met, even if it means compromising on some aspects of the debate. A mediator could help to build up support for a solution that would be acceptable to all parties, and could help parties generate international commitments to help with the implementation period. This is a tall order; finding an appropriate mediator acceptable to all parties would be, of course, a challenge in this case (as it is with almost all conflicts). It would take a special person or persons to be able to accomplish it. But as a possible "way out" of this intractable conflict, it might be well worthwhile to explore this option along with others that are on the table.

In closing, we have not sought to propose a policy or solution for the successful denuclearization of North Korea but rather to illustrate the complex negotiation dynamics at work over the years and identify factors that haveled to unsuccessful negotiations. There were many factors that explain why those negotiations were unsuccessful; some might argue that the United States held too strict a stance on North Korea's nuclear weapon program while others would point out that North Korea was never willing to give up its nuclear program. This book, though, has sought to explain that besides all those reasons that had been explored before (that is, even if all those factors were taken care of), from negotiation theory's point of view, these negotiations were bound to fail as there was no ripe moment or party cohesion, which are considered key to successful negotiations. To do so, in chapters 3–8, we identified the goals, strategies, and motives of each of the six parties involved in the North Korea nuclear negotiations over the years and then explained how international/domestic political/economic/social conditions in each country caused changes in the three variables. In chapter 9, while tracing how those changes in each party's goals, strategies, and motives altered the negotiation dynamics, we demonstrated that neither party cohesion nor ripeness formed over the years and proposed ways to achieve them. Such proposals might not be particularly easy to implement or popular enough to gain sufficient support, which explains why forty years of denuclearization efforts have not been fruitful. However, this demonstrates that without reframing the talking points or conditions/environments, a successful negotiation on North Korea's nuclear weapon program might remain a remote possibility.

Notes

1. Associated Press, "Talks on North Korea Nuclear Program End," *NBC news*, February 24, 2004, https://www.nbcnews.com/id/wbna4365670.

2. Kelsey Davenport, "The Six-Party Talks at a Glance," *Arms Control Association*, June 2018, https://www.armscontrol.org/factsheets/6partytalks.

3. Steven R. Weisman, "Discord on North Korea as Powell Finishes East Asia Trip," *New York Times*, October 27, 2004, https://www.nytimes.com/2004/10/27/world/discord-on-north-korea-as-powell-finishes-east-asia-trip.html.

4. Mark Silva, "U.S., South Korea Present United Front on Pyongyang," *Baltimore Sun*, June 11, 2005, https://www.baltimoresun.com/news/bs-xpm-2005-06-11-0506110237-story.html.

5. Scott Snyder, Ralph Cossa, and Brad Glosserman, "Whither the Six-Party Talks?" The United States Institute of Peace, May 17, 2006, https://www.usip.org/publications/2006/05/whither-six-party-talks.

6. Steven R. Weisman, "Lasting Discord Clouds Talks on North Korean Nuclear Arms," *New York Times*, March 14, 2004, https://www.nytimes.com/2004/03/14/world/lasting-discord-clouds-talks-on-north-korean-nuclear-arms.html.

7. I. William Zartman, "Ripeness: The Hurting Stalemate and Beyond," in *International Conflict Resolution after the Cold War*, ed. Paul Stern and Daniel Druckman (Washington, DC: National Academy Press, 2000), 225–50.

8. I William Zartman, "Mediation: Ripeness and its Challenges in the Middle East," *International Negotiations* 33, no. 3 (2015): 479–93.

9. Dean Pruitt, "The Evolution of Readiness Theory," in *Handbook of International Negotiation: Interpersonal, Intercultural, and Diplomatic Perspectives*, ed. Mauro Galluccio (Switzerland: Springer, 2015), 123–38.

10. Toby Dalton and Youngjun Kim, "Negotiating Arms Control with North Korea: Why and How?" *Korean Journal of Defense Analysis* 33, no. 1 (March 2021): 1–21.

Selected Bibliography

Abramowitz, Morton, and James Laney. "Meeting the North Korean Nuclear Challenge: Report of an Independent Task Force Sponsored by the Council on Foreign Relations." Council on Foreign Relations Independent Task Force, 2003.

Allison, Graham, and Philip Zelikow. *Essence of Decision: Explaining the Cuban Missile Crisis*. 2nd Edition. New York: Pearson Press, 1999.

Bae, Jung-Ho et al. *The Perceptions of Northeast Asia's Four States on Korean Unification*. Seoul: KINU, 2014.

Baldwin, David A. "The Power of Positive Sanctions." *World Politics* 24, no. 1 (1971): 19–38.

Bernauer, Thomas, and Dieter Rulo. *The Politics of Positive Incentives in Arms Control*. South Carolina: University of South Carolina Press, 1999.

Blank, Stephen. "How Can Russia Contribute to Peace in Korea?" *The Korean Journal of Defense Analysis* 32, no. 1 (March 2020): 41–63. https://www.kci.go.kr/kci-portal/ci/sereArticleSearch/ciSereArtiView.kci?sereArticleSearchBean.artiId=ART002561503.

Bolton, John. *In the Room Where It Happened*. New York: Simon and Schuster, 2020.

Brams, Steven, and Jeffrey M. Togman. "Camp David: Was the Agreement Fair?" *Conflict Management and Peace Science* 15, no. 1 (1996): 99–112.

Bülow, Anne Marie, and Rajesh Kumar. "Culture and Negotiation." *International Negotiations* 16 (2011): 349–59.

Buszynski, Leszek. *Negotiating with North Korea: The Six Party Talks and the Nuclear Issue*. Abingdon, UK: Routledge, 2013.

Buzo, Adrian. *The Guerilla Dynasty: Politics and Leadership in North Korea*. New South Wales, Australia: Allen and Unwin, 1999.

Cha, Donggil. "Research on Execution Strategy of Moon Jae-In Administration's 'Korean Peninsula Driver Theory.'" *Korea-Japan Military Culture Studies* 25, no. 1 (2018): 61–90.

Cha, Victor. *The Impossible State North Korea Past, and Future*. New York: HarperCollins, 2018.

Chinoy, Mike. *Meltdown: The Inside Story of the North Korean Nuclear Crisis*. New York: St. Martin's Press, 2010.

Cho, Min, and Jinha Kim. *Chronology of North Korea's Nuclear Development 1955–2014*. Seoul: Korea Institute for National Unification, 2014.

Cho, Min. "Roh Moo-hyun Government's Peace and Prosperity Policy: Prospects and Tasks." *Unification Policy Studies* 12, no. 1 (2003): 1–27.

Cho, Sung-ryol. "Huddles and Prospects of the Moon Jae-in Administration's North Korea Policy: Analysis of the Korean Peninsula Denuclearization and the Vision of the Peace Regime." *Unification Policy Studies* 26, no. 1 (2017): 1–28.

Choi, Wankyu. "The Kim Young-sam Administration's North Korea Policy: Assessment and Suggestions." In *Inter-Korean Relationship in the 21st Century*, edited by Baek Young-cheol, Seoul: Beopmoonsa, 2000.

Chun, Bong-Keun. "An Assessment and Lessons of the North Korean Nuclear Negotiations for the Past Twenty-Years." *Korea and World Politics* 27, no. 1 (2010): 183–212.

Chung, Ok-nim. *The North Korea Nuclear Crisis 588 Days*. Seoul: Seoul Press, 2015.

Clemens, Walter. *Getting to Yes in North Korea*. Boulder: Paradigm Publishers, 2010.

Cordesman, Anthony H. et al. *North Korean Nuclear Forces and the Threat of Weapons of Mass Destruction in Northeast Asia*. Washington, DC: CSIS, July 25, 2016.

Creekmore, Marion Jr. *A Moment of Crisis: Jimmy Carter, The Power of a Peacemaker, and North Korea's Nuclear Ambitions*. New York: Public Affairs, 2006.

Crocker, Chester A. "Lessons for Practice." In *How Negotiations End*, edited by I. William Zartman, 295–303. Cambridge: Cambridge University Press, 2019.

Crocker, Chester A. *High Noon in South Africa: Making Peace in a Rough Neighborhood*. New York: W. W. Norton, 1992.

Crocker, Chester A., Fen Osler Hampson, and Pamela R. Aall, eds. *Herding Cats: Multiparty Mediation in a Complex World*. Washington, DC: U.S. Institute of Peace Press, 1999.

Crocker, Chester A., Fen Osler Hampson, and Pamela R. Aall. *Taming Intractable Conflicts: Mediation in the Hardest Cases*. Washington, DC: U.S. Institute of Peace Press, 2004.

Crump, Larry, and A. Ian Glendon. "Towards a Paradigm of Multiparty Negotiation." *International Negotiation* 8, no. 2 (2003): 197–234.

Crump, Larry. "Multiparty Negotiation: What Is It?" *ADR Bulletin* 8, no. 7 (2006): 1–10.

Dalton, Toby, and Youngjun Kim. "Negotiating Arms Control with North Korea: Why and How?" *Korean Journal of Defense Analysis* 33, no. 1 (March 2021): 1–21.

Dalton, Toby, and Ain Han. *Elections, Nukes, and the Future of the South Korea–U.S. Alliance.* Washington, DC: Carnegie Endowment for International Peace, October 26, 2020.

DeLaet, James C., and James M. Scott. "Treaty-Making and Partisan Politics: Arms Control and the U.S. Senate, 1960–2001." *Foreign Policy Analysis* 2, no. 2 (April 2006): 177–200.

Dingman, Roger. "Atomic Diplomacy During the Korean War." *International Security* 13, no. 3 (Winter 1988–89): 50–91.

Dossani, Rafiq. *Engagement with North Korea: A Portfolio-Based Approach to Diplomacy.* Santa Monica: RAND, 2020.

Drezner, Daniel W. *The Sanctions Paradox: Economic Statecraft and International Relations.* Cambridge: Cambridge University Press, 1999.

Druckman, Daniel. "Linking Micro and Macro-Level Processes: Interaction Analysis in Context." *The International Journal of Conflict Management* 14, no. 3/4 (2003): 177–90.

Eberstadt, Nicholas. "North Korea's Interlocked Economic Crises: Some Indications from 'Mirror Statistics.'" *Asian Survey* 38, no. 3 (March 1998): 223–25.

Eden, Lynn. *Whole World on Fire. Organizations, Knowledge, Nuclear Weapons Devastation.* Ithaca: Cornell University Press, 2004.

Fearon, James D. "Rationalist Explanations for War." *International Organization* 49, no. 3 (1995): 379–414.

Fisher, Roger, William Ury, and Bruce Patton. *Getting to Yes: Negotiating Agreement Without Giving In.* 2nd Ed. New York: Penguin Books, 1991.

Fontaine, Richard, and Micah Springut. "Coordinating North Korea Policy—An American View." In *The US-ROK Alliance in the 21st Century*, edited by Jungho Bae and Abraham Denmark, 136. Seoul, South Korea: Korea Institute for National Unification, 2009.

Foote, Rosemary. "Nuclear Coercion and the Ending of the Korean Conflict." *International Security* 13, no. 3 (Winter 1988–89): 92–112.

Ford, Glyn. *Talking to North Korea: Ending the Nuclear Standoff.* London: Pluto Press, 2018.

Fravel, M. Taylor. "Regime Insecurity and International Cooperation: Explaining China's Compromises in Territorial Disputes." *International Security* 30 (Fall 2005): 46–83.

Freeman, Carla, ed. *China and North Korea: Strategic and Policy Perspectives from a Changing China.* New York: Palgrave Macmillan, 2015.

Fuhrmann, Matthew, and Michael C. Horowitz. "When Leaders Matter: Rebel Experience and Nuclear Proliferation." *The Journal of Politics* 77, no. 1 (2015): 72–87.

Fuhrmann, Matthew, and Sarah E Kreps. "Targeting Nuclear Programs in War and Peace: A Quantitative Empirical Analysis, 1941–2000." *Journal of Conflict Resolution* 54, no. 6 (2010): 831–59.

Garver, John W. *China's Quest: Foreign Relations of the People's Republic of China.* New York: Oxford University Press, 2016.

Garver, John W., and Fei-Ling Wang. "China's Anti-Encirclement Struggle: The U.S., India, and Japan." *Asian Security* 6, no. 3 (October 2010): 238–61.

Gilpin, Robert. *American Scientists and Nuclear Weapons Policy.* Princeton: Princeton University Press, 2015.

Goldstein, Lyle J. *Meeting China Halfway: How to Defuse the Emerging US-China Rivalry.* Washington, DC: Georgetown University Press, 2015.

Groves, Kevin, Ann Feyerherm, and Minhua Gu. "Examining Cultural Intelligence and Cross-Cultural Negotiation Effectiveness." *Journal of Management Education* 39, no. 2 (2015): 209–43.

Hampson, Fen Osler, with Michael Hart. *Multilateral Negotiations: Lessons from Arms Control, Trade, and the Environment.* Baltimore and London: The Johns Hopkins University Press, 1999.

Hampson, Fen Osler. "The Risks of Peace: Implications for International Mediation." *Negotiation Journal* 22, no. 1 (2006): 13–30.

Hassner, Ron E. "To Halve and To Hold: Conflicts Over Sacred Space and the Problem of Indivisibility." *Security Studies* 12, no. 4 (2003): 1–33.

Hecker, Siegfried S. "The Nuclear Crisis in North Korea." *Engineering and Foreign Policy* 34, no. 2 (June 1, 2004).

Heo, Uk, and Chong-Min Hyun. "An Analysis of South Korea's Policy towards North Korea." *Pacific Focus* 16, no. 1 (2001): 89–102.

Heo, Uk, and Chong-Min Hyun. "The 'Sunshine Policy' Revisited: An Analysis of South Korea's Policy Toward North Korea." In *Conflict in Asia: Korea, China-Taiwan, and India-Pakistan*, edited by Young-cheol Baek. Westport, CT: Greenwood, 2003.

Heo, Uk, and Terence Roehrig. *South Korea Since 1980.* Cambridge: Cambridge University Press, 2010.

Heo, Uk, and Terence Roehrig. *South Korea's Rise: Economic Development, Power, and Foreign Relations.* Cambridge: Cambridge University Press, 2014.

Hill, Christopher. *Outpost.* New York: Simon and Schuster, 2014.

Hopmann, P. Terrence. "When Is 'Enough' Enough? Settling for Suboptimal Agreement." In *How Negotiations End*, edited by I. William Zartman, 265–86. Cambridge: Cambridge University Press, 2019.

Huh, Moon-young, Jung-ho Bae, In-gone Yeo, Byung-gon Chun, and Woo-taek Hong. *Implementation Strategy of The Lee Myung-bak Administration's North Korea Policy and Unification Policy.* Seoul: Korea Institute for National Unification, 2010.

Hymans, Jacques E. "Veto Players, Nuclear Energy, and Nonproliferation: Domestic Institutional Barriers to A Japanese Bomb." *International Security* 36, no. 2 (2011): 154–89.

Hymans, Jacques E. *The Psychology of Nuclear Proliferation: Identity, Emotions and Foreign Policy.* Cambridge: Cambridge University Press, 2006.

Iklé, Fred. *How Nations Negotiate*. New York: Harper and Row, 1964.

Jeong, Ho-Won. *International Negotiation: Process and Strategies*. Cambridge: Cambridge University Press, 2016.

Kihl, Young Whan. "Seoul's Engagement Policy and US-DPRK Relations." *Korean Journal of Defense Analysis* 10, no. 1 (1998): 21–48.

Kim, Choong Nam. *The Korean Presidents: Leadership for Nation Building*. Norwalk, VA: East Bridge, 2007.

Kim, Il Sung. *With the Century*. Pyongyang: Foreign Languages Publishing House, 1992.

Kim, Samuel. "North Korea in 2000." *Asian Survey* 41, no. 1 (2001): 12–29.

Ko, Sangtu. "Geopolitical Motivations behind Russia's Active Engagement with North Korea." *The Korean Journal of Security Affairs* 24, no. 2 (December 2019): 144–61.

Koo, Bon-Hak. "Challenges and Prospects for Inter-Korean Relations under the New Leadership." *Korean Journal of Defense Analysis* 10, no. 1 (1998): 75–93.

Koo, Bon-Hak. "Process of the North Korean Nuclear Issue and Its Solution." *Unification Policy Studies* 24, no. 2 (2015): 1–24.

Kreps, Sarah, Elizabeth Saunders, and Kenneth Schultz. "The Ratification Premium: Hawks, Doves, and Arms Control." *World Politics* 70, no. 4 (2018): 479–514.

Lee, Chang-hun. "South Korean Government's Approach to the North Korean Nuclear Issue: An Evaluation." *Political Intelligence Analysis* 6, no. 2 (2003): 105–30.

Lee, Jung-bok. *Solution of the North Korean Nuclear Crisis and Its Prospect*. Seoul: Joongang M&B, 2003.

Lee, Seung-hyun. "The Moon Jae-in Administration's North Korea Policy based on Five Keyword." *Legislative Politics Review* 13, no. 1 (2018): 163–86.

Levite, Ariel E. "Never Say Never Again: Nuclear Reversal Revisited." *International Interactions* 28, no. 3 (2003): 237–60.

Lukin, Alexander, and Oksana Pugacheva. "Russia's Priorities and Approaches to Issues Regarding the Korean Peninsula." *The Korean Journal of Defense Analysis* 34, no. 1 (2022): 81–99. https://www.kci.go.kr/kciportal/landing/article.kci?arti_id=ART002818704.

Lukin, Artyom "Russia's Game on the North Korean Peninsula: Accepting China's Rise to Global Hegemony?," in *The China-Russia Entente and the Korean Peninsula*, edited by Jaewoo Choo, Youngjun Kim, Artyom Lukin, and Elizabeth Wishnick. The National Bureau of Asian Research, NBR Special Report No. 78, March 2019. https://www.nbr.org/wp-content/uploads/pdfs/publications/sr78_china_russia_entente_march2019.pdf.

Lukin, Artyom. "Why Did the Hanoi Summit Fail and What Comes Next?: The View from Russia," *Joint U.S.-Korea Academic Studies* 4, no. 3 (2019): 341–52. http://keia.org/sites/default/files/publications/kei_jointus-korea_2019_4.3.pdf.

Mazarr, Michael J. *North Korea and the Bomb: A Case Study in Nonproliferation*. New York: St. Martin's Press, 1995.

McManus, Roseanne W. "Making It Personal: The Role of Leader-Specific Signals in Extended Deterrence." *The Journal of Politics* 80, no. 3 (2018): 982–95.

Mehta, Rupal N. *Delaying Doomsday: The Politics of Nuclear Reversal.* Oxford: Oxford University Press, 2020.

Miller, Nicholas L. *Stopping the Bomb: The Sources and Effectiveness of US Non-proliferation Policy.* Ithaca: Cornell University Press, 2018.

Ministry of National Unification. *The Participatory Government's Peace and Prosperity Policy.* Seoul: Ministry of National Unification, 2003.

Moltz, James Clay, and Alexandre Y. Mansourov, eds. *The North Korean Nuclear Program: Security, Strategy, and New Perspectives from Russia.* New York: Routledge, 1999.

Monteiro, Nuno P., and Alexandre Debs. *Nuclear Politics: The Strategic Causes of Proliferation.* Ithaca: Cornell University Press, 2018.

Moon, Chung-in. "Understanding the DJ Doctrine: The Sunshine Policy and the Korean Peninsula." In *Kim Dae-jung Government and Sunshine Policy: Promises and Challenges.* edited by Chung-in Moon and David I. Steinberg. Washington, DC: Georgetown University Press, 1999.

Nam, Kwang Kyu. "The Moon Jae-in administration's North Korea Policy and Korea–US Relations." *Asian Education and Development Studies* 8, no. 1 (2019): 59–74.

Nincic, Miroslav. *The Logic of Positive Engagement.* Ithaca: Cornell University Press, 2011.

O'Neill, Barry. "International Negotiation: Some Conceptual Developments." *Annual Review of Political Science* 21 (2018): 515–33.

Obama, Barack. *A Promised Land.* New York: Crown Press, 2020.

Oberdorfer, Don, and Robert Carlin. *The Two Koreas: A Contemporary History* 2nd ed. New York: Basic Books, 1997.

Oberdorfer, Don, and Robert Carlin. *The Two Koreas: A Contemporary History* 3rd ed. New York: Basic Books, 2013.

Odell, John S. *Negotiating the World Economy.* Ithaca: Cornell University Press, 2000.

Olson, Mancur. *The Logic of Collective Action: Public Goods and the Theory of Groups.* Cambridge: Harvard University Press, 1971.

Pacheco Pardo, Ramon. *North Korea–US Relations under Kim Jong II: The Quest for Normalization?* London and New York: Routledge, 2014.

Park Ihn-Hwi. "A Theoretical Approach of the Korean Peninsula Trust Process and Proposal for Internationalization." *Unification Policy Studies* 22, no. 1 (2013): 27–52.

Park, Hwi-lak. "Contents and Directions of South Korea's North Korean Nuclear Strategy: Focus on Denuclearization." *Unification Strategy,* 18, no. 1 (2018): 28–39.

Park, Young-ho. "The Park Geun-hye Administration's North Korea Policy: The Korean Peninsula Trust Process and Its Policy Direction." *Unification Policy Studies* 22, no. 1 (2013): 1–25.

Park, Youngsoo. "Limits of the Kim Young-sam Administration's Response to the North Korean Nuclear Crisis Revisited." *Korean Political Studies* 20, no. 3 (2011): 55–78.

Pollack, Jonathan D. *No Exit: North Korea, Nuclear Weapons, and International Security*. New York: Routledge, 2011.

Pritchard, Charles L. *Failed Diplomacy: The Tragic Story of How North Korea Got the Bomb*. Washington, DC: Brookings, 2007.

Pruitt, Dean G. "When Is 'Enough' Enough? Approach-Avoidance." In *How Negotiations End*, edited by I. William Zartman, 256–64. Cambridge: Cambridge University Press, 2019.

Pruitt, Dean G. *Negotiation Behavior*. New York: Academic Press, 1981.

Pruitt, Dean. "The Evolution of Readiness Theory." In *Handbook of International Negotiation: Interpersonal, Intercultural, and Diplomatic Perspectives*, edited by Mauro Galluccio, 123–38. Switzerland: Springer, 2015.

Putnam, Robert D. "Diplomacy and Domestic Politics: The Logic of Two-level Games." *International Organization* 42, no. 3 (1988): 427–60.

Quinones, Kenneth C. "South Korea's Approaches to North Korea: A Glacial Process." In *Korean Security Dynamics in Transition*, edited by Kyung-Ae Park and Dalchoong Kim, 19–48. New York: Palgrave, 2001.

Radcliffe, William W. "Origins and Current State of Japan's Reconnaissance Satellite Program." *Studies in Intelligence* 54, no. 3 (Extracts, September 2010). https://www.cia.gov/static/aca9997a3231f8682380c970a5ab831a/Origins-and-Current-State.pdf.

Rathbun, Brian C., and Rachel Stein. "Greater Goods: Morality and Attitudes toward the Use of Nuclear Weapons." *Journal of Conflict Resolution* 64, no. 5 (2020): 787–816.

Ratner, Ely et al. *More Willing and Able: Charting China's International Security Activism*. Washington, DC: Center for a New American Security, 2015.

Roehrig, Terence. "Korean Dispute over the Northern Limit Line: Security, Economics, or International Law?" *Maryland Series in Contemporary Asian Studies* 2008, no. 3. https://digitalcommons.law.umaryland.edu/mscas/vol2008/iss3/1.

Roehrig, Terence. *From Deterrence to Engagement: the US Defense Commitment to South Korea*. Lanham, MD: Lexington 2006.

Roehrig, Terence. *Japan, South Korea, and the United States Nuclear Umbrella: Deterrence after the Cold War*. New York: Columbia University Press, 2017.

Rubin, Jeffrey Z., and Bert Brown. *The Social Psychology of Bargaining and Negotiation*. New York: Academic Press, 1975.

Saccone, Richard. *Negotiating with North Korea*. Elizabeth, NJ: Hollym Press, 2003.

Sagan, Scott. "Why Do States Build Nuclear Weapons? Three Models in Search of a Bomb." *International Security* 21, no. 3 (1996/97): 54–86.

Sartori, Ann. *Deterrence by Diplomacy*. Princeton: Princeton University Press, 2005.

Schelling, Thomas C. *The Strategy of Conflict*. Cambridge: Harvard University Press, 1960.

Segal, Leon V. *Disarming Strangers: Nuclear Diplomacy with North Korea*. Princeton: Princeton University Press, 1998.

Smith, Sheila. *Japan Rearmed: The Politics of Military Power*. Cambridge: Harvard University Press, 2019.

Snyder, Scott. "Lee Myung-bak's Foreign Policy: A 250-Day Assessment." *Korean Journal of Defense Analysis* 21, no. 1 (2008): 85–102.

Solingen, Etel. *Sanctions, Statecraft, and Nuclear Proliferation*. Cambridge: Cambridge University Press, 2012.

Suh, Jae Jean. *The Lee Myung-bak Government's North Korea Policy—A Study on its Historical and Theoretical Foundation*. Seoul: Korea Institute for National Unification, 2009.

Tabatabai, Ariane, and Camille Pease. "The Iranian Nuclear Negotiations." In *How Negotiations End*, edited by I. William Zartman, 27–45. Cambridge: Cambridge University Press, 2019.

Tan, Hongmei. "A Study on North Korean Policy in South Korea: Compare with Kim Dae Joong, No Moo Hyon, and Lee Myong Bak Government." *Global Political Studies* 3, no. 1 (2010): 93–115.

Toloraya, Georgy, and Vassily Gabets. "Solving the Korean Conundrum: Russia's Interaction with Major Actors in the Trump-Moon Era." *International Journal of Korean Unification Studies* 26, no. 1 (2017): 109–14. https://www.kinu.or.kr/pyxis-api/1/digital-files/16bd4162-9f47-47fe-8be5-d4624d0044db.

Toloraya, Georgy. "The Six Party Talks: A Russian Perspective." *Asian Perspective* 32, no. 4 (2008): 45–69.

Walton, Richard E., and Robert B. McKersie. *A Behavioral Theory of Labor Negotiations*. New York: McCraw-Hill, 1965.

Wang, Fei-Ling. "Between the Bomb and the United States: China Faces the Nuclear North Korea." In *The North Korea and Nuclear Weapons: Entering the New Era of Deterrence*, edited by Sung Chull Kim and Michael Cohen, 157–78. Washington, DC: Georgetown University Press, 2017.

Wang, Fei-Ling. "Changing Views: Chinese Perception of the United States–South Korea Alliance." *Problems of Post-Communism* (July-August 1996): 25–34.

Wang, Fei-Ling. "China and the Prospects of Denuclearization of North Korea." *Asian Journal of Peacebuilding* (Seoul, Korea) 6, no. 2 (2018): 267–88.

Wang, Fei-Ling. "Joining the Major Powers for the Status Quo: China's Views and Policy on Korean Reunification." *Pacific Affairs* 72, no. 2 (1999): 167–85.

Wang, Fei-Ling. "Looking East: China's Policy toward the Korean Peninsula." In *Engagement with North Korea: A Viable Alternative*, edited by Sung Chull Kim and David C. Kang, 47–72. Albany: State University of New York Press, 2009.

Wang, Fei-Ling. "Resisting, Reducing, and Replacing: China's Strategy and Policy towards the United States." In *China's Domestic Politics and Foreign Policies, and Major Countries' Strategies on China*, edited by Jung-Ho Bae, 155–86. Seoul: KINU, 2012.

Wang, Fei-Ling. *The China Order: Centralia, World Empire, and the Nature of Chinese Power*. Albany: State University of New York Press, 2017.

Wang, Fei-Ling. *The China Record: An Assessment of the People's Republic*. Albany: State University of New York Press, 2023.

Wang, Yuan-kang. *Harmony and War: Confucian Culture and Chinese Power Politics*. New York: Columbia University Press, 2010.

Whitlark, Rachel E. "Nuclear Beliefs: A Leader-focused Theory of Counter-Proliferation." *Security Studies* 26, no. 4 (2017): 545–74.

Wit, Joel S., Daniel B. Poneman, and Robert L. Gallucci. *Going Critical: The First North Korean Nuclear Crisis*. Washington, DC: Brookings, 2004.

Woodward, Bob. *Rage*. New York: Simon and Schuster, 2020.

Yi, Xiaoxiong. "China's Korea Policy: From 'One Kore' to 'Two Koreas.'" *Asian Affairs: An American Review* 22, no. 2 (Summer 1995): 128–31.

Yokota, Sakie. *Megumi, Okaasan ga Kitto Tasukete Ageru* [Megumi, Mom Will Rescue You No Matter What]. Tokyo: Soshisha, 1999.

Yoon, Hong-Suk. "The Peace and Prosperity Policy and the South-North Relationship: Evaluation and Future Tasks," in *Peace and Prosperity Policy and Peace Regime on the Korean Peninsula: The Limits of Coercive Diplomacy in Korean Peninsula*, edited by In-Duk Kang, Seoul: Institute for East Asian Studies, 2005.

Young, Oran R. *Bargaining: Formal Theories of Negotiation*. Urbana: University of Illinois Press, 1975.

Zartman, I. William. "Introduction." In *How Negotiations End*, edited by I. William Zartman, 1–24. Cambridge: Cambridge University Press, 2019.

Zartman, I. William. "Lessons for Theory." In *How Negotiations End*, edited by I. William Zartman, 287–94. Cambridge: Cambridge University Press, 2019.

Zartman, I. William. "Mediation: Ripeness and Its Challenges in the Middle East." *International Negotiations* 20, no. 3 (2015): 479–93.

Zartman, I. William. "Ripeness: The Hurting Stalemate and Beyond." In *International Conflict Resolution after the Cold War*, edited by Daniel Druckman and Paul C. Stern, 225–50. Washington, DC: The National Academies Press, 2000.

Zeng, Jinghan. *Slogan Politics: Understanding Chinese Foreign Policy Concepts*. London: Palgrave Macmillan, 2020.

Contributors' Biographies

Pamela Aall is senior advisor for conflict prevention and management at the U.S. Institute of Peace (USIP) and an adjunct professor at American University. She serves as board chair of Women in International Security (WIIS) and is a member of the World Refugee and Migration Council. She has co-authored and co-edited articles and books in the field of mediation and conflict management. Her most recent books are *Responding to Violent Conflicts and Humanitarian Crises: A Guide to Participants* (co-edited with Dan Snodderly) and *Diplomacy and the Future of World Order*, co-edited with Chester Crocker and Fen Hampson.

Paige Cone is assistant professor of strategy and security studies at the School of Advanced Air and Space Studies (SAASS). Her research focuses on issues of international security, nuclear security and nonproliferation, and strategic deterrence. Recent publications include articles on the impact of hypersonic weapons on nuclear deterrence, the role of positive and negative inducements in interstate relations, and an award-winning article on effective strategies for approaching North Korean nuclear weapons activity. She is currently working with the University of Chicago Press to publish her first book project, *Bribing the Bomb: Inducements in Arms Control*. Prior to coming to SAASS, Dr. Cone was an assistant professor with the Center for Strategic Deterrence Studies and was a postdoctoral fellow at The University of Chicago, serving as the Chicago Project and Security and Threats' first-ever nuclear proliferation fellow. Dr. Cone received an MA in international studies and a PhD in political science from the University of South Carolina and has a BA in political science from the University of North Carolina Wilmington where she double minored in English and international relations.

Uk Heo is University Distinguished Professor of Political Science at the University of Wisconsin-Milwaukee and editor-in-chief of *Asian Survey*. His research interests focus on Korean security and political economy, the North Korean nuclear crisis, defense economics, and democracy. Uk Heo has authored or coauthored five books, including three with Cambridge University Press: *South Korea Since 1980*; *South Korea's Rise: Economic Development, Power, and Foreign Relations*; and *The Evolution of the South Korea–United States Alliance*. He has also published more than sixty journal articles, which have appeared in *Asian Survey, British Journal of Political Science, Comparative Politics, Comparative Political Studies, International Studies Quarterly, Journal of Conflict Resolution, Journal of Politics, Journal of Peace Research, Political Research Quarterly*, and others. Uk Heo received his PhD in political science from Texas A&M University and is a former president of the Association of Korean Political Studies.

Su-Mi Lee is an associate professor at the University of Hawai'i at Hilo. Her research interests center around international conflict management, including mediation and negotiation. Her research appears in academic publications such as *International Interactions, Foreign Policy Analysis, Negotiation Journal, International Negotiation*, and *The Korean Journal of Security Affairs*. She has held a variety of fellowships including the Fellowship of Field Research of the Korea Foundation, the Fulbright-Hays Seminar Abroad Program of the US Department Education and the Fulbright Commission in Chile, and the Emergent Scholar Seminar of the Asia Pacific Higher Education Research Partnership in Thailand. Dr. Lee received her PhD in political science from the University of Kentucky, MA in political science from the University of Missouri, and BA in political science from San Jose State University.

Terence Roehrig is professor of national security affairs at the U.S. Naval War College and a nonresident expert with the Center for Korean Legal Studies at Columbia University. He was a research fellow at the Kennedy School at Harvard University and is a past president of the Association of Korean Political Studies. He has published several books, including his most recent *Japan, South Korea, and the U.S. Nuclear Umbrella* (Columbia University Press) and *The Evolution of the South Korea–United States Alliance* (Cambridge University Press), co-authored with Uk Heo. Roehrig has also published numerous articles and book chapters on Korean and East Asian security issues, North Korea's nuclear weapons program, the

Northern Limit Line dispute, the South Korean Navy, deterrence theory and the U.S.–South Korea alliance. Dr. Roehrig received his PhD from the University of Wisconsin-Madison and an MA from Marquette University, both in political science.

Scott A. Snyder is senior fellow for Korea studies and director of the program on U.S.-Korea policy at the Council on Foreign Relations (CFR). Mr. Snyder is the author of *South Korea at the Crossroads: Autonomy and Alliance in an Era of Rival Powers* (January 2018). Mr. Snyder also served as the project director for CFR's Independent Task Force on policy toward the Korean Peninsula. Prior to joining CFR, Mr. Snyder was a senior associate in the international relations program of the Asia Foundation, where he founded and directed the Center for U.S.-Korea Policy and served as the Asia Foundation's representative in Korea (2000–04). He was also a senior associate at Pacific Forum Center for Strategic and International Studies. Mr. Snyder has worked as an Asia specialist in the research and studies program of the U.S. Institute of Peace and as acting director of Asia Society's contemporary affairs program. He was a Pantech visiting fellow at Stanford University's Shorenstein Asia-Pacific Research Center during 2005–06. Mr. Snyder received a BA from Rice University and an MA from the Regional Studies–East Asia program at Harvard University.

Yuki Tatsumi is a senior fellow and co-director of the East Asia Program and director of the Japan Program at the Stimson Center. Before joining Stimson, Tatsumi worked as a research associate at the Center for Strategic and International Studies (CSIS) and as the special assistant for political affairs at the Embassy of Japan in Washington. She is an author of *Lost in Translation? U.S. Defense Innovation and Northeast Asia* (Stimson Center, 2017), *Opportunity out of Necessity: The Impact of U.S. Defense Budget Cuts on the U.S.-Japan Alliance* (Stimson Center, 2013) and *Japan's National Security Policy Infrastructure: Can Tokyo Meet Washington's Expectations?* (Stimson Center, 2008), as well as co-author of *Global Security Watch: Japan* (Praeger, 2010). Tatsumi was awarded the Letter of Appreciation from the Ministry of National Policy of Japan for her contribution in advancing mutual understanding between the United States and Japan in 2012. A native of Tokyo, Tatsumi holds a BA in liberal arts from the International Christian University in Tokyo, Japan and an MA in international economics and Asian studies from the Paul H. Nitze School of Advanced International Studies (SAIS) at Johns Hopkins University in Washington.

Fei-Ling Wang is a professor at Sam Nunn School of International Affairs, Georgia Institute of Technology. His research interests are comparative and international political economy, U.S.–East Asian relations, and East Asia and China studies. He has published eight books (two co-edited) in two languages including *Organization through Division and Exclusion: China's Hukou System* (Stanford University Press, 2005), *The China Order: Centralia, World Empire, and the Nature of Chinese Power* (SUNY Press, 2017), and *The China Record: Assessment of the People's Republic* (SUNY Press, 2023). He has also published dozens of book chapters and journal articles in four languages. Dr. Wang taught at the U.S. Military Academy (West Point) and U.S. Air Force Academy (Colorado Springs), and held visiting and adjunct/honorary positions in institutions such as European University Institute in Italy, Sciences Po in France, National Sun Yat-sen University and National Taiwan University in Taiwan, National University of Singapore, Renmin University and Anhui Normal University in China, University of Macau, University of Tokyo, and Sungkyunkwan University and Yonsei University in Korea. He has appeared in many national and international news media such as Al Jazeera, AFP, AP, BBC, CNN, *The Financial Times*, *The New York Times*, Radio China International, *South China Morning Post*, VOA, *The Wall Street Journal*, and the Xinhua News Agency. He has had numerous research grants including a Minerva Chair grant, a Fulbright Senior Scholar grant and a Hitachi Fellowship. He is a member of the Council on Foreign Relations.

Richard Weitz is a senior fellow and director of the Center for Political-Military Analysis at Hudson Institute. Before joining Hudson in 2005, Dr. Weitz worked for several other academic and professional research institutions and the U.S. Department of Defense. His current research includes regional security developments relating to Europe, Eurasia, and East Asia as well as U.S. foreign and defense policies. In addition to many articles and op-eds, Dr. Weitz has authored or edited several books and monographs, including *The New China-Russia Alignment: Critical Challenges to U.S. Security* (2022); *Assessing the Collective Security Treaty Organization*; *Promoting U.S.-Indian Defense Cooperation*; *China and Afghanistan after the NATO Withdrawal*; *Turkey's New Regional Security Role: Implications for the United States*; *War and Governance: International Security in a Changing World Order*; *The Russian Military Today and Tomorrow*; *Global Security Watch—Russia*; and two volumes of *National Security Case Studies* for the Project on National Security Reform. Dr.

Weitz received his PhD in political science from Harvard University, MPhil in politics from Oxford University, MSc in international relations from the London School of Economics, and BA with highest honors in government from Harvard College, where he was elected to Phi Beta Kappa. He is proficient in Russian, French, and German.

Index

www.ingramcontent.com/pod-product-compliance
Lightning Source LLC
Chambersburg PA
CBHW030401270326
41926CB00009B/1209